The Critical Path
to
Corporate Renewal

The Critical Path
to
Corporate Renewal

Michael Beer
Russell A. Eisenstat
Bert Spector

Harvard Business School Press

94   93   92   91   5   4   3   2

The paper used in this publication meets
the requirements of the American National
Standard for Permanence of Paper for
Printed Library Materials Z39.49-1984.

Library of Congress Cataloging-in-Publication Data

Beer, Michael.
    The critical path to corporate renewal / Michael Beer, Russell A.
Eisenstat, Bert Spector.
        p.   cm.
    Includes index.
    ISBN 0-87584-239-9
    1. Corporate turnarounds.   2. Corporate reorganizations.
I. Eisenstat, Russell A., 1955–   . II. Spector, Bert. III. Title.
HD58.8.B438   1990
658.4'063—dc20   90-37570
                                                                      CIP

To Cynthia, Tom, and Shannon
To Stephanie, Ben, and Sam
To Maureen, Kate, and Tess

Contents

Acknowledgments

The authors would like to express their appreciation for the generous research support provided by the Harvard Business School Division of Research under the direction of Professors Raymond Corey and Jay Lorsch. One of the authors also received research support from the Research and Scholarship Development Fund and the College of Business of Northeastern University, and we extend our thanks for that support.

Part of the funding from the Harvard Business School provided us with the indispensable assistance of John Junkerman. In addition to conducting some of the field research, John was a regular contributor to the ongoing discussions and analysis that finally resulted in this book. Thanks, John, for your help. Our appreciation goes also to Nicole Steckler and Molly Schmitt for their assistance in analyzing our quantitative data. Special thanks is due Maria Van Nuysenburg for her patience and commitment in providing administrative support for the production of the manuscript.

We also take this opportunity to recognize the invaluable assistance of many of our colleagues who read all or parts of the manuscript and offered guidance, suggestions, criticisms, and support. Special thanks, then, to Chris Argyris, Joseph Bower, Robert Eccles, Richard Hackman, Jay Lorsch, Gary Loveman, Robert McKersie, Frank Spital, Richard Walton, and Shoshana Zuboff.

Eliza Collins and Carol Franco at the Harvard Business School Press provided steady hands, an unflagging commitment, and insightful voices in the ongoing development of the book. We are indebted to them and the staff at the press for their support.

Finally, we should acknowledge our deepest debt and gratitude to a group without whom there truly could have been no book: the men and women of the corporations that we studied. Hundreds of individuals—shop-floor workers, union leaders, managers, staff specialists, consultants, presidents, and chairmen—gave unselfishly of their time and insights, asking for nothing in return. We have agreed not to name them here and will, of course, honor that agreement. But we would be remiss if we failed to express to every one of them our most sincere sense of appreciation. Our only hope of repayment for their contribution lies in our ability to learn from their experiences and to communicate that learning to our readers.

Boston, Massachusetts

May 1990

Michael Beer
Russell A. Eisenstat
Bert Spector

The Critical Path
to
Corporate Renewal

Introduction

"Managing organizational change is a topic American business needs to examine and understand, because fundamental change will be the order of the day for the foreseeable future. And, obviously, the company that can adapt its culture to change, quickly and successfully, will have a powerful competitive advantage." [1]*

Zane E. Barnes, CEO
Southwestern Bell

The Critical Path is about a journey, a journey undertaken by American corporations in search of renewal. Over the past decade, the competitive environment in which American business operates has undergone nothing short of a sea change. Companies that once enjoyed easy command of their markets now find themselves engaged in a raging battle to reestablish their dominance, regain their market share, and even, in some cases, ensure their very survival. In responding, these businesses have at their disposal a number of approaches: acquisition and divestiture, trimming excess costs, rationalizing assets. In today's environment, businesses ignore any of these responses at their own peril.

In the battle to reclaim competitiveness, there is, however, another powerful approach that is being used by an increasing number of American companies—Ford Motor, Scott Paper, Xerox, AT&T, McDonnell Douglas, Rockwell

International, Procter & Gamble, and Cummins Engine among them. That approach is organizational revitalization. In search of renewed strength, leaders in these and similar companies look beyond the need to manage financial assets wisely by recognizing that competitiveness is inexorably linked to the abilities and effectiveness of their employees.

THE CHALLENGE OF REVITALIZATION

Revitalization involves enhancing the abilities of, and contributions made by, managers, workers, and the organization as a whole to cope with an increasingly competitive environment. To this end, corporations are reducing their exclusive reliance on the authority of management, on rules and procedures, and on strict and narrow divisions of work. Instead, employees at all levels are involved in decision making; teamwork is encouraged among functions, business units, union and management; information concerning performance and the competitive environment is shared and communicated throughout the corporation; and responsibility and accountability are pushed far down the hierarchy.

These changes are resulting in a flatter, less hierarchical, and more flexible organization. They empower employees to take initiative in reducing costs, improving quality, and responding to customer needs. In turn, this new organization demands different patterns of management and employee commitment plus a redefinition of the corporation's culture. Such changes are fundamental, and they never occur easily.

SIZING UP THE CHALLENGE OF REVITALIZATION

In order to better understand the process of revitalization, we embarked on an in-depth study of six large corporations engaged in a conscious effort to make fundamental change in their patterns of management. The companies were selected on a number of criteria: the need for a variety of industries, for representation in the manufacturing and service sectors, for inclusion of both single and multibusiness firms, and, of course, their willingness to provide open research access. The companies' sales ranged from $4 to $10 billion. Five were in the manufacturing sector, and one was a large international bank.[2]

The way to learn about the revitalization process, we reasoned, was to study a number of companies actually undergoing revitalization, determine from that study what did and did not work, and then develop a theory of corporate revitalization consistent with those determinations. To collect the data and arrive at the judgments presented in *The Critical Path,* we conducted hundreds of interviews in the six companies. We also made use of primary source documents relating to revitalization efforts.

We then ranked the companies according to the success with which they had managed their revitalization effort. This ranking was based on the extent to which their cultures were changing in four substantive areas that managers typically cited as objectives for revitalization efforts: significantly improved interfunctional coordination, decision making, work organization, and concern for people.

It is important to note that we did *not* define success as improvement in financial performance of the companies. In the short run, corporate financial performance is influenced by many situational factors, including market share, cost-cutting initiatives, and financial strength, as well as by past investment decisions in new product development and manufacturing technology. The quality of those decisions, themselves a function of the decision-making process and managerial competence the organization fostered in the past, influence performance for many years.

Although we did not try to establish a link between successful revitalization and financial performance, other research has done so. That research has demonstrated a long-run positive relationship between the types of corporate culture dimensions we used to rank our six companies and financial performance.[3] So while our understanding of re-

vitalization assumes a long-run relationship with performance, our definition of success focuses on the immediate impact of the change effort on *how* the company was being
managed.

To corroborate our rankings of the companies, we administered a standardized questionnaire in each company.[4]
With one exception, managers' perceptions of how much
their companies had changed were identical to ours. We, as
well as the employees, designated General Products as the
clear revitalization leader, with Fairweather Corporation a
distant second. U.S. Financial and Continental Glass & Container were clearly revitalization laggards. Our rank ordering
of the six companies is presented in Table I-1. It also shows
the extent of the cultural transformation in each company as
rated by employees.

Table I-1: The Revitalization Effort Rated

	Extent of Revitalization		
	Ranked by Researchers	Rated by Employees	
Company		Average	Standard Deviation
General Products	1	4.04[a]	.35
Fairweather	2	3.58	.45[b]
Livingston Electronics	3	3.61	.76
Scranton Steel	4	3.30	.65
Continental Glass	5	2.96	.83
U.S. Financial	6	2.78	1.07

a. A 1-to-5 scale was employed. A rating of 3.0 meant no change. A rating
   below that meant that the culture had actually moved away from the direction sought by the revitalization effort.
b. Based on researchers' knowledge of the companies, Fairweather was
   judged to have changed more than Livingston, despite the fact that employee ratings placed it third by a small margin. A much smaller standard
   deviation suggests greater consensus among employees about the extent of
   revitalization at Fairweather than at Livingston and supports researcher
   judgment.

Top management at each of the six companies wanted to change how the *total* company was being managed. We quickly found, however, that corporate revitalization typically started in individual units and that progress had to be measured by the number of organizational units that undertook and ultimately succeeded in revitalizing themselves. By "unit" we mean a discrete, identifiable organizational entity such as a manufacturing plant, a branch, or a division or business unit devoted to making and/or delivering products or services. Corporate staff groups, R&D centers, and the corporate top-management team were also considered discrete units.

Because we concluded early in our investigation that corporate revitalization depends on successful renewal in many organizational units, we had to explain what factors caused some units to renew successfully and others to fail. To arrive at that explanation, we used the previously described standardized survey to rank all the units we visited in the six companies on the extent of their success in managing change. Our findings about what differentiated successful unit-level revitalization efforts from less successful ones will be presented early in the book and provide the foundation on which our theory of corporate revitalization rests. (Appendix II contains the survey results concerning unit-level change and a more detailed discussion of the methodology of this study.)

THE CRITICAL PATH: AN OVERVIEW

The extent of organizational change at both company and unit levels provided the key to understanding the revitalization process. From our observations and from survey responses we could identify the factors that separated successful from less successful revitalization efforts. To put it simply, we could answer the question, "What did the leaders do that the laggards failed to do?"

Our answers contain more than a few surprises and

5

run contrary to much of the conventional wisdom and practice regarding the management of large-scale organizational change. We concluded the following:

- Change efforts that begin by creating corporate programs to alter the culture or the management of people in the firm are inherently flawed even when supported by top management.
- Formal organizational structure and systems are the *last* things an organization should change when seeking renewal—not the first, as many managers assume.
- Effective changes in the way an organization manages people do *not* occur by changing the organization's human resource policies and systems.
- Starting corporate renewal at the very top is a high-risk revitalization strategy *not* employed by the most successful companies.
- Organizations should start corporate revitalization by targeting small, isolated, peripheral operations, not large, central, core operations.
- It is not essential that top management consistently practice what it preaches in the early stages of renewal, although such action is undoubtedly helpful.

As *The Critical Path* unfolds, we will present and develop a series of propositions relating to exactly how effective corporate revitalization does occur. These propositions will appear in the following chapter order.

Chapter 1. The external environment has changed in such a way that traditional organizational arrangements (hierarchical structures and top-down decision making) that worked well in stabler times no longer suffice to keep American firms competitive. The demands of the competitive environment for simultaneous achievement of high quality, low cost, and product innovation require a new type of task-driven organization.

For the task-driven organization to function effectively, far higher levels of coordination and teamwork—across functions, borders, business units, organizational levels, as well as between management and union—will be needed. To achieve that co-ordination, higher levels of employee commitment and competence will be required at all levels of the organization.

Chapter 2. The initial response of many corporations to the recognized need for change were programs driven from the top. These have been inadequate at best; at their worst, such programs are detrimental to the long-run success of renewal. Successful corporate revitalization starts in plants or divisions.

Chapter 3. Successful unit-level renewal occurs only when units directly align a call for new employee behaviors and skills with an urgent response to the unit's central competitive challenge. *Task alignment* is the term we use to designate this all-important wedding of behavioral and business concerns.

Chapter 4. While task alignment can be achieved by mandating changes in formal systems and structure, that approach reduces commitment and fails to develop the competence people need to function effectively within the newly aligned organization. We propose a sequence of interventions we identify as *the critical path,* which creates task alignment in a way that increases coordination as well as commitment and competence.

Chapter 5. For revitalization to move beyond isolated units and spread throughout the corporation, top management must develop a corporate climate in which renewal can flourish. Developing that climate involves six strategies that must be carefully sequenced and orchestrated.

Chapter 6. The development of a corporate climate that demands revitalization depends on two conditions: Top management must be philosophically attuned to balancing short-term demands for cost reduction with sustained long-term investment in the firm's human resources. It must also provide support in the form of skilled professional resources—a change-oriented human resource function, and external consultants.

7

Chapter 7.   Whether it be at the unit or corporate level, leadership is the key propellant to renewal. Effective leaders have certain convictions and skills that unfortunately are extremely scarce, raising the all-important question of how such leaders might be developed.

Chapter 8.   The first several years of effective corporate renewal are focused on plants and divisions, not on corporate headquarters and top management. To sustain revitalization, the top management unit must ultimately confront its own organization and behavior. Pressures from capital markets have the potential to spur this development, but we found that in several of our companies such pressures diverted top management from the revitalization effort.

Chapter 9.   *The Critical Path* has action implications for a wide range of corporate actors: the CEO, line managers, human resource managers, and union leaders all can have a significant impact on renewal by taking action consistent with their roles. At the same time, they must work together to reinforce one another's actions. We conclude with practical recommendations for each actor in the drama of revitalization.

This book describes a comprehensive theory of corporate revitalization that will help managers develop an adaptive organization, one in which people and groups possess the commitment and competence to coordinate effectively. Like a superior basketball team, organizational members understand all the plays (plans and strategies), know and anticipate one another's moves (roles and responsibilities), and are eager to work selflessly (look at the business rather than their function or job) to win the game.

Of course, revitalization is not the only way to make a corporation more competitive. Cost reduction, acquisition and divestiture, asset rationalization, and the introduction of new manufacturing systems are also ways to create a more competitive corporation. They change the economics of the company and introduce new and valuable technology. They do not necessarily improve coordination and teamwork, however. Nor do they create the commitment and competence employees must have to sustain high levels of coordination. Indeed, they often cause a decrease in these valued human and organizational sources of competitive advantage, ones we argue later are essential for managing continuous improvements in quality, cost, and products/services. These are the business outcomes essential to compete in the 1990s and beyond.

NOTES

1. Z.E. Barnes, "Change in the Bell System," *Academy of Management Executive* 1 (1987), pp. 43–46.
2. While the stories of the renewal efforts in these companies will unfold in detail throughout the book, the reader can turn to Appendix I for a brief overview of each company, as well as a listing of the key units and employees. The reader should understand that although the companies and individuals in our study are real, all names used in this book are fictitious.
3. Three important studies that demonstrate a long-term linkage between the organizational characteristics sought through revitalization and financial performance are P.R. Lawrence and D. Dyer, *Renewing American Industry* (New York: Free Press, 1983); D.R. Dennison, "Bringing Corporate Culture to the Bottom Line," *Organizational Dynamics* 13 (Autumn 1984), pp. 4–22; and M.E. Dertouzos, R.K. Lester, and R.M. Solow, *Made in America: Regaining the Productive Edge* (Cambridge, MA: MIT Press, 1989).
4. See Appendix IV for the dimensions and items on the standardized questionnaire. Four of its dimensions—interfunctional coordination, work organization, decision making, and concern for people—were taken from the Survey of Organizations, a widely used measure of organizational climate developed at the Institute for Social Research, University of Michigan. These dimensions were found by Dennison to be correlated with long-term financial performance. See Dennison, "Bringing Corporate Culture to the Bottom Line."

1

The Need for Revitalization

While the six companies we studied differed in the nature of their leaders, the products or services they provided, and the markets they served, they nevertheless shared a common goal of revitalization. Like other corporations, they faced the difficult challenge of transforming their organizations to regain positions of leadership suddenly threatened by a far more demanding competitive environment.

In this chapter we lay the foundation for the critical path by considering the popular approaches to organizing and managing corporations in the post–World War II era and why those approaches have made revitalization both necessary and difficult. We begin by examining the connection between a firm's competitive position and how it organizes and manages people.

ORGANIZATIONAL SOURCES OF COMPETITIVE ADVANTAGE

Firms create value for their customers through a series of individual activities that are necessary to design, produce, market, distribute, and support a product or service. If a firm is able to perform each of these activities and exploit the linkages among them in a way that gives it an edge over its rivals in cost, quality, or innovativeness, it has created a source of competitive advantage.[1] Thus a firm's ability to succeed in the marketplace is a result not only of the technical skills of its employees, but also of how well those employees coordinate with one another in accomplishing these core "value-creating" tasks. Why is coordination important and what is required to achieve it?

- *Coordination*. Teamwork is especially important if an organization is to find and act on cost, quality, and product improvement opportunities. The production and sale of a high-quality, low-cost product depend on close coordination among marketing, product design, and manufacturing as well as between labor and management. As we shall explain, that is why revitalization focuses on enhancing coordination.
- *Commitment*. High levels of motivation are essential if the effort, initiative, and cooperation needed for coordinated action are to be achieved.
- *Competence*. Knowledge about the business as a whole, analytical skills, and interpersonal skills are required for people to identify and solve problems as a team.

Employees' levels of coordination, commitment, and competence are shaped by various aspects of the organization's design, which is made up of the following:

- The formal structure of jobs and reporting relationships defined in written job descriptions and organizational charts.

- The people chosen to fill the jobs.
- Employees' informal understandings of their assigned roles, responsibilities, and working relationships.
- The organizational systems that recruit, evaluate, train, and promote employees, provide them with financial rewards, and supply them with the information needed to do their jobs.

How these organizational variables affect the human resource attributes of coordination, commitment, and competence—and in turn the performance of the business—is illustrated in Figure 1-1, which places the organization's ability to achieve desired cost, quality, and innovation dead center. The degree to which an organization can achieve those outcomes is affected by the extent to which it has the necessary level of coordination, commitment, and competence. These human resource attributes are in turn determined by elements of the organization's design: structure, people, roles/responsibilities/relationships, and systems.

The relationships we have just described apply generally. Coordination, commitment, and competence are always needed. The key question is how widely spread in the organization these human attributes have to be. Is it sufficient for coordination to occur primarily at the top of the organization, thus making it essential for high-level managers to possess special levels of commitment and competence; or must lower-level employees possess these attributes as well? The answer depends on the nature of the business environment.

Both the rate of change and the level of complexity in the business environment have important effects on how organizations achieve necessary coordination.[2] Under conditions of environmental certainty, when technology and customer needs do not change rapidly, coordination of decisions about product/market strategies can occur among a few top managers who then direct lower levels to implement them. Because these businesses are relatively simple and stable, conflicts among functions can be resolved directly through top-management intervention or indirectly through administrative rules and standard operating procedures. This pattern

13

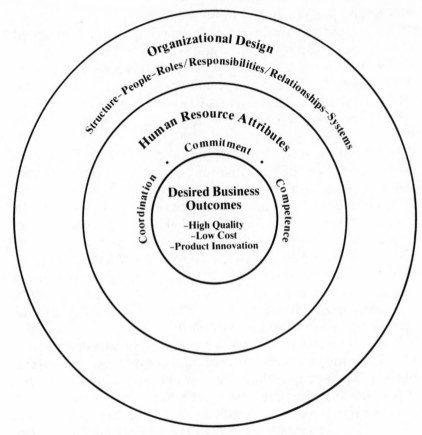

Figure 1-1: The Target of Revitalization: The Organizational and Human Sources of Competitive Advantage

of coordination is most consistent with a "tall" functional organizational structure, a combination that has been called a *mechanistic* or *command-and-control* organization.[3]

Command-and-control organizations require only modest levels of coordination at lower levels and therefore demand less competence and commitment from most members. Because the scope of most jobs in such organizations is quite narrowly defined within each function, it is fairly easy to recruit or train individuals who have the necessary technical skills. Because both business decision making and coordination among groups occur at the top of a mechanistic organization, it is only top management that requires such competencies as broad business perspective, initiative to identify problems beyond a job or specialty, interpersonal skills to negotiate and resolve conflict, and analytical skills to solve emerging business problems.

Similarly, because general management decision making is concentrated at the top, only these same few individuals need to have a high level of commitment to the overall success of the firm. It is sufficient that most employees are willing to do as they are told in exchange for pay and continued employment.

COMMAND AND CONTROL IN THE POST–WORLD WAR II ERA

As we talked with managers in the six firms under investigation, it became clear they had institutionalized a command-and-control approach to organizing and managing in the 1950s and 1960s. The business environment, lack of management talent, and low worker commitment were the reasons.

All these companies, along with many other American corporations, were preeminent in their markets in the post–World War II era because of the ravaged state of economies in Japan and Western Europe. When one considers the advantage that natural resources and technology gave the United States, it is not surprising that American corporations enjoyed a competitive edge well into the 1970s. With few competitors to cause concern, the general manager in the postwar years kept track of changes in the external marketplace with relative ease. Likewise, the slow pace of technological change made it easy for people at the top to make sensible internal decisions in such areas as manufacturing and new product development.[4] A regulated industry created virtually the same competitive conditions for the only bank in our sample, U.S. Financial, and also allowed top management to concentrate decision making at the top without penalty.

While a relatively simple environment made a command-and-control organization viable, the shortage of effective managers that resulted from the war and the demands of rapid growth made it almost inevitable. General Products' chief operating officer described the organization that evolved in his early years with the company:

> Our number one problem [in the 1950s and 1960s] was to get enough [management] talent, and quite frankly we didn't have enough. So . . . what you did, you built a total system and structure under you. You had people checking on people to make sure the jobs and the assignments were carried out. . . . We built organizations and really almost were ruling the thing with an iron hand.

This elaborate system of corporate oversight continued into the 1980s. Managers of subsidiaries in far-flung parts of the world talked about daily calls from headquarters requesting detailed numbers about cost, orders, and, shipments. The same managers were required to obtain approval for the smallest expenditures. This pattern caused middle to upper-middle managers to complain about being overmanaged and to describe themselves as "technical specialists" rather than "business generalists." Consider also the complaints of a plant manager at Scranton Steel. "Every morning at eight o'clock I reported in to headquarters only numbers: costs, production schedules, things like that. Corporate strategy or where our plant fit into it all—no, that was never on the agenda."

Built on the assumption that most managers were not dependable, the elaborate oversight systems developed by these command-and-control organizations reinforced the very conditions that caused them to be installed in the first place. They increased employee frustration and thus decreased commitment, while providing few opportunities for management development. Typically, managers remained in the function through which they entered the company, creating what one top executive called the "elevator-shaft approach to management development." The result was the development of managers who possessed technical skills and functional expertise but lacked a broad business perspective and managerial skills.[5]

If top managers were concerned about whether lower-level managers would perform their jobs effectively, they were even more worried about the commitment of hourly employees. This concern was particularly evident in five of our companies with large numbers of unionized workers. The lack of faith in employees was deeply rooted in the adversarial history of union-management relations, a history that bred a generation of managers who were antiunion and pessimistic about the ability and willingness of employees to cooperate.

A past official of the United Steelworkers of America, described the management system and how it affected the extent to which workers' talents were utilized in solving quality and cost problems:

> Forty years ago when I was working in a steel mill in Youngstown, Ohio, and became president of my local, one of the things that became clear to me was the great inefficiency in the plant and the nonuse of workers, of their potential knowledge and experience. It was a totally controlled environment. I would talk to managers about quality and production, and they viewed this as a violation of their prerogatives.
>
> What became clear to me as I continued to negotiate with management was that one of the great barriers to its willingness to allow us to have a say-so in the production quality end of the business was the fact that it looked on the workers as if they were expendable. Management's way of running the plant—and this comes from Scientific Management—was that you

ran it according to the system of production, not according to the needs of the people. You break every job down to its lowest component. You don't have to train workers, then. You can give them any job. You can hire anybody to do it. You have a bunch of foremen standing around telling workers how to do their jobs, and if the workers don't do it right, you discipline them. Or you fire them. And you hope that somehow out of all this comes a quality product.

Because companies like Scranton Steel had only limited competition, the system of production described above worked in its time. However, it gave rise to unions and to adversarial union-management relationships. As the conflict between union and management increased in intensity, each party saw the other in more negative terms. Employee commitment declined further; management became more staunchly antiunion; and union leaders became less inclined to work collaboratively with management. An internal survey at Scranton Steel, for instance, revealed that over 70 percent of unionized workers agreed with the statement "You can't *trust* management to look after the interests of workers." [emphasis added]

These adversarial conditions resulted in escalating wage demands, rigid work rules, and bureaucratic grievance procedures. The result in industries such as autos and steel was very high labor costs and poor productivity. Without competitive pressures, however, the system held together. Workers were highly controlled but well paid. Shareholders received dividends, although at a sacrifice of investment in plant, equipment, and R&D.[6]

The confluence of a stable environment, coordination through command and control from the top, and resultant low commitment and general management competence led to a formal and rigid organization at the corporate, division, and plant levels. The organization had been adequate to the competitive challenges of the post–World War II period, although there were human and social costs. However, it was totally

inadequate for coping with the new competitive environment. "We're a company made of bricks and mortar," said one executive as a way of describing that rigidity. "We're a two-ton baby that doesn't bob to the top very fast," observed another.

THE TASK-DRIVEN ORGANIZATION

Today's intense global competition and deregulation has created much higher uncertainty for firms in virtually every industry.[7] Increased competition mandates a constant response to initiatives by other firms. It calls for the continuous improvement of quality and products, while controlling costs.[8] These new external demands are overwhelming the capacity of command-and-control organizations to respond. That was certainly true of the six companies we studied.

The new competitive environment requires a flexible and adaptive organization, as well as a different pattern of work behavior. Managers and workers must be aware of what the customer wants and what competitors are doing. They must translate this knowledge into effective decisions about improvements in product, service, quality, and cost, and they must implement these decisions at all levels. Markets, products, and technologies are changing too rapidly for top management to master all the necessary information to make these decisions. Instead, the competitive environment requires using the skills and abilities of a much larger number of employees than ever before.

Managers are becoming aware that it is impossible to respond rapidly to changing customer demands and meet lower cost and higher quality requirements without radically improving coordination and teamwork. They have become aware that manufacturing costs are influenced by R&D's product design, just as R&D's understanding of the value it is designing into the product or service is influenced by marketing's communication about the customer. Within a function such as manufacturing, firms have discovered that cost and quality are a result of how well manufacturing engineers work with production employees in designing an effective production process, and how well different departments along the "value-creation chain" coordinate and exchange information. Thus continuous improvements in productivity and quality require closer coordination among functions at all levels, as well as between labor and management. Lower-level employees from various functions must communicate directly with one another and coordinate activities with respect to particular products, defined market segments, or large and important customers.

It has become increasingly clear to managers that they cannot create the needed levels of coordination within their old, relatively stable, bricks-and-mortar functional hierarchies. When these managers look at newer high-technology firms, which have always functioned in a complex and rapidly changing environment, they see a different set of organizational arrangements. There the functional structure is overlaid with teams of lower-level people from different departments who come together to solve business problems and make coordinated decisions. The number and focus of these teams change fairly often in response to the rapidly evolving business environment.

This kind of quick responsiveness and adaptability is possible because the task, rather than hierarchy, is the basis for assigning roles and responsibilities. Knowledge replaces formal authority as the basis for influence. We call a firm that uses this approach a *task-driven* organization.[9]

For coordination to be improved by the task-driven organization, the transformation must be accompanied by equivalent changes in employee commitment and competence. Without commitment to the business as a whole, horizontal coordination among functional departments with different orientations and goals is impossible. Without commitment and a cooperative spirit, vertical coordination among management, employees, and unions is difficult, particularly given their different interests.[10] As for needed competencies, closer coordination requires that employees at all levels learn interpersonal skills and develop a generalist's rather than a specialist's perspective of the business.

These requirements pose a dilemma. The command-and-control organization actively discourages the development of the attitudes and behaviors necessary to move to a responsive task-driven organization.[11] Mired in rigidity and inflexibility, the companies we studied and many others like them experienced major shortfalls in the key performance outcomes necessary for survival: improved quality, decreased costs, and more effective new product development.[12]

Given these shortfalls, it is not surprising that corporate leaders realized their organizations were simply not up to the competitive challenge. Such a realization does not amount to a sufficient response, however. The more fundamental challenge lies ahead: how to develop corporations that demand of employees and instill in them the capacity for coordination and teamwork, as well as the commitment and competence this requires. In other words, how to achieve corporate renewal.

NOTES

1. This definition of value-adding activities comes from M.E. Porter, *Competitive Advantage: Creating and Sustaining Superior Performance* (New York: Free Press, 1985).
2. See P.E. Lawrence and J.W. Lorsch, *Organization and Environment: Managing Differentiation and Integration* (Boston: Harvard Business School, 1967); J.R. Galbraith, *Organization Design* (Reading, MA: Addison-Wesley, 1977); R. Duncan, "What Is the Right Organization Structure?" *Organizational Dynamics* (Winter 1979), pp. 59–80.
3. The concept of a mechanistic organization is from T. Burns and G.M. Stalker, *The Management of Innovation* (London: Tavistock Publications, 1961). The control/commitment dichotomy is from R.E. Walton, "From Control to Commitment in the Workplace," *Harvard Business Review* 64 (March–April 1985), pp. 77–84.
4. This view of the shifting general management role is consistent with the view presented in J.P. Kotter, *The Leadership Factor* (New York: Free Press, 1988).
5. For a discussion of the impact of functional career development on a number of American industries, see P.E. Lawrence and D. Dyer, *Renewing American Industry* (New York: Free Press, 1983).

6. Ibid.
7. See President's Commission on Industrial Competitiveness, *Global Competition: The New Reality* (Washington, DC: U.S. Government Printing Office, January 1985); B.R. Scott and G.C. Lodge, eds., *U.S. Competitiveness in the World Economy* (Boston: Harvard Business School Press, 1985); and M.L. Dertouzos, R.K. Lester, and R.M. Solow, *Made in America: Regaining the Productive Edge* (Cambridge, MA: MIT Press, 1989).
8. See R.H. Hayes, S.C. Wheelright, and K.B. Clark, *Dynamic Manufacturing: Creating the Learning Organization* (New York: Free Press, 1988).
9. This type of organization has also been called an *organic organization;* see Burns and Stalker, *The Management of Innovation.*
10. Lawrence and Dyer, *Renewing American Industry.*
11. Recently a good deal of attention has been paid to the time and cost-saving benefits that can accrue from an organic organization. See, for example, G. Stack, Jr., "Time—The New Source of Competitive Advantage," *Harvard Business Review* 66 (July–August 1988), pp. 41–51; and J.L. Bower and T.M. Haut, "Fast Cycle Capability for Competitive Power," *Harvard Business Review* 66 (November–December 1988), pp. 110–118.
12. The importance of quality as a source of competitive advantage has been documented by D.A. Garvin, *Managing Quality: The Strategic and Competitive Edge* (New York: Free Press, 1988); and R.D. Buzzell and B.T. Gale, *The PIMS Principles: Linking Strategy to Performance* (New York: Free Press, 1987). The barrier posed by tall, functional, command-and-control organizations to product innovation and the need for coordinating mechanisms and roles has been widely documented. See, for instance, R.M. Kanter, *The Change Masters: Innovations for Productivity in American Corporations* (New York: Simon and Schuster, 1984); R.M. Kanter, "The Middle Manager as Innovator," *Harvard Business Review* 60 (July–August 1982); R. Katz and M.L. Tushman, "A Longitudinal Study of the Effects of Boundary Spanning Supervision on Turnover and Promotion in Research and Development," *Academy of Management Journal* 26 (1983), pp. 437–456; J.R. Galbraith, "Human Resource Policies for the Innovating Organization," in C. Fombrum, N. Tichey, and M.A. Devane, eds., *Strategic Human Resource Management* (New York: Wiley, 1984); R. Katz and T.J. Allen, "Organizational Issues in the Introduction of New Technologies," in P.R. Kleindorfer, ed., *The Management of Productivity and Technology in Manufacturing* (New York: Plenum Press, 1985); and W.E. Souder, "Stimulating and Managing Ideas," *Research Management* (May–June 1987), pp. 13–17.

2

Programmatic Change: False Starts to Renewal

Understanding the need for change is a far cry from the successful renewal of an organization. As we learned time and time again, the initial steps taken by corporate leaders proved to be false starts. A variety of programs not only failed to make a significant change in the corporate culture, but also instilled cynicism, making future efforts even more difficult.

The first individuals with whom we spoke in each company were executives from the corporate human resource function. Invariably they greeted us with enthusiastic descriptions of major change programs under way, efforts to redefine corporate culture, development of a mission or philosophy statement, introduction of a new appraisal or pay-for-performance system, corporatewide education and training, broad use of quality circles, or a change in organizational structure. To these human resource executives, such programs were obvious evidence that their corporations were undergoing major change.

As our interviews broadened to include line managers at the business unit and plant levels, we encountered a different view of the programs, one also echoed by several union leaders. To them, these highly touted programs were at best irrelevant and at worst detrimental to the corporation's change objectives.

What do we mean by a human resource change "program"? Whatever the specific content, a program for change has some, if not all, of the following characteristics:

1. It is imposed on the organization from the top.
2. It serves as a centerpiece for launching and driving change throughout the whole organization in the early stages of revitalization.
3. Its off-the-shelf standardized solutions are not customized to meet the individual needs of different subunits.
4. Its focus is on one particular human resource management issue: employee skills, leadership style, performance evaluation and compensation, organizational structure, or organizational culture.

In the companies we studied, these programs were usually developed and administered by the human resource function and supported by top management. Occasionally they were initiated and administered by other staff groups; rarely were line managers the primary agents of change. Most often the programs were used to stimulate corporatewide change, but some were found at the group, division, and plant levels. The response by line managers was uniformly negative and skeptical about their impact.

Significantly, an analysis of the six companies indicated that General Products—the revitalization leader—had initiated only one minor programmatic change. The two revitalization laggards, U.S. Financial and Continental Glass, how-

Table 2-1: The Relationship between Extent of Revitalization and the Use of Programs

	Company					
	General Products	Fair-weather	Livingston Electronics	Scranton Steel	Continental Glass	U.S. Financial
Revitaliza-tion Rank	1	2	3	4	5	6
Use of pro-grams	Minor	◄—.Considerable—►			Central	Central

ever, had introduced several corporatewide programs and relied almost exclusively on them to stimulate change and move it along. Although Fairweather Corporation, Livingston Electronics, and Scranton Steel did implement programs, those programs were not central to their revitalization efforts as were the programs at U.S. Financial and Continental Glass (see Table 2-1).

This chapter describes some of the programs these companies utilized in their unsuccessful attempts at corporate renewal. We then address questions about why programs are used so frequently and how and why they actually can be detrimental to the objectives they are intended to achieve.

To begin, let us turn to the efforts of U.S. Financial to bring about renewal through a well-supported, well-financed culture program.

CULTURE CHANGE AT U.S. FINANCIAL

When Henry Lester became chief executive officer of U.S. Financial he realized the newly deregulated, highly competitive environment would require a new responsiveness to the marketplace and, at the same time, cost effectiveness. It was an adaptation for which U.S. Financial was particularly ill suited. Multiple organizational layers made accountability difficult to assign; many loan officers lacked adequate knowledge of the industries they served; even knowledgeable loan officers often were unable to exercise their own judgment. Not surprisingly, many observers both inside and outside the bank considered the institution to be stodgy and unresponsive to the changing marketplace.

Lester announced his intention to launch a direct attack on U.S. Financial's "cautious and conservative style," telling employees that the role of manager is to be an agent of change and the role of the chairman is to be *the* agent of change. "My job," he told them, "is to bear the pain of transition from one environment to another."

Shortly thereafter, Lester held a retreat for his top 15 executives. One of the participants described the retreat:

> Henry asked us to come together to discuss U.S. Financial: its origins, its meaning, its current purpose, its future role. We were told ahead of time to mail in a short statement—thirty words or less—on "What is U.S. Financial?" At the retreat we discussed all those replies, then took a vote on which seemed most relevant. Henry said, "Now we start the process of getting the bank ready for the future." He then told us to go back to our offices and come up with four words which summed up what this bank was all about. This was the beginning of our culture study.

To promote change in the culture of U.S. Financial, Lester hired Ben Tutt from another company well known for its excellence in management to be vice president of human resources. Tutt's goal was to promote a cultural change that would focus on the values of the bank:

> We undertook an assessment of the current culture to determine if our vision of what we stand for and intend to achieve was sufficiently clear and well understood. We also analyzed the values which were driving our employees' daily behaviors to see if they were sufficiently linked to our heritage as well as appropriate to achieve the goals of the organization for the future.

26

With the enthusiastic backing of the CEO, Tutt and an outside consultant began the formal corporate culture study. The first phase involved an attitude survey of current employees as well as a detailed study of U.S. Financial's archival history to identify the original culture of the bank. The result was a profile contrasting the bank's early values—values that had led to success—with its current belief system. At its inception, the bank's founder had espoused the idea that the customer was "in the center of the universe"; innovation and risk taking were qualities to be rewarded in the early days, and U.S. Financial's policy emphasized friendliness, openness, and informality. Now, however, employees believed that risk taking and conflict were to be avoided, short-term profits were of overriding importance, and customer service was a low priority.

Tutt presented the findings to Lester and the nine-member management committee. Then, with Lester's backing, he involved the group in a series of meetings designed to articulate a new U.S. Financial culture. The group met two or three days per quarter. Over the next year, Lester's strong public support kept these top executives on board even when their interest began to flag. By 1984, the management committee had produced an elaborate statement of the bank's Vision, Values, and Strategy. Among those values were: "Place the customer first," "Respect, recognize, and reward," "Make the most of technology," and "Share our strategy, strengthen our team."

A number of executives understood that beneath the statements was a dramatic call for new managerial behavior at U.S. Financial. Said one, "We're trying to take conservative, comfortably situated, nonrisk managers and turn them into risk takers. We're trying, quite literally, to turn this place upside down."

In order to move that understanding of the need for radical change down beyond the management committee, Tutt and Lester initiated a process of "rolling out" the Vision, Values, and Strategy statement. At a meeting of the bank's top 250 executives, Lester clearly charged his top managers with the responsibility for spreading the word:

27

> The most difficult task is the one that will consume us as we go forward—to close the gap between vision and reality . . . . That's where the management task comes in . . . . I expect you to read the material [the statement] and understand it. To share it. And sell it. To have very candid discussions about these issues with your direct reports. And then to develop a workable approach to make these ideas a way of life in every aspect of our enterprise.

Thousands of copies of the statement were printed and distributed, as was a detailed handbook informing managers how to handle the process of cascading the values down through the organization. Convinced U.S. Financial's revitalization effort was on track, Tutt continued to seek ways of pushing the Vision, Values, and Strategy statement throughout the organization. The values were incorporated into performance evaluation forms and training programs and were widely communicated through videotapes.

As the rolling-out process continued, managers wondered openly what, if any real, impact it was having on the way managers functioned and U.S. Financial operated. One key issue, admitted the human resource manager assigned to oversee the culture program, was the failure of upper management in general, and members of the management committee in particular, to identify and eradicate barriers to coordinated action on the bank's major problems. Although the group spent a lot of time defining the culture (past, present, and future), they never examined how the bank might be organized and managed differently to achieve its strategic and performance goals and how they would modify the management process at the top. "That seemed to escape them," said the culture program coordinator.

Two years after the rolling-out process had begun, the entire culture study intervention ground to a halt, with an ambiguous record of accomplishment. "We spent a lot of time discussing what values we should have," admitted a human resource executive, "but not enough time discussing how to make them real in the organization. So a lot of people ended up viewing the Vision, Values, and Strategy stuff as being just a lot of words.''

PROGRAMMATIC CHANGE—A FLAWED RESPONSE

U.S. Financial's attempt at cultural revolution seems, at first glance, to have all the earmarks of a successful revitalization effort. Important competitive challenges—for example, the deregulation of the banking industry—created a need for changing the way the bank operated. Furthermore, the new CEO understood that need. Then, with his full support, abundant resources, and a key human resource executive in place to oversee the intervention, the process of change began at the top of the organization, something textbooks suggest is key to successful change. U.S. Financial also established sophisticated techniques both for pushing the desired change down through the organization and for measuring the effectiveness of the effort on an ongoing basis with employee surveys. All the necessary elements appeared to be in place, yet virtually nothing happened. What went wrong?

U.S. Financial's emphasis on values or culture did not take into account the organization as a total system.[1] Its culture program failed to focus on how work was being done, who was accountable, and how the efforts of different parts of the bank could be coordinated—elements that had to be reshaped to fit the new demands of the competitive environment. Only when employees are involved in aligning these interdependent elements can simultaneous change occur in coordination, commitment, and competence.

U.S. Financial's culture-change effort built no new technical or general management competencies. It may well have generated slightly higher levels of commitment on the part of employees who reported for the first time they were given information about the strategic directions of the organization. According to U.S. Financial's internal attitude surveys, however, those gains were eradicated by the bank's continued poor performance. More important, the culture program failed to stimulate new coordinated actions at lower levels to manage product/market segments more effectively. This might have helped U.S. Financial improve profitability and speed up the introduction of much-needed new products and technology. These changes would have improved performance and sustained, perhaps even increased, commitment. Changes in how U.S. Financial operated would also have exposed people to fresh experiences, broadening their perspectives and developing new skills.

U.S. Financial's programmatic approach to renewal, while ultimately unsuccessful, represented a pattern that we saw in the companies we studied and many others as well. In order to create rapid revitalization, corporate management mandated programmatic change. We now look at several of the most common programmatic efforts in use today. Each was heralded at the time of its implementation as the centerpiece of corporate renewal and was typically driven by top management. Each received generous allocations of money, time, and resources. And each intervention was ultimately dismissed by most line managers either as inconsequential—having little to do with what was really important in their business unit, plant, or branch—or as actually harmful to the organization.

Training Programs

Training programs proliferated in the companies we studied. Perhaps no company relied more heavily on training as an intervention designed to bring about organizational change than Continental Glass. With the help of academics, the company instituted an Advanced Management Program (AMP). It was designed to expose high-potential middle managers to ideas about business strategy, organizing and managing people, leadership, and interpersonal relations. To increase the chances that AMP would have an impact on the company and to enrich the learning experience, participants formed task teams to study a major corporate issue identified by top management. With guidance from the faculty they collected data, analyzed the problem, and delivered a report to top management at the conclusion.

The program was so well received that participants asked senior management to go through a similar experience, noting that change would not occur without their bosses' active involvement. Approximately 100 senior managers participated in a shortened version called the Senior Management Program (SMP). The mood in the company was one of excitement and ferment. Several divisions called on the AMP faculty to consult on strategy and organizational problems. Everyone, including the faculty, felt that the company was undergoing a cultural transformation. Five years after the initiation of AMP, many participants reported learning a significant amount about strategy, organization, and management. They acknowledged, however, that AMP and SMP had little impact on the company's culture. At about the same time, a top manager who had been through the training and wholeheartedly supported its aim, volunteered that "the program had absolutely no impact on the company." The CEO, Jim Taylor, who as executive vice president had called for change in the first place, agreed. In an interview he admitted that his vision of a new corporate culture had never been achieved.

To overcome the deficiencies of traditional educational programs that impart knowledge without necessarily changing actual behavior, several training efforts we encountered attempted to involve participants in examining their own actions and attitudes. If revitalization requires behavioral changes, why not focus education directly on them?

The most extensive such intervention involved the head of Fairweather's computer operation, Hugh Dorsey. The program, known as Lee's Point after the remote rural setting where it took place, brought Dorsey and his top 150 managers together in groups of 20 to 30 for a week-long workshop. Dorsey and his key staff went through the program first, and Dorsey appeared at all subsequent programs to talk about his vision. Participants moved through story-telling and role-playing exercises, examined feedback from subordinates about their management style, climbed a steep cliff to experience teamwork, and developed action plans detailing what would happen when they returned to work.

Among many participants, the program released enormous energy and positive commitment, much more than is generated in conventional education programs. Nevertheless, a number of trainees complained about the "brainwashing" nature of the experience. Dorsey was unapologetic, however. "What we're trying to do is to have everybody look at themselves," he noted, "and decide what it means to play on a team, what it means to work in such a fashion that you accomplish your objectives, what it means to feel like part of a whole."

The brainwashing charge, although perhaps somewhat overstated, does reveal a fundamental weakness in the Lee's Point process. Learning was imposed on managers in a setting far removed from their work and organizational lives. Therefore, instead of being seen as an essential tool for performing work and organizational duties more effectively, the session was viewed as something exotic, peripheral, and unconnected to the core requirements of their jobs. The fact that the program was personally threatening, as are all attitude and behavioral changes demanded by revitalization, probably reduced its participants' motivation to discover the program's relevance to the business. That sense of irrelevancy lies at the heart of the brainwashing charge. It also underlies descriptions such as "weird" and "crazy," which some of Dorsey's immediate subordinates applied to the Lee's Point experience. The coordinator of the effort acknowledged that Dorsey had never been able to translate the energies and learnings of the week-long sessions into enduring changes in participants' behavior once they returned to work.

These findings pose the same questions about the efficacy of powerful personal learning experiences as were raised in the 1960s about sensitivity training, a widely used program to develop interpersonally competent managers. Today we can ask those questions about a new generation of powerful personal learning programs, among them the outdoor survival programs that have become a fad in many companies undergoing renewal. Our finding that training programs, regardless of how personally powerful, do not change organizational behavior is reinforced by previous research that points to serious problems in the transfer of learning from management training to the job.[2] These programs simply do not affect enough elements in the system—roles and responsibilities at work, the boss, rewards, and structure, for example—to change organizational behavior.

Quality Circles

In an effort to stimulate employee concern for continuous improvement, many U.S. corporations have introduced a variety of quality programs. Two of our companies, Fairweather Corporation and Livingston Electronics, relied extensively on the creation of quality circles. The Livingston quality circle program grew out of numerous trips made by top executives and union officials to Japan, where they discovered the extraordinary involvement of Japanese workers in identifying and solving quality problems.

Livingston created a productivity center with the mission to introduce quality circles in the corporation. Training programs and internal consultants supported by top management pushed quality circles. Managers throughout the company were required to report on the number of quality circles they had introduced. Not surprisingly, quality circles began to proliferate, eventually numbering well over two thousand.

The reaction of managers in both companies was far from positive. One Fairweather manager reported the following:

> The first quality circle program was very political; everybody noticed who participated and who didn't. Any problems we had in implementing it had to be swept under the rug; all management wanted to know was how many teams had been formed and how much money they had saved.

33

Thus the *quantity* of circles implemented became more important than the *quality* of implementation. A business unit manager at Livingston told us that the program forced him to expend considerable energy introducing quality circles in his plants, whereas he thought customer relations was the most pressing competitive issue. The program drained energy away from the organization's most significant problem, thus reducing that manager's and his staff's commitment to quality circles. This left first-level supervisors without the support they needed to implement quality circles effectively. It left quality circles isolated from the main task of the organization. Research shows that when quality circles are embedded in an unsupportive environment, they typically fail.[3] Again, a programmatic intervention failed to consider the organization as a system. In this instance, the interdependence ignored by the corporate program was between lower levels where quality circles were mandated and upper-middle managers who ran the business unit and set its agenda.

New Appraisal and Pay Programs

Many companies attempt renewal by introducing a performance appraisal system and/or a pay-for-performance system. Several of our companies did just that. At Continental Glass, one of the first acts of a new human resource manager, hired to help improve organizational effectiveness, was to introduce a new appraisal system. Livingston Electronics did likewise. Employees we spoke with did not feel that either program had any impact on their behavior or on the overall competitiveness of their company.

Ben Tutt's efforts at U.S. Financial went further. In order to create a more aggressive, performance-oriented institution, Tutt introduced a pay-for-performance program that involved tightening the performance evaluation system, eliminating "guaranteed" bonuses for executives, and moving toward a forced-curve performance ranking of employees. "Top management is finally saying, 'What have you done for me lately?' " explained Tutt. The pay-for-performance program called for jointly developed performance plans, significant differentials between top and bottom performers, a suggested distribution curve, and a review of employee evaluations by upper management. The result of this change, Tutt insisted, would be increased employee satisfaction with rewards and increased motivation to strive for excellent performance.

New pay programs like the one at U.S. Financial, we found, typically fail to transform organizational culture. A lot of new words and phrases are uttered on their behalf: "pay-for-performance," "what have you done for me lately?," "performance distribution curve." Little new behavior actually results. At U.S. Financial, some managers complained about the rigidity of the system; others indicated performance differentiations were not taking place, at least not on a large scale. U.S. Financial's in-house employee attitude surveys indicated a widespread sense that clear performance goals were not being set nor was excellent performance being rewarded, and this view became stronger as the bank's performance continued to flag. If the objective was to increase employee motivation and satisfaction, the program was a failure. Managers who had lacked the competence to make and communicate individual performance evaluations did not suddenly develop it. Perhaps most important, the pay-for-performance program did little to influence patterns of coordination that might have actually improved business effectiveness.

Reorganizations

Companies often use changes in organizational structure to initiate or influence a revitalization process. Continental Glass & Container hoped to improve coordination between staff and line, increase accountability, and reduce cost by decentralizing its staff functions. At U.S. Financial, a matrix structure was created to manage product/market segments more effectively than when each of 100 retail branches made its own decisions about selling and servicing the bank's diverse product lines. In both instances the intention of the structural change was consistent with the revitalization objective of improving coordination. Yet these companies were the revitalization laggards in our study. Obviously, structural change by itself is not the answer to effective renewal.

The problems with structural change became apparent at General Products, where this was the only example of programmatic change. Convinced of the need for a worldwide marketing and advertising strategy, and concerned about the lack of coordination between domestic and international operations, General Products' CEO asked the corporate human resource department to design an organization that consolidated the international division's marketing and advertising departments into corporate marketing. When word of the planned consolidation got out, morale in the international division sank. John Merrow, international's president, had already made considerable progress in revitalizing his organization, pushing responsibility down to the regions and countries and clarifying global strategy. The corporate reorganization, Merrow said, undercut some initiatives that were effectively under way to develop a coordinated marketing strategy with domestic.

Even more troubling, according to Merrow, the new organization ignored subtle differences between product lines and countries. For some product lines, local advertising and pricing were needed. For others, regional and perhaps even worldwide pricing and advertising made sense. Merrow's managers feared the corporate marketing department, headed by someone with little international experience, would not recognize these subtleties. Merrow shared their fears when we talked with him a full year after the reorganization.

The frustrations of General Products executives after an imposed reorganization unleashed dysfunctional consequences were not unique. A disillusioned veteran of one too many corporate reorganizations at Livingston had the following sign in his office:

Every time we were beginning to form up into teams, we would be reorganized. I was to learn later in life that we tend to meet any new situation by reorganization . . . and a wonderful method it can be for creating the illusion of progress while producing confusion, inefficiency, and demoralization.

Petronius Arbitor, 210 BC

Why do efforts to revitalize through reorganization fail? The reorganization at General Products was intended to affect coordination. In contrast to other programs, the structural change focused on behavior critical to competitiveness—the relationships between domestic and international marketing. Unfortunately, reorganizations conceived at the top and designed by a corporate human resource function may miss subtleties known to lower-level managers closer to the business. Moreover, as illustrated by the General Products case, such efforts may actually frustrate initiatives under way. The managers in General Products' international division became passive and fatalistic and, we think, contributed little to mitigating the dysfunctional effects of the new structure.

Finally, changes in boxes and lines on a chart conceived at the top do not develop the skills and orientation needed to function in the new structure. Having had changes imposed on them from the top, employees have little motivation to adopt new attitudes or learn new skills. This is particularly true when the new structure is a nontraditional departure from the command-and-control model. This was the case at U.S. Financial, where managers told us they were experiencing difficulty learning how to function within the new matrix structure.

WHY PROGRAMS ARE "FALSE STARTS"

We label programmatic change a "false start." We do not say training, pay system changes, changes in structure, or new statements of corporate philosophy are worthless, nor do we contend that they should never be used. In fact, each of these interventions can play an important role in supporting an integrated change effort. They become problematic only when used in isolation as a "magic bullet" to create renewal.

To state it succinctly, programs cannot change coordination, commitment, and competence simultaneously. Without mutual reinforcement of these three interdependent targets of renewal, it is difficult to develop sustained change.

While top-down reorganizations attempt to change the pattern of coordination, they frequently fail because they are unable to instill the skill and motivation necessary to make the new structure work. Culture programs and new pay systems are usually intended to increase employee commitment and, to varying degrees and lengths of time, may achieve this. However, neither program changes patterns of coordination in ways relevant to the problems and needs of the business.

Nor do these programs develop the competence needed to carry out the behaviors they espouse. Managers do not become more skilled at confronting performance problems when a pay-for-performance system is installed. Employees do not become more skilled at teamwork when a new philosophy statement is issued. Thus, because they affect neither skill nor behavior, such programs have little impact on ultimate competitive performance.

Finally, training and education are targeted primarily at increasing competency levels. Occasionally they may increase commitment as well for short periods of time, as we saw in Fairweather Corporation's Lee's Point program. They do not, however, enable new patterns of coordinated behavior in either the corporation or the participants' business unit or plant. Consequently, the training is soon viewed as irrelevant, reducing any commitment the program may have aroused.

Even when behavior, motivation, and skill are affected simultaneously by a program such as quality circles, interdependencies among organizational levels may be ignored. Programs like quality circles are mandated from the top and aimed at shop-floor employees. Because they bypass the middle managers who run business units and plants, these managers are less likely to be committed to their support.

A final problem with almost all corporate programs is that they attempt to impose a uniform solution across a wide range of operating units. To decree that all managers "should" undergo this training program, change their culture, and use certain new forms and systems is dangerous. Such universal application ignores elements that create diversity among the operating units in any large corporation, including differences in markets, in key task demands, in work forces, and in unit histories. Applied universally across organizational boundaries, programs usually lack the specific relevancy needed to help managers in a given unit solve their real and immediate business problems.

WHY THE PROGRAMMATIC APPROACH?

Surprisingly, we have found that programmatic change, despite its inadequacy, is the method most commonly used by organizations in their attempts to bring about renewal. How do we explain this seeming paradox?

First, programs represent actions that can be put into place quickly. Top managers faced with a competitive crisis want to make changes immediately. Pressures for quarterly earnings coupled with impatience and task orientation drive management to search for a lever that will influence a vast bureaucracy. Programs offer a visible but simplistic response to the complex task of improving corporate effectiveness. Their appeal is that of the quick fix.

Second, managers like to emulate well-known success stories. The lessons of "excellent" companies or of Japanese competitors are often oversimplified in the business press and by consultants. Quality circles, educational programs teaching the latest "truth," cultural programs to instill values of successful companies, pay programs to motivate, and new organizational structures are the latest corporate fads. An executive at Continental Glass explained to us that his company started the AMP training program because "It seemed to be a kind of trendy thing thing to do. We were one of the *Fortune* 500 companies and we are all into this buzzword kind of stuff, and so let's get with a program here. We don't want to be left behind!"

Third, programs are tangible and therefore easy to measure, an attribute that makes it possible to hold managers accountable for directing change. Both top management and the human resource function have an interest in that approach. Earlier we noted how Fairweather and Livingston executives took great pride in pointing to the number of quality circles generated on their watch. Equally measurable is the number of people going through a training program or the existence and administrative implementation of a new appraisal system or pay system. Human resource executives have a particularly strong interest in tangible programs and measurable results: such statistics enable them to cite clear accomplishments in persuading top management of their effectiveness.

We do not maintain that the motivation of top management or human resource executives in these and other cases was cynical. They believed the programs they promoted could benefit their organization in a significant way. Their actions, however, indicated that they thought measuring compliance was equivalent to measuring change.

A fourth reason why programs are so often used to manage change has to do, at least in some cases, with top management's proclivity against being involved directly in the change process. Top-management time is a scarce resource. Programmatic change helps by delegating the implementation of change to the human resource function.[4]

Not all top managers distanced themselves from the change process. Lester and his top management team at U.S. Financial worked actively in the culture program. Hugh Dorsey at Fairweather chose to go through the program with his staff before anyone else. However, top management in many other firms was less involved.

40

INOCULATING AGAINST RENEWAL

Unfortunately, the costs of continued reliance on pro-grammatic change efforts go far beyond the inefficient use of management resources. Each unsuccessful and discarded program makes it that much harder for any future effort to effect organizational renewal.

When one failed program leads to another, managers begin to discount and ignore all programs. Because line managers have no ownership of these efforts, their initial commitment is often low and diminishes further with each successive program. Such declining support has deeper implications, however; it indicates a growing cynicism about the corporation's commitment to renewal. Thus over-reliance on programmatic change can seriously damage a re-vitalization effort.

Programmatic change demands a significant commitment of time and resources. Consider, for instance, U.S. Finan-cial's culture change. When the programmatic effort led to little real change, line managers naturally questioned its value. One summed up the skepticism this way: "So often these programs were seen as gimmickry by the working people and as magic by [upper] managers. In most cases, they were implemented through management edicts and di-rectives. I am just not interested in another short-lived program."

In order to live with the demands of programmatic change placed on them from above, line managers commonly adopt one of three familiar postures:

- They tolerate the efforts, carry out procedures to the best of their ability, but fail to provide any lasting support for program continuation.
- They complete the minimal requirements expected of them; that is, they fill out the proper forms or attend the required conference but disdain and criticize all aspects of the effort.

41

- They avoid the effort entirely, if they can get away with it.

When efforts fail to generate the anticipated change, top managers implicitly assume they have tried the wrong program. When one "people program" simply faded from view at Fairweather, Hugh Dorsey tried another. This conclusion leads to a succession of flawed programs leaving a company mired in frustration. At some point, top management decides it simply cannot change the way people behave in their organization. This flawed conclusion leads to increased emphasis on other strategic responses to the competitive challenge such as divestiture or massive personnel reductions, measures that may improve financial performance in the short run but do not necessarily revitalize the organization for long-term effectiveness. When alienation increases, new "people programs" are instituted. The company can easily get caught in a "pendulum swing" between concern for people and concern about costs.[5]

BEYOND PROGRAMMATIC CHANGE

Corporate revitalization requires simultaneous change in coordination, commitment, and competence in a way that is geared to the particular needs of an individual business unit. How did our change leader, General Products, manage such a feat?

Instead of a companywide program, General Products created systemic change in a series of targeted smaller units such as individual manufacturing plants and divisions. In fact, it led all companies in the number of successful business units and plants that were undergoing change (see Table 2-2). Fairweather Corporation, Scranton Steel, and Livingston Electronics, the next tier of relatively successful revitalization efforts, did use programs. That reliance on programmatic

Table 2-2: The Relationship between Extent of Revitalization, Number of Units Undergoing Revitalization, and Use of Programs

	General Products	Fair-weather	Livingston Electronics	Scranton Steel	Continental Glass	U.S. Financial
Revitaliza-tion Rank	1	2	3	4	5	6
Units under-going re-vitalization	Many	Many	Several	Several	Few	None
Use of pro-grams	Minor	◄——— Considerable ———►			Central	Central

change was offset, however, by other initiatives at the plant and business-unit levels. Fairweather, in particular, instituted a number of visible and successful unit-level revitalization efforts. At the lower end of the scale, Continental Glass had a few isolated units attempting to revitalize, but one of these was a well-known failure. U.S. Financial, at the bottom, had no unit-level revitalization efforts.

It became increasingly apparent to us that in order to understand successful revitalization, we needed to turn our attention to unit-level interventions.

NOTES

1. The concept of organizations as social systems has a long history in organizational theory. See D. Katz and R.L. Kahn, *The Social Psychology of Organizations* (New York: Wiley, 1978); J.P. Kotter, *Organization Dynamics: Diagnosis and Intervention* (Reading, MA: Addison-Wesley, 1978); M. Beer, *Organization Change and Development: A Systems View* (Glencove, IL: Goodyear, 1980); R.H. Waterman, T.J. Peters, and J.R. Phillips, "Structure Is Not Organization," *Business Horizons* 23 (June 1980), pp. 14–26.
2. Substantial literature exists on the limitation of training in changing managerial behavior on the job. See E.A. Fleishman, E.F. Harris, and H.E. Burtt, *Leadership and Supervision in Industry: An Evaluation of a Supervisory Training Program* (Columbus, OH: Ohio State University Bureau of Educational

Research, 1955); R.J. House, "T-Group Education and Leadership Effectiveness: A Review of the Empiric Literature and A Critical Evaluation," *Personnel Psychology* 20 (Spring 1967), pp. 1–32; M. Beer, "The Technology of Organization Development," in M.D. Dunnette, ed., *Handbook of Industrial and Organizational Psychology* (New York: Wiley, 1976), pp. 937–993.
3. Our observations about the limitations of quality circles are consistent with other research. See, for instance, E.E. Lawler and S.A. Mohrman, "Quality Circles: After the Honeymoon," *Organizational Dynamics* 15 (Spring 1987), pp. 42–54; W.J. Abernathy, K.B. Clark, and A.M. Kantrow, *Industrial Renaissance: Producing a Competitive Future for America* (New York: Basic Books, 1983), pp. 85–86; R.H. Hayes, "Why Japanese Factories Work," *Harvard Business Review* 59 (July–August 1981), pp. 57–66.
4. Other observers of organizational change have noted that top management's tendency to delegate responsibility for change to lower levels impedes progress. See L.E. Greiner, "Patterns of Organizational Change," *Harvard Business Review* (May–June 1967), pp. 119–128; M. Beer and J.W. Driscoll, "Strategies for Change," in J.R. Hackman, and J.L. Suttle, eds., *Improving Life at Work* (Santa Monica, CA: Goodyear, 1977), pp. 364–453.
5. The concept of a pendulum swing in concern for production and concern for cost was originally formulated by Robert Blake and Jane Mouton. See R.R. Blake and J.S. Mouton, *The New Managerial Grid* (Houston, TX: Gulf Publishing, 1964).

3

Task Alignment

By now it should be clear how difficult it is to revitalize a corporation. However, we have also learned that fundamental change can be achieved. In the same companies where wave after wave of programs rolled across the corporate landscape with little positive impact, more successful transformations were under way at the plant and divisional levels.[1] In virtually all cases of successful revitalization, management focused on the business's central competitive challenges as the means for motivating change and developing new behaviors and skills. We call this successful approach *task alignment*.

By task alignment we mean a redefinition of work roles, responsibilities, and relationships within a unit, in a way that will enhance the coordination required to accomplish the tasks critical to the success of the business. A process of realigning how people and departments should work together

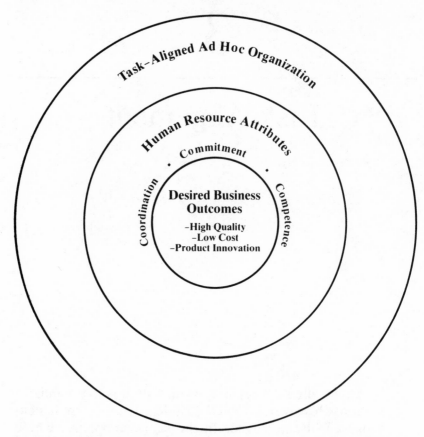

**Figure 3-1: The Target of Revitalization: The Role of Task Alignment
in Revitalization**

might occur in Plant A around reducing excessive inventory
levels, in Division B around increasing the speed of new product development, and in the top management team for Corporation C around defining strategy, allocating resources, and
developing policies for the corporation as a whole.

By changing how people work together around core
tasks without changing the organizational chart, a commonly
understood and legitimated ad hoc team organization
emerges. As Figure 3-1 depicts, this new organization resulting from the task alignment process (outer ring) changes the

extent and manner of coordination, commitment, and competence.[2] These changes make it possible in turn for the organization to achieve the target of revitalization, the levels of quality, cost, and product innovation required to compete.

TWO CASES OF TASK ALIGNMENT

Because it focuses on the most important problem facing a business, task alignment occurs within units small enough for a group of individuals to have responsibility for a common goal, not within a large and diverse corporation as a whole. Two cases serve as illustrations of task alignment.

Continental Glass & Container's Crawfordsville Plant

When Richard Vanaria arrived at Continental Glass & Container's Crawfordsville plant, he found an operation dedicated far more to reducing cost than to producing a quality product. Vanaria replaced a more experienced manager who had been quite effective over the past decade in pushing results to the bottom line. According to Vanaria, the division expected the plant to "get the bottom line as high as you can. . . . Quality was never a very high issue. It was always productivity."

The marketplace, however, had changed. International competitors were able to produce consumer glassware at lower cost and higher quality than Continental. Vanaria understood only too well that meeting the demands of radically improved quality and low cost would require not just higher standards but fundamental redefinition of plant operations and management. The culture stood in the way.

Crawfordsville had been characterized by the centralization of information and decision-making responsibilities. Almost all decisions came from the plant manager, and little competitive information filtered down to lower levels. There was little incentive for employees in different parts of the

47

plant to work collaboratively. According to Vanaria, "Everyone spent all their energy fighting among themselves." The lack of coordination plagued the plant manager's staff as well as the employees on the shop floor. Particularly strong tensions existed between those who molded the molten glass on "the hot end" of the shop floor and those on "the cold end" who inspected for quality once it cooled.

Vanaria began his quality improvement effort with the creation of a Quality Committee chaired by the manager who had ultimate responsibility for the cold end. Members included heads of staff departments having direct effects on product quality and the supervisors for both the hot and the cold ends. Through discussion with Continental's sales force, the Quality Committee first determined the 20 quality problems that most affected the marketability of the plant's products; then it concentrated on resolving the top three.

At the same time, Vanaria and his staff took a number of other initiatives:

- A survey was made of employee attitudes to pinpoint internal impediments to quality. Not surprisingly, the results focused on poor interdepartmental coordination and cooperation.
- Examples of competitors' glassware were placed in locations throughout the plant to make workers more aware of the economic challenges facing the plant. "What we find," noted a committee member, "is that once we start emphasizing quality and show them [hourly operators] competitive ware, they kind of get defensive about it. That is when we start finding out where the problems are."
- Committee members met periodically with hourly operators to keep the operators informed of the committee's work and elicit suggestions on how to improve quality.

The Quality Committee's efforts showed results that speak for themselves. The number of products held for quality defects in 1984 was 14 percent lower than in 1983. Quality improvements were not made at a sacrifice to production: job efficiencies were 5 percent better in 1984 than in 1983, and reinspection costs dropped $57,000. Overall, it was estimated that the improvements would result in a savings of approximately $1.25 million annually.

The quality improvement effort also led to major changes in the organization and management of plant employees. The manager for the hot end reported the following:

> The Quality Committee has helped to improve relations more than anything else we have done. We feel like we are working together on this problem. It is not like it was in the past where they set the [quality] limits without us [in the hot end] being involved, and it was up to us to sink or swim. We feel like we are committed along with them, which is what we wanted to be anyhow. . . . We want to be able to say we took part in this decision to improve quality, we agree with it, and we are going to do it, and we get some of the credit for it too.

Perhaps the most important change in the plant, evident from the preceding quote, was how individuals on the Quality Committee began to see their roles, responsibilities, and relationships.

- Instead of the head of Quality Control feeling isolated and alone in the role, all members of the Quality Committee began to take on that role. They were extensions of the plant manager, worrying about the same things that worried him and taking the initiative on quality problems as needed.
- Previously, committee members felt responsible for achieving specific departmental production goals, such as tons melted per day or number of items produced. Now they were also responsible for making and delivering on time a quality product at a given cost, and they learned to think about problems in these terms.

49

- Once almost totally isolated from one another, supervisors on the hot and cold ends were virtually forced into mutual relationships. The same could be said of the managers of production, quality, and engineering.

These changes permeated lower levels as members of the Quality Committee began to exhibit more positive attitudes about other departments, the plant, and the importance of quality. The redefined roles, responsibilities, and relationships resulted in improved coordination and communication among the different parts of the plant. Rather than continuing to blame one another, workers at the hot and cold ends began working together to solve lingering quality problems. The Crawfordsville revitalization effort had produced exactly the behaviors, motivation, and skills needed to compete more effectively.

General Products' Technical Center

Task alignment was not limited to manufacturing facilities like Crawfordsville. Top management at General Products' white-collar, professional-level Technical Center also achieved a successful renewal. Success did not come easily, however. Several false starts occurred as Technical Center management at first relied on programmatic interventions.

Convinced that the corporation's future competitive edge lay in a continuous stream of extensions to its major product line, top management of General Products built a new technical facility and urged its management to undertake an "employee involvement" initiative modeled on successful revitalization initiatives in manufacturing. Presentations to Technical Center management were made by William Bryant, executive vice president of manufacturing, and plant managers who had led successful revitalization efforts. These encounters stimulated a search for ways to involve Technical Center employees.

With the help of an external consultant who was an expert in career development, a survey of employee satisfaction with the center's development and promotion policies was taken. Committees were formed to discuss results and make recommendations. Another committee was set up to make recommendations about what art work should be displayed in the center's atrium. Operating under the belief that corporate management supported greater employee involvement, the center's top management met many times to develop a consensus on what employee involvement meant. That consensus turned out to be elusive. Managers argued about philosophy, values, and the applicability of employee-involvement efforts to professionals who, some insisted, were already "involved" in their jobs. The group's capacity to achieve consensus and move renewal forward was further hampered by the center's director, who was ambivalent about how directive he should be in moving the organization toward participation.

Two years later, many managers expressed frustration with the meager results their efforts had yielded. Managers in the Technical Center and top corporate management believed that the revitalization effort was in trouble.

What began to turn around the Technical Center's effort was the need to introduce a CAD/CAM system as an aid in product and process formulation. With the help of yet another consultant, a cross-discipline task force of lower-level managers identified poor cross-functional coordination as a central organizational problem that would block effective utilization of the new technology. Enthusiastic about that discovery, the task force broadened its focus and looked at the general inability of the center to meet customer needs for timely delivery of effective product prototypes. The task force recommended that a project team be formed to integrate decision making among functions and ensure timely delivery of a prototype to the company's major customer. Management agreed, and a team was formed.

Quite independently, another consultant confronted management with his own diagnosis of the Technical Center's effectiveness. The core task of the center—the development of product extensions—was impeded by strict functional lines and a lack of teamwork throughout the organization. A project team organization was a possible design solution the consultant discussed with the center's managers. They in turn undertook to verify the diagnosis and recommendations by commissioning a lower-level management task force to gather more data and make its own recommendations. The result was the implementation of several product development teams modeled after the first team, which by now was operating successfully.

According to the human resource manager and top management, the revitalization effort was finally moving forward. Engineers and scientists who had previously seen themselves as functional experts began to view themselves as members of teams with a clear and important mission measurable in business terms, not just technical terms. As teams began to produce results, relationships among functions improved, engineers and production specialists began to feel empowered, and demands for skills in team management were met with a training program. Of course, new problems arose as well. The center's management had to grapple with its own ineffectiveness as a team and with the director's management style.

MAKING TASK ALIGNMENT WORK

The quality improvement effort at Continental's Crawfordsville plant, like the product development teams at General Products' Technical Center, illustrates a very different approach to revitalization from the programmatic efforts that organizations more typically engage in. Dick Vanaria did not make a speech to his management staff about the importance of cooperation, participation, and teamwork. He did not call for an in-depth study of Crawfordsville's culture, nor did he send employees off to a training program.

Instead, Vanaria engaged his management group around an issue—improving product quality—identified as critical to the economic viability of the plant. Service on the various task forces demanded changes in the roles, responsibilities, and relationships of the plant's top management team and of those involved in similar cross-functional teams below them.

The alterations in the interaction patterns among managers enabled by an ad hoc structure—the Quality Committee—led to further changes in the organization and management of the plant. These changes included increased employee participation, collaboration, and information sharing—characteristics needed for a more adaptive organization. Thus the plant introduced behaviors, attitudes, and skills required for employee participation and involvement without using those terms and without using programs.

To achieve task alignment within a unit, a manager must lead a process (to be described in Chapter 4) that will decide who needs to work together on what tasks, in what ways, to solve the most important business problem facing the organization. Fundamental changes in roles, responsibilities, and relationships made at Crawfordsville and the Technical Center can be made without first modifying the formal organizational structure. That is what distinguishes task alignment from programmatic reorganization. Task alignment focuses on developing ad hoc structures such as project teams, task forces, or committees. By avoiding top-down change in formal reporting relationships before new interaction patterns are established, resistance is reduced and the opportunity for people to develop necessary skills and motivation is enhanced. Changes in formal structure may eventually follow such changes in ad hoc structure as a way of firming up and institutionalizing renewal, but by then commitment to the new approach and the competence needed to enact the required behaviors are firmly in place.

Structural overlays are not a new idea. Their utility in developing needed coordination in businesses that operate in uncertain and complex environments has been well documented.[3] Our findings provide new insights, however, about how to create the patterns of behavior, motivation, and skill required for such structures to work.

These insights are supported by statistical analysis of the

Table 3-1: Correlation of Researcher Ratings of Unit Change Strategies and Revitalization Success

Change Strategy Employed	Correlation of Strategies with Revitalization Success[a]	Ratio of Leaders to Laggards Using Strategy[b]
Alignment with business issue	.47**	100%:56%
Roles, relations, and responsibilities redefined	.45*	100%:66%

a. N = 26 units; Statistically significant at *p<.05; **p<.01; See Appendix II for details.
b. The 9 units with the highest scores on the extent of revitalization measure are compared to the nine units with the lowest scores.

revitalization strategies employed in the 26 cases of unit change. Table 3-1 shows that those units that had changed the most were more likely than lagging units to have

- Established a clear and broadly understood link between business problems and the need for change (alignment with business issues).
- Changed organizational roles, responsibilities, and relationships by means of ad hoc organizational mechanisms aimed at improving effectiveness and financial performance.

WHY TASK ALIGNMENT WORKS

The objective of revitalization is the development of the organization's human resources. In contrast to the command-and-control organization, a less hierarchical task-driven organization requires a larger number of employees at all levels who have the commitment and competence to initiate and coordinate. Why is task alignment so effective in developing these human assets, particularly when compared to traditional human resource programs? An analysis of General Products' Technical Center and Continental Glass's Crawfordsville cases—two different organizations with radically different tasks—revealed some common elements.

Motivation to Change

Revitalization is a painful process. It demands changes in traditional behaviors and attitudes that employees often find personally threatening.[4] The task-aligned organization challenges the power and status that the hierarchy may have bestowed on employees; change challenges their subjective sense of competence as well as their career paths. Consequently, revitalization occurs only when there is a consensus among key organizational members that its benefits outweigh its obvious risks. We have found that it is easiest to create this consensus when there is a "clear and present danger": a tangible and immediate problem that must be confronted if the organization is to remain economically competitive.[5]

Confronted with such a business problem, human resource programs are at a disadvantage. At best, programs provide elusive and long-term solutions, but their costs are real and immediate. When employees are sent to a management training program, the tangible costs of that programmatic intervention appear on this month's income statement. The intangible benefits in upgraded employee skills will accrue to the organization gradually over a period of years, if they accrue at all.

Sometimes the advocates of these programs sell them as long-term investments in human capital. This approach still implicitly asks managers to make trade-offs of time, energy, and capital between the programs and the more immediate demands of running the business. When the demands intensify, the programs are often relegated to a secondary status.

However they are sold, investments in human resource programs are simply not as compelling to managers as investments in physical assets. While the payback period for a new machine may be a few years, at least one can see both the machine and its outputs. It is often more difficult to see tangible results of a human resource development activity.

Furthermore, direct links can often be drawn between investments in physical assets and the quality of the product produced. The consequences of investments in human capital are usually more indirect. At most, the programs improve employee skills and motivation, which in turn may improve the quality of the product or the service.

Finally, line managers tend to be more experienced in accurately assessing the returns on investment in physical assets than they are in assessing returns on investment in human assets.

Task alignment works by aligning the organization's ad hoc structure with its critical business problems. It is not only a long-term human resource development strategy, but also an immediate response to a tangible business problem. Task forces were not introduced into the Crawfordsville plant and the Technical Center primarily as a means of increasing participation and collaboration. Rather, they were intended and understood as a way of addressing problems in product quality and new product development.

The payoffs of task alignment interventions are not nearly as elusive or as long term as those of human resource programs. Has the quality of the Crawfordsville plant's product improved or not? Are new products being developed more quickly and effectively by the Technical Center? These are questions all managers can understand, appreciate, and answer. Moreover, as changes are enacted in response to the most critical business problem, the return on the organization's investment can begin relatively quickly.

The task alignment approach possesses an important advantage over human resource programs. There is a greater agreement in most organizations on the need to confront core business issues than on the need to manage people differently. Consider the difficulty managers at the Technical Center had coming to agreement on the meaning and need for an employee involvement program. After two years of debating the question they were no closer to consensus, and the revitalization effort at the Technical Center was stalled. The recognition that new product development could be enhanced and accelerated through an ad hoc team structure made coming to a consensus easier, despite the fact that teams were likely to involve employees as much or more than previously debated programs or philosophy.

While the managers on Dick Vanaria's staff at Crawfordsville did not all agree that the plant would benefit from a move to participative management, they did see the need to improve product quality. Consequently, Vanaria minimized the resistance to his efforts by initially focusing on the latter rather than the former issue. The Quality Committee in Crawfordsville gave participants direct and immediate evidence that alternative approaches to managing interdependencies would have a positive effect on the plant's quality problem. It was a short step from that consensus to the recognition that the new approach and patterns of behavior could positively influence other performance problems as well.

Task alignment, then, begins with a generally shared agreement on the need of the unit to confront core business issues. In addition, the support for change created through task alignment is likely to build. It will be a support based not on abstract theories or the popularity of a new management fad, but on organizational members' personal experience. When managers hear words such as "participation" for the first time in training programs, top management speeches, or corporate mission statements, they can assign any meaning they want to the concept. In contrast, managers who are involved in a task alignment process—like the managers at Crawfordsville and, after some false starts, those in the Technical Center—are given an actual example of what participation could mean to them. When they talk about participative management in the future, they are not likely to mouth platitudes. They will refer to a specific set of behaviors. Because they experienced the new behaviors and the benefits that flowed from them, they will understand the value of employee participation as a means of accomplishing the organization's task more effectively, not as a style of management that has suddenly become fashionable.

However, not all changes that improve a business's competitiveness create widespread motivation to change. Cost reduction efforts may be good for the business, but they put employees' jobs at risk. In fact, our survey data show that units in which employees perceived cost reduction or improvement of business results as the primary purpose for organizational change were not necessarily those that changed the most as perceived by the same employees. Support for, and actual success in, revitalization were more apt to occur in units where employees perceived that change would result in real improvements in their own well-being (see Appendix II for more detail).

Thus, for revitalization to succeed, employees need to believe that organizational change will improve not only the business, but also their own well-being. The Crawfordsville and Technical Center cases illustrate that task alignment is uniquely suited to achieving these dual objectives. Participation in the Quality Committee at Crawfordsville left people feeling more effective, challenged, and empowered. The same sense of competence and efficacy was felt by members of the product development teams in the Technical Center. Task alignment is a change strategy that integrates concern for people and concern for task, something that previous research has shown improves both organizational effectiveness and employee well-being.[6]

Developing Human Assets

Task alignment is not only a response to immediate business problems; it is also a highly effective human resource development strategy. Immediate problems are addressed in a manner that leads to long-term development of the organization's human assets. The Crawfordsville Quality Committee improved product quality as well as enhanced the three human resource attributes necessary for competitiveness: coordination, commitment, competence.

> *Coordination.* Communication channels were improved between the manufacturing and sales organizations, among functional areas in the plant, and between management and hourly employees. The top management team felt there were fewer "turf issues" in the plant, as well as fewer individual attempts to

protect oneself. In short, there was much more team-work.

Commitment. By participating in the committee's problem-solving efforts (overcoming long-standing, bitter feuds among functions or working directly with the sales force to rectify customer service problems), members of the committee developed a real commitment to the implementation of solutions. Members of Vanaria's staff told us they were working harder and having more fun since the formation of the Quality Committee.

Competence. Through participation in clarifying the nature of the organization's core tasks and determining how best to accomplish them, all key stakeholders learned by doing. For example, members of the committee learned much about business, team management, and their new roles and responsibilities; they also developed skills in problem solving and management.

These are precisely the human outcomes hoped for from more traditional human resource development programs. They should allow the Crawfordsville organization to engage in a process of continual improvement in quality, cost, and product innovation.

Why do changes in ad hoc organization that occur in the task alignment process lead to the development of human resource and organizational capabilities? The Quality Committee at Crawfordsville and the product teams at General Products' Technical Center altered three significant elements of the context in which people did their jobs:

1. The individuals with whom they routinely interacted
2. The information to which they became exposed
3. The actions for which they were socially and intrinsically rewarded

These changes in interaction, information, and psychological reward create an ongoing set of demands for new behavior. In both cases, teams were held accountable for performance: improved quality at Crawfordsville and more rapid and effective product development at the Technical Center. Team members could not achieve their objectives without learning to interact with one another in new ways. These modified interactions in turn developed trust and understanding of problems not possible through such means as new compensation systems or training programs.

Task alignment capitalizes on the power of social context to change individual behavior. It makes simultaneous changes in a network of interrelated roles, thus announcing new expectations to all role occupants at once. Concurrent changes in roles reduce the probability of individuals encountering resistance from those who are not changing. Even if some individuals resist change, that resistance is less likely to dampen efforts to fill new roles. Support from the top for the changes in ad hoc structure gives employees confidence that resisters will be dealt with in time. In Crawfordsville, each member of the Quality Committee knew that he or she was accountable for achieving quality objectives, not just to one another, but also to Dick Vanaria.

PROGRAMMATIC CHANGE AND TASK ALIGNMENT CONTRASTED

So far, we have dealt with many of the specifics of how task alignment works and why it is more effective than traditional human resource programs as a strategy for renewal. Now we want to take a broader view of these two approaches. Programmatic changes differ from the task alignment approach not in purpose but in the assumptions made about how to change the behaviors of large numbers of interdependent people in an organization.

Most programmatic changes start with the assumption that the problem in changing organizations is one of changing individual knowledge, attitudes, and, in a few instances, behavior. Such changes, it is assumed, will ultimately lead to large-scale organizational transformation.

60

Table 3-2: Contrasting Assumptions About Renewal

Programmatic Change Assumptions	*Task Alignment Assumptions*
Problems in behavior are a function of individual knowledge, attitudes, and beliefs.	Individual knowledge, attitudes, and beliefs are shaped by recurring patterns of behavioral interactions.
(consequently)	(consequently)
The primary target of renewal should be the content of attitudes and ideas; actual behavior should be secondary.	The primary target of renewal should be behavior; attitudes and ideas should be secondary.
Behavior can be isolated and changed individually.	Problems in behavior come from a circular pattern, but the effects of the organizational system on the individual are greater than those of the individual on the system.
(consequently)	(consequently)
The target for renewal should be at the individual level.	The target for renewal should be at the level of roles, responsibilities, and relationships.

Our research into effective renewal, however, has led us to a different construction regarding how patterns of organizational behavior are set and changed. We concluded that after behavior is changed, then attitudes and knowledge will change. Since behavior is powerfully shaped by the roles individuals play in the larger organization, the means for changing the behavior of many interdependent people is to change the network of interdependent roles.

Consider the role changes imposed on members of the Crawfordsville Quality Committee. Individuals were expected to achieve a quality-improvement objective through cooperative problem solving. That effort required many new behaviors, which in turn demanded new attitudes and knowledge. Table 3-2 further elaborates our contrasting assumptions about renewal.

Our findings about the importance of role changes in inducing behavioral changes are supported by considerable evidence from other research, which has shown that changing roles can powerfully modify individuals' behavior and in turn their attitudes. For example, union leaders who were promoted to supervisory positions adopted the attitudes of management in a relatively short period of time.[7] Similarly, experience with work-system innovations has shown that people are capable of living up to radically redesigned roles. They make attitude adaptations and have been found to possess competencies far exceeding management's assumptions.[8]

TASK ALIGNMENT COMPARED WITH OTHER CHANGE STRATEGIES

To help the reader understand task alignment as an organizational revitalization strategy, we have contrasted it with human resource programs. Both approaches, however, share one assumption: revitalizing the human side of the enterprise is the way for organizations to respond to the new competitive environment.

Examination of other approaches to improving corporate performance should clarify why task alignment is such a powerful strategy for regaining competitiveness.

All the companies we studied attempted to become more competitive by rationalizing physical and human assets. They closed and consolidated manufacturing and administrative facilities and reduced their work force at every level of the corporation. These were clearly necessary actions to meet the short-term demands of capital markets for financial performance. However, the asset rationalization approach ignores the development of coordination, commitment, and competence that we have argued is needed for corporations to become adaptive and capable of competing in the long run. Change strategies such as portfolio management and strategic planning, while important elements in an effort to develop a com-

Table 3-3: A Comparison of Three Change Approaches

		Long-Term Development of Human Attributes	
		Ignored	Incorporated
Short-term business demands	Ignored		Programmatic change
	Incorporated	Rationalization of assets	Task alignment

petitive corporation, also aim primarily at meeting business demands. At Continental Glass we were frequently told that advocates of asset rationalization said, "Let me straighten out the business first, then we can worry about the people."

If asset rationalization ignores long-term developmental needs in favor of short-term business gains, then human resource programs move to the other extreme. "If we do a good job of developing people," human resource people maintain, "then the business will take care of itself." The long-term development of employee skills, in other words, becomes the raison d'être of these programs. Unfortunately, most human resource programs do nothing to address short-term business demands. As a consequence, they are easily dismissed by line managers as inconsequential, peripheral, and a distraction from the "real" order of business.

If asset rationalization and programmatic change represent the extremes vis-à-vis the incorporation of short-term business demands and long-term human resource development concerns, then task alignment can be said to reside in a "sweet spot" between the two (see Table 3-3). It is the approach that reconciles the short and the long term; that is, short-term business demands are dealt with in a way that develops human resource capabilities essential to compete in the long run.

IMPLEMENTING TASK ALIGNMENT

While task alignment may combine the best of both worlds, it is also difficult to implement. Without the requisite skill in implementation, even task alignment interventions can degenerate into the programmatic reorganizations we described in Chapter 2. When that happens, the approach will have little positive impact on organizational effectiveness. We emphasize this point because so many companies rely on reorganization as the means for achieving organizational alignment with key tasks or strategies. Consider how William Bryant, executive vice president of worldwide manufacturing at General Products and our corporate revitalization leader, described the traditional approach to realignment practiced in the company's sales department:

> Historically in General Products, there has been a reorganization of the sales department about every six months. Every time they [the sales department] are in trouble, they reorganize. The solution is always a reorganization whatever the hell the problem is. And the reorganizations are never thought out. They are, "God damn, that didn't work. Let's try a new [organization]."

At first glance, reorganization may seem to share many of the attributes of task alignment. Structural change does, after all, modify the organizational context in a way that simultaneously affects the responsibilities of many interdependent people. While new structure can be said to specify new responsibilities, it fails to specify exactly how people are supposed to behave within the structure, the roles they are expected to play, and the relationships they are expected to develop. Employees often flounder in a new structural context, returning to old, ineffective patterns of behavior. Changing the skeleton of formal organizations simply does not shape adequately the fine-grained details of informal interactions and information exchange that are necessary to support and reinforce an effective pattern of new behaviors.

To obtain the benefits of task alignment and avoid the pitfalls of programmatic reorganization, it is crucial that the general manager involve organizational members in the process of realigning the organization with the new competitive realities. It is to this process of implementation that we now turn.

NOTES

1. The 26 units on which our conclusions in this chapter are based were older existing organizations that faced the problem of changing an entrenched pre-existing culture. We visited eight other units that had incorporated innovative management practices from the beginning. Much has been written about the development of such innovative "greenfield" plants. See, for instance, E.E. Lawler, "The New Plant Revolution," *Organizational Dynamics* (Winter 1978), pp. 3–12; R.E. Walton, "Establishing and Maintaining High-Commitment Work Systems," in J.R. Kimberly and R.H. Miles, eds., *The Organizational Life Cycle: Issues in the Creation, Transformation and Decline of Organization* (San Francisco: Jossey-Bass, 1980).
2. In Figure 1-1, the outer ring of the target represented the overall organizational design. Here we focus on the specific aspect of that design—roles, responsibilities, and relationships—that is affected by task alignment.
3. See T. Burns and G.M. Stalker, *The Management of Innovation* (London: Tavistock Publications, 1961); P.R. Lawrence and J.W. Lorsch, *Organization and Environment: Managing Differentiation and Integration* (Boston: Harvard Business School, 1967); D. Zand, "Collateral Organizations: A New Change Strategy," *Journal of Applied Behavioral Science* 10 (1974), pp. 63–89; W.G. Bennis and P. Slater, *The Temporary Society* (New York: Harper & Row, 1968); A. Toffler, *Future Shock* (New York: Random House, 1970).
4. See B.M. Staw, "The Escalation of Commitment to a Course of Action," *Academy of Management Review* 6 (1981), pp. 577–587.
5. Robert Schaffer has found that commitment to fundamental organizational change is best motivated when managers successfully solve short-term problems using innovative approaches to organizing and managing people. See R. Schaffer, *The Breakthrough Strategy* (Cambridge, MA: Ballinger, 1988).
6. See B. Bass, *Stogdill's Handbook of Leadership: A Survey of Theory and Research* (New York: Free Press, 1981); R.R. Blake and J.S. Mouton, *The New Managerial Grid* (Houston, TX: Gulf Publishing, 1978); R.M. Stogdill, *Individual Behavior and Group Achievement: A Theory, the Experimental Evidence* (New York: Oxford University Press, 1959).
7. For a general discussion of how roles come to be perceived by their occupants and their pervasive influence on the behavior, see G. Graen, "Role-Making Process Within Complex Organizations," in M. Dunnette, ed., *Handbook of Industrial and Organizational Psychology* (Chicago: Rand McNally,

1976), pp. 1201–1245. For the effects of supervisory roles on the attitudes of former union members, see S. Lieberman, "The Effects of Changes on Role Occupants," *Human Relations* 9 (1956), pp. 385–402.

8. J.R. Hackman and E.E. Lawler, "Employee Reactions to Job Characteristics," *Journal of Applied Psychology Monograph* 55 (1971), pp. 259–286; M.D. Dunnette, R.D. Arvey, and P.A. Banas, "Why Do They Leave?" *Personnel* 50 (May–June 1973), pp. 25–39; J.R. Hackman, "Work Design," in J.R. Hackman and J.L. Suttle, eds., *Improving Life at Work: Behavioral Science Approaches to Organizational Change* (Santa Monica, CA: Goodyear, 1977), pp. 96–162.

4

The Critical Path
to Renewal

The story is told of two engineers assigned the task of designing sidewalks for a busy campus quadrangle. One engineer studies the terrain, the slopes and plains of the area. She draws a plan that recognizes the aesthetics of the quadrangle, the ecology of the grass and plant life, and the ease and quickness with which the new sidewalks can be constructed. The other engineer says, "Forget all that. Watch where students and faculty are actually walking and lay the sidewalk there."

Managers who want to revitalize their plant or business unit face the same alternatives to managing change as did the two engineers. Should organizational change be led by a top-down alteration of "hard" organizational elements, formal structure, and systems? Or should it be led from the bottom up by changes in the "soft" elements: how people interact and work with one another to accomplish the task? Managers who choose the first course assume people must be directed to walk in new ways; managers who choose the second assume that given the freedom to walk, employees will find the best paths and a formal design will emerge from observing them.

The metaphor of sidewalk design captures some of the choices faced by managers in the pursuit of task alignment. Perhaps the most fundamental choice relates to the hard-versus-soft dilemma. How unilaterally directive will management be in pursuing task alignment? To what extent will it rely on changes in systems, structure, and formal policies to transform the organization? How much employee participation will management invite in shaping the organization's response?

The top-down approach possesses some allure. It holds the promise of producing rapid change toward an elegantly conceived end state that is symmetrical and complete. Thus managers can lead their employees in the desired direction. But the unilaterally directive approach also has traps into which renewal can fall. Employee commitment to the newly aligned organization may be low, and employee knowledge of how things get done in the organization may not be considered in the solution.

A bottom-up approach that allows, even demands, participation by employees seems to address many of the failings of unilateral top-management direction. But it can suffer from a different set of problems. A participative approach to change may be too slow and ill defined to respond effectively to short-term business demands. It presents top managers with the problem of how to incorporate their perspective and knowledge into new solutions. It raises questions about the motivation and skill of employees to develop an ambitious solution that will "force" them, the employees, to change their ways. Even worse, participative approaches to change can be derailed by resistant managers, unions, and workers.

Our examination of revitalization efforts in 26 plants and business units across the six companies reveals that effective renewal occurs not when managers choose one alternative or the other. Instead, effective revitalization occurs when man-

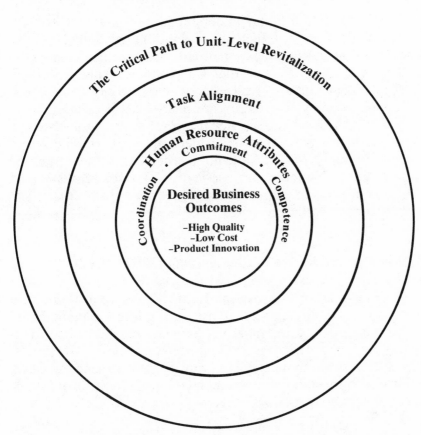

Figure 4-1: The Target of Revitalization: The Role of the Critical Path in Revitalization

agers follow a critical path that obtains the benefits of top-down as well as bottom-up change efforts while minimizing their disadvantages. The critical path integrates and synthesizes hard and soft approaches to change by a careful sequencing of interventions. Unsuccessful completion of any of the six interdependent and overlapping steps along the critical path—or a significant reversal in them—slows revitalization and, on occasion, halts it.

We can now add another ring to the target of revitalization, a ring that shows the critical path for achieving task alignment (see Figure 4-1).

To provide a better understanding of how and why the critical path is so effective in obtaining revitalization, we will look at the organizational unit that was most successful at revitalization: Fairweather Corporation's Navigation Devices.[1] That unit's overall effectiveness score on our questionnaire survey eclipsed all the rest of the 26 business units studied. These results do not mean, of course, that Navigation Devices' process was perfect, and we certainly do not mean to imply that we have not learned a great deal from the other units. Nonetheless, Navigation Devices represents an excellent starting point as we endeavor to explain the critical path to renewal at the unit level.

THE CRITICAL PATH IN NAVIGATION DEVICES

Fairweather Corporation formed Navigation Devices in the hopes of moving its Defense Group into the commercial and business aviation markets. Several years after its formation, however, that venture was proving to be a risky investment. Fairweather decided to bring in a new general manager, Jerome Simpson, who immediately began the task of revitalizing Navigation Devices.

The Scope of the Problem

Navigation Devices faced technological, customer, and financial problems. The design and production of reliable avionic navigation systems proved more difficult than anticipated. Additional product development and design costs, combined with recurring production costs that were higher than projected, meant that the operation was losing money. Even if the operation could turn the corner on profitability, return on investment would likely remain low.

The environment Jerry Simpson found at Navigation Devices did not make it any easier to address these problems. Management styles were characterized as "autocratic." Supervisors managed the production work force through fear, a mode of operation also reflected at the very top of the unit. As one manager recalled:

> The vice president [who preceded Simpson] set up competitive, adversarial relationships on his own management team. This attitude carried through the entire unit. I remember tension-filled meetings in those days with people yelling, swearing, and pounding the table.

Employee commitment and motivation at all levels were low. Interdepartmental coordination, particularly between design engineering and production, was poor. A senior production manager reported the following:

> Whenever engineering ran out of their budget, they would release whatever existed at the time, throw it over the fence into production, and then complete the design later with production money and lots of change orders. So it was throw the design over the fence, we don't talk to each other very much, engineering does the design, production does the build, quality does the inspection. We knew it was a very costly process, in time and dollars. We grew up that way, but we knew there were ways to do it better.

The production force was unionized, and the union contract called for higher wages and stricter work rules than at Fairweather's nonunion manufacturing operations. The relationship between union and management was generally uncooperative. Customer relations had also deteriorated. Lines of responsibility and accountability were not clear. There were too many levels. In short, many of Navigation Devices' problems were similar to those facing the rest of American industry.

Finding a Direction

Simpson began his revitalization effort by calling a number of lengthy meetings with his key executives where the weaknesses of the division were openly admitted and discussed. The conclusion: "There has got to be a better way to do it than this swamp we are in." During this period, Simpson and his staff spent a day away from the office working on relationships among themselves. At the meeting, the directors discussed their views of themselves, how they viewed their jobs, and their approaches to managing.

Simpson also targeted for discussion the basic business questions faced by Navigation Devices: What markets should the operation serve? What products and technology would be required? What levels of quality, services, and cost needed to be achieved? It was determined that initial market share would come from providing technologically superior products and services. Cost effectiveness would ensure long-term financial success.

The process of identifying business goals differed significantly from that of the previous administration. Prior to Simpson's arrival, all important business decisions came from the general manager and his marketing director. Simpson involved the entire management team. Initially, those newly involved managers reported some difficulty grappling with the cross-functional perspective demanded by the process. Involvement in the process, however, allowed them to develop that generalist perspective.

A visit by a cross-section of employees, including a number of union stewards, to a high-performing Fairweather plant organized entirely around teams built support for a new organizational approach. "My visit to that plant convinced me," recalled a production supervisor, "that a team approach could result in better management and improved productivity. The attitude and pride that the [plant's] employees show toward their job at Fairweather is unbelievable. You have to see it to believe it."

Not all employees reacted with quite the same enthusiasm, of course. Simpson himself reported that it took a while for him to realize the value of the team approach. He also found that his own staff was "nervous as hell. Some said that the team idea was the dumbest thing they had ever heard of."

A Velvet Glove

After becoming convinced himself, Simpson built support by applying what many called a velvet glove. He made clear to his managers that the division was going to apply employee involvement, that they must find ways to try it, and that he would help them learn to delegate and manage under the new approach. Off-site team-building sessions facilitated by external consultants spread the word that employee involvement was the "new religion" because "it is good for our business and our people." To those managers who wanted to help him reach the goal, Simpson offered support. To those who did not, he offered outplacement and counseling.

One of the initial skeptics regarding Simpson's thrust was the president of Navigation Devices' Teamsters local. "You can count me and the union out," the president insisted. "We've had enough of all these damned programs! When you get the support of my people and can prove it to me, then I'll back you." Simpson made sure that the union was amply represented on all planning and oversight groups, and members of the local union leadership eventually became staunch supporters of Simpson's revitalization effort.

Developing a Vision

Now two years into his tenure with Navigation Devices, Simpson created a 20-member planning team composed mainly of those managers, workers, and union representatives who had visited the innovative plant a year earlier. He charged the team with developing and implementing a plan to mobilize all employees to accomplish Navigation Devices' business goals. The planning team determined that for the unit to become effective, barriers to cross-functional coordination needed to be overcome. "We decided that no single, measurable piece of work gets accomplished within a single, functional area," said one of the team members.

Recognizing the need to further broaden involvement, the planning team created a 90-member core group. Representatives selected by peers would develop a vision for Navigation Devices. Concerned about being overpowered by top management, the core group initially did not invite a top manager to join it. Eventually, Simpson became a member at the group's request but played a low-key role. When it completed its deliberations, the core group called Navigation Devices' 650 employees together for a single meeting in a nearby theater.

The vision presented by the core group committed the organization to "establish a climate which encourages people to participate in decisions affecting them, and personally commit to profit, productivity, and growth objectives for the business." The vision stressed the central importance of quality in all areas, including the development of "superior, cost-competitive products, excellence in customer service, minimal scrap and rework, personal pride in the product," as well as "open communication and interpersonal relationships."

Finally, the core group called for the creation of a number of multilevel, cross-functional teams that would be organized around identifiable, measurable units of work. Among them were a business management team composed of Simpson and his staff to set the unit's strategic direction, business area teams to develop business plans for specific markets, product development teams to manage the development of new products from initial design to ultimate production, production process teams composed of engineers and production workers to identify and solve quality and cost problems in the plant, engineering process teams to examine engineering methods and equipment, and a number of job family teams focused on bringing together employees in similar jobs.

Simpson also created a bridge team made up of his staff and key stakeholders—a union steward, a secretary, a manager of finance, and a human resource facilitator—to monitor the revitalization effort and resolve issues that could not be handled within the team structure. Team leaders also came together in so-called team leader teams, and worked closely with the bridge team to oversee and facilitate the unitwide effort.

A Unit Revitalized

The team structure was implemented in stages, starting in the production area, a site volunteered by its manager. Business management and product development teams soon followed, but engineering process teams lagged by two years. All teams were aided by facilitators from the division and corporate human resource departments.

The changes did not modify Navigation Devices' organizational chart. They did affect behaviors. Members of teams were brought into relationships with interdependent functions and levels: production with engineering and marketing, shopfloor workers with engineers. Enforced interaction enhanced members' understanding of the roles of their functional counterparts and underscored their joint responsibilities in achieving mutually accepted goals for which they would be held accountable. Operational information was shared, and problems were identified long before they matured into crises. As once rigid barriers to interfunctional cooperation fell, even more information flowed throughout the organization.

Navigation Devices' performance in the years following the changes was dramatic. The quality of products and service rose. Operating measures of organizational performance—value-added per employee, scrap reduction, quality, customer service, gross inventory per employee, and profit—increased substantially.[2]

Employees reported a significantly improved organizational climate, as well. One employee made the following observation:

> I certainly have seen relationships improving. We have people from that other department on our team. They are recognizing that they have an obligation to make early contributions to the development process

75

as opposed to evaluations downstream, when it's too late to do anything. I also see a stronger orientation in design toward making product cost a driving force in design.

The outlook and competence of individuals were also affected by the changes. Employees developed a broader business perspective, a capacity to solve problems, and improved people skills. Said one employee:

> I've changed as a person. I am a different person than I was four years ago. My attitudes toward things are completely different. I reason better, I look at the other side better. I want a win-win situation, I don't want people hurt.

On a standardized measure of employee attitudes that Fairweather administers periodically, Navigation Devices scored among the highest in the corporation, a dramatic change from its lower standing five years earlier.

Simpson's earlier offer to outplace those who did not fit into the new vision of Navigation Devices proved not to be idle. Several managers, including two key executives on Simpson's staff, sought opportunities in other divisions of Fairweather. With Simpson's help, they were transferred or promoted elsewhere. Simpson used their departure to eliminate two hierarchical levels near the top, a move wholly consistent with the emergence of the task-driven team organization.

Remaining Challenges

Despite enormous progress, the organization still had problems to address five years into the revitalization effort, many arising from the changes made. "Factory supervision feel like they are not an important part of the picture. And so they find all kinds of excuses not to help the team," reported one manager. Though performance had improved significantly, some perceived the shift from a hierarchical organization to a task-driven team organization had reduced discipline and goal orientation.

> Before we had an autocratic management style, out of the military avionics group. Now some people think we've swung too far in the other direction. We've become too permissive. . . . Some people are taking advantage of it, taking breaks, longer lunches; the supervisors aren't supposed to be looking over their shoulders as much. I think we have to find some middle ground.

These observations led management to consider the introduction of a more formal information and control system for teams, one that formalized the goal-setting process and would make teams more accountable.

KEY STEPS ALONG THE CRITICAL PATH

Navigation Devices' revitalization experience followed a sequence of steps that we have come to recognize in other successful unit-level revitalization efforts and found missing in less successful ones. It is not surprising that General Products, the revitalization leader in our study, had many units at various stages along the critical path. Conversely, the revitalization laggards, U.S. Financial and Continental Glass, had few or no such units. That is why we concluded that skilled execution of the steps in the critical path by unit managers of a large corporation is essential to corporate renewal.

We became convinced that following, approximately, the sequence of overlapping steps along the critical path was as important as the content of the steps themselves. This approach allowed unit managers to obtain the benefits of participation—high motivation and developing skills—as well as the benefits of top-down change—a sharp business focus.

77

The critical path is a general manager-led process that implements task alignment at the unit level by doing the following:

1. Mobilizing energy for change among all stakeholders in the organization by involving them in a diagnosis of the problems blocking competitiveness.
2. Developing a task-aligned vision of how to organize and manage for competitiveness.
3. Fostering consensus that the new vision is "right," competence to enact it, and cohesion to move change along.
4. Spreading revitalization to all departments of the unit in a way that avoids perception that a program is being pushed from the top, but at the same time ensures consistency with the organizational changes already under way.
5. Consolidating changes through formal policies, systems, and structures that institutionalize revitalization.
6. Continually monitoring and strategizing in response to predictable problems in the revitalization process.

We now look in greater detail at each of the six steps to help explain and "operationalize" the effective implementation of revitalization within business units.

Step 1. Mobilizing Energy

The transformation at Navigation Devices challenged fundamental assumptions about organizing and managing. It is not surprising that leaders who contemplate such a transformation need to find a source of energy for change. The nature of human beings, and therefore of organizations, is to avoid change. At Navigation Devices, first-line supervisors as well as middle and upper managers were threatened by the task-driven, egalitarian organization that was emerging.

Virtually all the organizational units we studied began the revitalization process as a result of pressures for improved performance. At Navigation Devices, it was large losses and slower-than-expected introduction of new products. At Continental's Crawfordsville glass plant, it was inadequate product quality. Such external pressures present the potential for motivating change in all of an organization's stakeholders.[3] That potential must be developed by the general manager, however.

The general manager may feel performance pressures acutely, whereas other employees may be only dimly aware of them. That lack of awareness was often perpetuated by managers who failed to share with employees relevant information regarding costs, quality, and profits. The average worker knew nothing about the customer's needs or competitive costs, let alone the actual cost and quality of the product he or she was making. It is not surprising that many employees had not developed much of an understanding of the competitive environment or the need for change. Employee support for change is critical; our survey data revealed an extremely strong relationship between employee support and the extent of revitalization (see Appendix II).

Each revitalization leader had to find a way to translate external pressures into internalized dissatisfaction with the status quo and/or excitement about a better way. Dissatisfaction is fueled by awareness that the organization is no longer meeting the demands of its competitive environment. Excitement can be stimulated by imagining an approach to organizing and managing that eliminates many current problems or appeals to fundamental values.[4] Such energy was mobilized in several ways.

Sharing Data and Discussing Its Meaning. At Navigation Devices, Jerry Simpson worked to develop consensus that the competitive environment demanded new ways of operating and managing. The several meetings he held with his staff resulted in that consensus. Those meetings gave Simpson an opportunity to present data on the reality of the competitive situation and to share information about internal problems.

They led to an understanding of the root causes of the problems and the likely consequences if problems went uncorrected.

The most common method for creating a shared dissatisfaction with the status quo involved dissemination of data concerning competitive performance and feedback from internal surveys of employees. Data about business performance consisted of profit-and-loss information, comparative price and cost information, comparative wages, and information on the unit's position in the marketplace vis-à-vis that of competitors.

The urgency and reality of a problem was conveyed most effectively by putting employees in direct touch with the source of the information. Dick Vanaria at Crawfordsville did that when he displayed samples of superior glassware made by a competitor. Visits to customers and suppliers or presentations by them at the company's facility were other means for giving employees direct contact with the external environment.

Demanding Improved Performance and Behavior.   General managers typically augmented the employees' growing awareness that the organization was in trouble with demanding objectives for ends and means. Jerry Simpson's low-key role in the planning meetings reflected a desire to avoid controlling the outcome, but it did not indicate his failure to be directive about the parameters that were to guide all deliberations and actions. He made clear that all proposed changes must be based on two assumptions:

1. All interventions had to enhance the ability of the unit to meet the business objectives established by Simpson and his staff.
2. Employee involvement and enhanced teamwork had to be the means for achieving those objectives.

The importance of demanding both results and behavior was supported by our quantitative survey data, which showed that while most leaders of revitalization efforts set goals for results, leaders of successful transformations set goals for behavioral change significantly more often than did leaders whose efforts proved less successful.

Exposing Employees to Model Organizations.   Dissatisfaction with the status quo can also be raised by exposing employees to radically different and better ways of managing a business. The visit to the team-oriented Fairweather plant offered an alternative model to Navigation Devices employees. That model convinced the visitors that a team approach based on cooperation and trust produced superior performance and made for a more satisfying work environment. Of course, seeing an innovative, high-performing organization also contributed to their dissatisfaction with conditions at Navigation Devices. That the plant was within Fairweather and the visitors could talk directly with its managers and workers made the demonstration even more credible.

Throughout the 1980s, many companies arranged visits to Japan to achieve the same purpose. Livingston Electronics, for example, sent teams of executives and union leaders to tour Japanese manufacturing facilities. Both admiration and dissatisfaction were aroused by these visits, according to a senior executive at Livingston.

When There Is No Clear and Present Danger.   It might be said that Jerry Simpson held a natural advantage in his efforts to mobilize energy. Navigation Devices faced a clear and present danger: it simply was not making money. Does this mean a leader must wait until his or her unit is in serious difficulty before mobilizing energy for renewal? Even if the unit is currently profitable, can the awareness that there might be future problems be enough to mobilize energy?

Our empirical evidence tells us that the greatest change occurred in units that faced a dire competitive situation. Yet we see no reason that this has to be so. If the leader believes that fundamental changes are called for in order to meet the future demands of the environment, he or she can mobilize energy around that understanding. The key is to make sure all stakeholders are privy to the same information that has convinced the leader of the need for change.

Step 2. Developing a Task-Aligned Vision

Navigation Devices responded to the competitive crisis it faced with more than piecemeal, programmatic initiatives. Under Simpson's leadership, an ad hoc team structure provided a map of just how the division would operate to achieve high-quality products in the future. Employee involvement and teamwork were the underlying tenets of the vision.

The essential role of developing a vision or model of the future state for moving renewal forward has often been noted.[5] Without a vision, employees do not have an understanding of how the organization will function in the future or a clear rationale for the changes in roles, responsibilities, and relationships they are being asked to make. Just as important, the vision allows revitalization initiatives to be integrated as they unfold over time. The result should be a "high-fit" organization in which new roles, management style, employee attitudes and skills, structure, and the management process mesh and reinforce desired behavior.[6]

How to develop a consistent vision? Like many other unit leaders, Simpson himself did not have a clear vision initially, and no single factor produced a full-blown one. We can trace the steps by which a vision emerged:

- The business goals of technological leadership and high-quality service, which emerged from the strategic planning process, made teamwork an imperative.
- After visiting Fairweather's innovative plant, Simpson developed the general notions of employee involvement and teamwork, and that notion fit the lingering dissatisfaction Simpson had with Fairweather's bureaucracy.
- The planning team concluded that all work, particu-

larly new product development, involved cross-functional interdependencies.

- The involvement of more than 100 employees in the planning team and core group shaped these general ideas into a specific vision for the team structure and management process of Navigation Devices.

It would be a mistake to conclude that envisioning the future state of an organization undergoing renewal was left entirely in the hands of representatives of employee groups. Simpson's leadership was both directive and nondirective. He was highly directive about the values for his emerging vision and where renewal ought to take Navigation Devices. When the core group issued its own statement of values, those values reflected a high degree of consistency with Simpson's.

One manager who was a member of the core group recalled chafing under what at the time seemed like a highly directed "participative" process:

> I was asked to become involved in a planning process, yet it looked to me like all the important decisions had already been made by Jerry. I didn't feel like it was a very participative process.

Simpson was far less directive in determining precisely how those values would be implemented within Navigation Devices.

Articulating a vision and encouraging the organization to move toward it was done more frequently by managers of successful subunit transformations (63 percent) than by managers of less successful transformations (25 percent) when data from the total sample of 26 subunits were analyzed.

Widespread Involvement. The question remains: why involve so many individuals in a process designed to produce answers that are already—at least in a broad way—known by the general manager? The number of employees involved at Navigation Devices was large—certainly larger than any other example we came across—admittedly making the envisioning process both slow and awkward. A facilitator of the core group's meetings described the process as "teaching a baby dinosaur how to walk." That slowness must seem particularly naive, even dangerous, to managers facing a tough competitive situation.

Broad involvement, however, was important. We found in our statistical analyses that those units using a more participative process in developing a vision were more apt to have been successful in revitalization.

Involvement served a number of purposes at Navigation Devices. It built commitment to the new organization that the core group proposed. Since representatives of the various stakeholders were involved, the process by which the vision evolved ensured that the content of the vision would meet the needs of those stakeholders.[7] The same manager who originally felt Simpson had made all the "important decisions" became committed to them after extensive involvement in shaping their implementation as part of the core group.

If participation in the envisioning process produces commitment to renewal, it also improves competencies. Members of the core group practiced, experienced, and learned listening and communication skills, nondestructive ways to deal with conflict and reach consensus, and skills in analyzing and thinking about abstract problems. These interpersonal and cognitive skills are the ones necessary to make the interfunctional team structure successful.

Finally, core group participation began to improve Navigation Devices' coordination problems. The inclusion of representatives from the design, engineering, production, and sales functions created relationships among employees who ultimately formed teams. Their involvement also ensured that the design solution—the team structure—would speak to the need for coordinated action of these formerly isolated operations. The people who lived daily with the organizational problems had a voice in designing solutions to them.

Creating Meaning. Navigation Devices' vision was far more than a description of a new approach to running the business. By closely aligning business goals with new roles, relationships, and responsibilities among employees, the vision of a revitalized Navigation Devices held a significant meaning for employees.

Effective visions are not only practical statements about how the management process will change and how that change is related to business goals; they also express values that allow employees to identify with the organization. In short, they contribute to the business and to employee well-being, something financial goals alone do not do. Most of those with whom we spoke agreed with the Continental Glass manager who suggested, "It's hard to get excited about 15 percent return on equity."

In contrast, revitalization efforts that emphasized producing a high-quality product were generally seen as enormously meaningful by employees. Consequently it is not surprising that the vision at Navigation Devices focused on product quality. As a general manager at one of Livingston's divisions told us:

> Quality is like apple pie, motherhood, and the American flag. People experience it in their work lives and outside. They know what bad quality is when they buy a poorly made product or get poor service.

Since improving product quality usually strengthens a company's competitive position, employees' desire to make a meaningful contribution is aligned with the financial objectives of shareholders and the job-security objectives of employees.

Step 3. Fostering Consensus, Competence, and Cohesion

The process of overcoming resistance and fostering necessary skills always requires greater intervention and support than is provided by merely letting employees participate in vision development. Why? Not everyone can take part in the design of the new organization. Those who do participate do not fully appreciate the demands for change until the new organization is in place.

Thus change leaders typically take a number of other specific steps to further strengthen employee support and skills. **Team Building.** One of the first steps Jerry Simpson took in dealing with his top staff group was to hold an off-site team-building session. Simpson was not alone in discovering that team-building sessions were an important intermediary step to improving coordination and mutual problem solving. The ability to include others in decisions, to share information openly, to admit to mistakes, and to offer help for the good of the overall organization does not always come easily.

Outside facilitators—usually corporate human resource staff or professional consultants who specialize in third-party facilitation and dynamic team building—help move a team-building process along. They are able to solicit honest views from members about problems the group may have working as a team. At meetings away from the workplace, these views can be presented to the manager and subordinates in a way that will facilitate open discussion. Work groups are often amazed to find they can discuss the previously undiscussable and agree on a process for communication and decision making. In turn, each member has a better understanding of how he or she must behave in order to fit into the team, sometimes causing significant personal reevaluation.[8]

The team-building process has been used by companies to improve union-management relationships as well. It is not surprising that attempts to form a collaborative relationship with a union often stumble over the behavioral patterns of both management and labor representatives. Years, even decades, of conflict build layers of distrust that must be addressed and overturned.

One plant manager in an especially successful revitalization effort taken in collaboration with his local union pointed to these team-building sessions as the key step in the process:

> I would say that there was nothing as important, or as valuable to the plant [revitalization effort] as when I

86

took my top six or seven managers and met with the top guys of the union. We went to their [international union's] training center. At first, the management guys sat on one side of the room and the union people on the other. But that changed as we started talking. We talked about the things we didn't like about each other, and even some of the things we did like about each other. Pretty soon, we were mixing in pretty well.

Once new patterns of behavior are established, the focus of team-building sessions changes. Instead of looking directly at behaviors, the sessions attack real business problems. At the previous commentator's plant, the sessions had evolved by the third day to discussions of how to reduce labor costs to make the plant more competitive while ensuring job security for union members. At Navigation Devices, Jerry Simpson's team began to analyze their business position and develop a strategy for regaining a competitive advantage. In both cases, the patterns of behavior learned through team building served the unit well as it focused more directly on the task.

Consulting and Training Support.   Jerry Simpson did not lead the renewal of Navigation Devices by himself. Like most other unit-level leaders of successful revitalization efforts, he benefited from the counsel and advice of consultants both internal and external. Those consultants brought with them new ideas about how to organize and manage as well as useful methodologies for collecting data. They also coached managers and workers about new behaviors demanded by redefined roles, responsibilities, and relationships, and facilitated interactions between interdependent individuals and groups.

For example, Navigation Devices' divisional human resource function played a major role in providing facilitators to each team. The teams viewed the facilitators as temporary members who were there to provide feedback and encourage permanent members to monitor group processes. They also worked to model the kind of behaviors that would lead to effective teamwork, such as drawing quiet group members into the discussion or asking whether the group had reached consensus.

Once business teams were up and running, formal training was provided. Team members then participated in leadership effectiveness training. What kept this training from becoming just another program was that revitalization did not *begin* with it. Only after energy was mobilized, a model of the new approach to organizing and managing developed, and employees placed in a situation that demanded new skills of them was training offered. That training was designed to impart the skills being demanded by the new arrangement. Simpson started by creating a demand for training, then offered formal training programs.

Despite the skills and usefulness of the facilitators at Navigation Devices, they were not a substitute for Simpson's leadership. Our experience would lead us to suggest that effectiveness is probably enhanced by striking a balance between overreliance and underreliance on consultants. Underreliance—particularly at the early stages of renewal—can lead to problems and difficulties caused by the lack of skills and knowledge concerning the management of a revitalization process. However, we found that overreliance on consultants or human resource personnel was usually a strong sign that a general manager was uncomfortable in the essential role of spearheading the revitalization process.

Replacing Resisters.   Despite all efforts, not all employees become committed to the goals of renewal or develop the requisite skills to carry out those goals. The replacement of key personnel characterized 50 percent of our more successful units, but only 17 percent of the less successful units. The process of replacement could occur, in fact, at all organizational levels as the revitalization process unfolded. First-line supervisors, who can be particularly hard hit by a redefinition of their roles and responsibilities, were often moved out if they could not adapt.[9]

When managers declined to replace resisters, supporters of the revitalization effort read those inactions as a sign management was not fully supportive of fundamental change. Our survey data revealed the replacement of resisters was directly correlated with perceived support for revitalization and on-the-job behavioral change. The removal of resisters is essential if the general manager is to build a cohesive team committed to renewal.

The Local Union. As committed allies, union leaders can be extremely helpful in moving renewal along; as adversaries, they can mobilize resistance to the transformation. Obtaining the commitment of local union leaders is therefore critical. It merits special mention because of the traditionally adversarial relationship that has existed between union and management and because of the extremely delicate three-way relationship that must be sustained among management, union, and workers.

Considering that Navigation Devices (with production workers organized by the Teamsters) obtained cooperation of the local union and achieved the highest level of effectiveness in its revitalization effort among 26 units studied, it may seem incongruous to devote special attention to the problem of the union. What we discovered, however, was that not all managers were as effective in obtaining union consensus as was Jerry Simpson. In those cases, it was not so much the presence of a union itself that offered the roadblock, but the approach that management took to the union.

To illustrate this point we need to look outside Navigation Devices. Scranton Steel's work force was heavily unionized by the United Steelworkers. Managers in two Scranton Steel plants, both seeking to revitalize their operations, approached the union locals in significantly different ways. The impact was obvious. At Plant A, workers talked knowledgeably and sincerely about the competitive crisis in the American steel industry and the need for fundamental change in the way the plant was managed and shop-floor work was done. In contrast, workers at Plant B insisted almost unanimously that the so-called steel crisis was a contrivance of upper management to drive up the price of steel and force concessions from the union. They had read newspaper articles, even heard directly from management about the dimensions of the crisis: international competition, the high cost and low quality of domestically produced steel, overcapacity, and slack demand. They just did not believe what they read and heard.

In large part, the revitalization effort at Plant B stumbled over the assumptions of the plant manager. He understood he needed shop-floor employees willing to work harder and smarter and demonstrate flexibility and commitment to new approaches. However, he also looked at the plant's long history of conflict between union and management and assumed that the union would be a roadblock. So, he reasoned, why not go around the union and appeal directly to workers for their support and commitment? Management newsletters signed by the plant manager and his director of labor relations heralded the decline in the domestic industry and the need for renewal.

Contrast that approach with the management effort at Plant A, where management did not spread the word directly but worked through the union. The local union in turn presented the dimensions of the crisis and the need for revitalization to the workers. All types of information—results of attitude surveys, reports of various department-level activities, even minutes of the joint union-management plant steering committee—came to the workers of Plant A either through a newsletter entitled *Participation Team Update,* issued jointly by plant management and union leadership, or from the local president speaking at union meetings.

The differing responses of the workers at these two plants in turn directly affected the ability of plant management to bring about change. Fundamental work restructuring at Plant A spread quickly and relatively easily from department to department. Conversely, since employees at Plant B saw no legitimate reason for uprooting their traditional ways of operating, revitalization efforts there immediately bogged down and never took hold.

Not all union-management relationships, even in relatively successful unit-level efforts, proceeded as cooperatively as those at Scranton Steel's Plant A or at Navigation Devices. Where union leadership was weak and external pressures were strong, unit-level managers occasionally obtained some advances with only limited union involvement. Even in these cases, however, the ability of management to make changes in shop-floor work rules was limited.

If management attempts to undermine the union's role as the representative of the work force, as happened at Scranton's Plant B, then the result will be even higher levels of distrust and resistance. If management attempts to work collaboratively with the union in a renewal effort, then the union leadership can serve as an extraordinarily helpful partner in consolidating support and commitment.

Step 4. Spreading Revitalization Through Process

Revitalization does not occur in all parts of a plant or business unit at the same time. Within Navigation Devices, some departments began their revitalization even before the formal teams were put into place. Other departments lagged significantly behind. In particular, the production function led the effort, while engineering, marketing, and customer service lagged. Engineers were vocal in complaining that Simpson's team concept was a "force fit," an idea that might work well for production but was being "jammed down the throat" of engineering. Engineers were made uneasy about how their interactions would change with individuals and departments over whom they had felt more power and control in the past. Bringing production people in at all stages of product development, for instance, represented a loss in power and prestige to the engineers.

Directed Participation. Participation in the process became the tool that allowed revitalization efforts to overcome most departmental resistance. Each department at Navigation Devices was allowed to take the general concepts of coordination and teamwork and apply them to its particular

91

situation. In effect, each department followed its own critical path process.

Navigation Devices' engineering department spent nearly a year agonizing over exactly what the team concept meant to it. Top staff held off-site meetings with outside consultants. Surveys tapped employee attitudes. The engineering manager held an open meeting to discuss alternative organizational structures for the department as part of an effort to develop a task-aligned vision of how to organize. When employees failed to reach a consensus, the manager announced the direction in which he wanted to go, but the process began all over again with a group of engineers assigned to develop recommendations for implementation.

This painstakingly slow process is bound to frustrate managers in a hurry to make their organizations more effective. In essence, it amounts to allowing each department and unit to "reinvent the wheel." Yet failure to allow for such up-front time often costs the organization time in the long run.

A graphic example of the increased costs of bypassing a participative process was provided by a Scranton Steel plant superintendent. He recalled the anger, frustration, and resistance caused by his plant manager who, in the middle of a renewal effort, introduced by fiat a new maintenance program:

> About a year ago, right after we started discussing the need for greater trust and communication, we were introduced to a new program called Operational Maintenance Concept. It grew out of the maintenance department, but it would have affected every superintendent in the plant by giving us new responsibilities.
>
> The plant manager introduced the idea to us at lunch, and it was handled the way things are always handled. We were told it was going to be put in. The immediate response of the superintendents was that it wouldn't work. The plant manager asked what the problems were, and in ten minutes, it was obvious that

a number of major problems had not even been considered by the mechanical people who had sold the idea to the plant manager.

People got defensive. I lost my temper, said there were major problems that hadn't been considered, and that the new concept wouldn't work. The plant manager got angry and jumped all over me. Immediately all other discussion stopped. . . .

Well, then the whole thing blew sky high. We had to ask why. We said, first of all, they didn't get our input before the fact. Finally, at this point, the plant manager sat down with all his superintendents. We did sensing groups and brainstorming, flip charts, and votes. We formed a representative steering committee and put a union representative on that committee. Of course we could have saved six months if we had done this in the first place.

In this story we see a characteristic error made by managers inexperienced in spreading revitalization. They confuse insisting on a particular solution to a problem with insisting on a *process* for finding a solution. Spreading renewal requires the management of a paradox. The revitalization leader must be directive about his or her desire to see all departments engage in a process that will move them toward an emerging vision, but he or she must be nondirective about the particular way each department chooses to implement that vision. This careful balancing act is important not only to build commitment, but also to ensure that revitalization is customized to meet the particular needs of each new area.

Looking for Readiness.   Even with an understanding of this basic principle, renewal can be spread more quickly if it is allowed to emerge in those functions and departments that are most ready. That readiness has a lot to do with the manager. In Navigation Devices, renewal started in the production function when a manager volunteered his department as a starting place. Such managers exist in every organization.

Readiness is also conditioned by the extent to which the function or department is likely to gain or lose power by its involvement.

Step 5. Consolidating by Formalizing

Revitalization at Navigation Devices modified how employees saw their roles and responsibilities. Members of product development teams were expected by team leaders to be as committed to the success of the team as they were to meeting functional objectives. They were expected to share information openly about potential delays in product development that might come from problems encountered in their department.

Initially, these modifications did not include many formal changes in reporting relationships, information systems, evaluation, compensation, or control systems. The changes were sustained by the general manager's expectations and by the changing norms of the organization. After several years of the unfolding process, however, Jerry Simpson contemplated possible changes in the compensation and information systems to support the emerging new patterns of behavior.

Modifications in formal policies, structure, and systems can certainly help ensure the long-term success of a revitalization effort, particularly given the inevitability that managers like Jerry Simpson will move on to other jobs. William Bryant, executive vice president of manufacturing at General Products, learned from an earlier experience as a plant manager the importance of formalizing new patterns of behavior:

> We put this concept [employee participation] into the plant. The only reason it worked to start with was because I personally was overriding the system. I was in the plant every damned day . . . so I personally made it work.
> The minute I took myself out [of my plant] . . . bingo, it was right back to where it was. . . . After that

happened it took me about a year and a half to realize that no matter how much training you do, how much teaching you do, no matter what the hell you do, if you don't permanently change the organization's structure, the infrastructure to force behavior change, it isn't going to happen. The organization, that structure, is stronger than anything else you can do and it's going to pull it right down to the old environment unless you permanently change it.

It is these "harder" interventions, such as structure and systems changes as well as alterations in staffing practices, that can help prevent regression by locking in behavioral changes that were initially obtained by "softer" means, such as leader expectations, an ad hoc team structure, and changing norms. In the long run, the softer means appear insufficient. Not surprisingly, William Bryant encouraged General Products' plant managers to make changes in structure and systems in order to consolidate their initial revitalization gains.

Step 6. Monitoring and Strategizing

The critical path is effective, but it is not problem free. The experience of revitalization uncovers strengths and weaknesses in an organization. Since organizations are interdependent systems, changes in one part of an organization lead to stresses and strains in other parts.

It is the ultimate responsibility of the general manager to monitor and strategize continually to ensure that problems become opportunities. Unilateral response to problems, though, may end up undermining the very commitment and coordination that revitalization seeks to create. Navigation Devices put into place several mechanisms that allowed key constituents to play a role in monitoring the revitalization effort. The bridge team, composed of Simpson, his staff, and key constituent representatives, kept a continual watch over the change process in the unit. Regular employee attitude surveys monitored patterns of behavior. Planning teams were formed and reformed in response to new challenges.

Many of the problems faced by Simpson and his employees were unique to Navigation Devices. However, there are predictable classes of problems that all revitalization efforts eventually face. These problems are not signs of failure. Rather, they represent dilemmas to be addressed and managed.

Loss of Power. Organizational revitalization broadens the number of employees who influence decisions. This can be difficult for some. One manager experienced in revitalization offered the following:

> The thing that seems to be toughest for managers I think is to get through the knothole. There is a feeling they're going to lose power. . . . People who have worked for many years and have the ability to now begin to make some decisions that can change the way things get done, all of a sudden are told, "No, that's not going to be your decision, it's going to be somebody else's."[10]

The engineers and supervisors at Navigation Devices certainly perceived a threat to their personal authority. Decisions previously made unilaterally—engineers' control over product design or supervisors' control over scheduling and organizing work—now included other functions and departments, even subordinates. Factory managers described supervisors whose traditional roles and power were being threatened as "finding all kinds of excuses not to help the teams."

There are no magic solutions to a perceived threat. Attention, empathy, and help in redefining the role of supervisors are answers. Many organizations have reassigned supervisors to roles as technical experts, facilitators, and trainers. Others have reduced levels and increased spans of control so that remaining supervisory jobs have more challenge and significance. Perhaps most important, involvement by the threatened parties in shaping the renewal process helps alleviate their fears. Involvement may well convince managers that their redefined roles allow them and the organization to gain power. That realization is one way managers can pass through the knothole. The experienced revitalization manager had this to add:

> What's really happening in this kind of process . . . is that the amount of power that's there increases. . . . You've got the power of the creative ideas of a whole work force rather than a small group at the top. So there's a great deal of power to be shared.

Loss of Discipline.   While some supervisors refuse to give up any control, others create difficulties by abdicating their responsibilities as leaders. Disciplinary problems are the most obvious indicator of this problem. For example, at Navigation Devices some worried about employees taking longer breaks and lunch hours. These concerns may appear trivial, but they may be symptoms of a deeper problem: a loss of goal orientation.

When managers become so focused on throwing out the "old" ways of managing, they can confuse participation with democracy and self-management with laissez-faire management. They forget that the critical path calls for a balance between top-down authority and bottom-up autonomy. They simply lose sight of their essential role in setting clear direction, defining the task, and holding individuals and teams accountable for results.[11]

The manager of one plant we visited was ultimately replaced because he was unable to focus the energies of his subordinates on the core tasks of his operation. As he explained:

> One of the strategic errors I made was the democratic concept. Every book I read kept spelling it out: Regardless of how heavy the pressure gets, don't give in and go back to being supposedly autocratic, sup-

posedly directive, supposedly the things that professional managers are supposed to be when they don't come from an innovative work system. So I hung on to that concept, way too long, where I tried to have the group determine what they wanted to do.

His replacement understood, as had Jerry Simpson, that to follow the critical path successfully, an effective leader must be clear about ends but flexible on means. A subordinate to the new, successful plant manager described the manager's style as follows:

> Alan [the plant manager] . . . points at the mountain and says, "Charge." And a lot of the other[s] . . . wanted to know which footpath are we going to take, and where are we going to rest. And Alan says, "We will figure that out as we go. I know which mountain we want to take and that is the most important thing. We are going to take that mountain, and we will figure out the details as we go."

Maintaining Realistic Expectations.   As the culture shifts to participation, as subordinates taste freedom of action and influence, employees are apt to develop the belief that all decisions, regardless of scope or content, should have everyone's input. This happened at Navigation Devices when employees complained about not participating in an organizational change to which they could contribute little.

If employee expectations about participation do not rise dramatically, it probably means that they have not been empowered and a significant cultural shift has not occurred. That is why the appearance of this predictable problem is, in a sense, a sign of the transformation effort's success in creating a new organizational way of doing business.

It is important, however, that the issue of management prerogatives and employee rights not become a contest for power and a source of distrust. A consensus about criteria for who will participate in what decisions needs to be developed. Employees correctly understand that in a task-driven organization, the old rule that all decisions get made at the top is no longer adequate. However, they must also understand that the old ways are replaced not with universal participation, but with flexible involvement in decisions by those individuals who have relevant knowledge and skills.

Making Midcourse Corrections. It is virtually assured that changes in business strategy, economic conditions, operating methods, and technology will challenge management to maintain the original vision while adapting to new circumstances. Successful renewal should dramatically improve an organization's ability to adapt to the changing conditions. However, unit leaders must manage the changes in a way that respects the integrity of the revitalized organization. Just-in-time manufacturing, statistical process control, customer service initiatives, and quality programs can easily be experienced by employees as disconnected efforts unless managers (and union leaders where there is a union) achieve the goals of these initiatives in ways that are consistent with the original vision and process. Since participation in problem solving is one of the central principles of a revitalization effort, employees must be involved in redesigning the organization to meet the new challenge. This ensures that the redesign is consistent with the original principles.

Organizational Learning. As this catalogue of predictable problems should make clear, the critical path is continuous and never ending. As problems are identified, they give rise to new initiatives. These initiatives require a reinfusion of energy, a modified vision that integrates them with the larger vision that started it all. The modified vision requires a new consensus, new skills, and it too must be spread by managers committed to renewal. New systems and structures to reinforce the initiatives may also be required.

As the process of continuous renewal unfolds, managers and workers learn more than merely how to solve the current operating problems facing the organization. They learn a process for analyzing performance problems and making changes in organizing and managing that eradicates the root causes of the problems.[12] In addition they learn attitudes and skills that

99

make them more effective managers and workers who will initiate continuous improvement. In sum, the organizational changes transcend the immediate problems solved—they have helped create an organization that has learned how to learn.

WHY THE CRITICAL PATH WORKS

We have addressed the issue of management impatience. Eager, pressured managers are tempted to leap ahead; tempted to build a vision before energy for change has been mobilized; tempted to force renewal without a process that ensures support, fit, and consistency; tempted to consolidate by making structure and systems changes before the intricacies of the task are understood or people have the motivation and skills to make them work. "If all this is going to help me meet my competitive demands," these managers seem to be saying, "let's get to it!"

We caution against such impatience because the sequence by which the critical path unfolds is as important to successful revitalization as the specific content of the interventions. Navigation Devices followed the sequence of steps on the critical path. The sequence should not be thought of as a rigid one—at Navigation Devices and in other successful revitalization efforts, the steps overlapped substantially. However, we saw no examples of effective revitalization that did not follow the general sequence we have described. Moreover, unsuccessful revitalization was often explained by improper sequencing.

In order to understand how and why revitalization requires a particular sequence of interventions, it is important to classify interventions into two dimensions: those that focus on the individual versus the organization as a whole and those that focus on informal behavior versus formal organizational design. Figure 4-2 classifies interventions typically used in organization change into four groups.

The number in each quadrant corresponds to the order in

Figure 4-2: Sequencing Interventions for Learning

	Level of Focus	
	Unit level	Individual or group level
Intervention seeks to modify	(1) Redefinition of roles	(2) Coaching/counseling Training
Informal behavior	responsibilities relationships	Process consultation Team building
Formal design	(4) Compensation system Information systems Organizational structure Measurement system	(3) Replacement Recruitment Career pathing Succession planning Performance appraisal

which interventions are applied when the critical path is followed. As the figure illustrates, the sequence moves from quadrant 1—modifying informal behaviors for the whole organizational unit—clockwise through quadrants 2, 3, and 4. The power of the sequence lies in the fact that each group of interventions creates the necessary preconditions—the levels of motivation, skills, and information—to allow the organization to move to the next step. We will now discuss the quadrant concept in greater depth.

In quadrant 1, the motivation for change developed in the mobilizing energy step is further enhanced by the participative process of creating a task-aligned vision. The ad hoc structure implemented at this stage specifies the patterns of coordination needed to respond to the competitive crisis. This informal structure also modifies roles, responsibilities, and relationships across the whole organizational unit. Employees are placed into a new organizational context that demands behaviors they may not be sufficiently skilled to execute or emotionally ready to accept. They are now motivated to learn by the need to live up to a new way of operating, which they see clearly as relevant to the success of the business. The fact that they were part of creating this new demanding organization prevents resistance as the reality of what it all means sets in. Resistance is also minimized by the fact that titles and compensation are not altered by the ad hoc structure. Moreover, because the ad hoc structure can be modified relatively easily based on early experience, the final organization that emerges fits the task and the people far better than any a priori formal structure would.

The demands for new behavior that occur in quadrant 1 lead directly into the quadrant 2 interventions. Quadrant 1 has brought to the surface deficiencies in knowledge, skills, and personal and interpersonal behavior. The coaching, training, team building, and facilitation occurring in quadrant 2 are designed to help individuals and groups overcome those deficiencies. They help the general manager develop consensus, competence, and cohesion, the third step on the critical path.

If those same interventions preceded quadrant 1—that is, if coaching, training, and facilitation came before the process of discovery and learning—employees would not understand or believe these interventions were in fact directly related to making the organization more effective. These interventions would simply be viewed as programs and, as a consequence, dismissed.

Now it is time for the "harder" interventions, which fall into quadrant 3: formal policies and practices with regard to staffing. Replacement decisions are made for individuals who have not modified their behavior or developed the requisite skills. Recruitment, career pathing, succession planning, and performance appraisal policies and practices (part of the consolidating change step) can now all be informed by the emergent understanding of just what kind of individual the organization needs in order to be effective.

Why are staffing interventions most effective when they follow interventions in quadrants 1 and 2? The transfer of managers, supervisors, and workers who do not adapt to the new pattern of management are perceived as fair only if these individuals have been given an opportunity to learn and develop. Immediate replacement appears arbitrary and leads to questions by employees about whether the organizational transformation will contribute to their well-being, a perception we found was requisite for successful revitalization.

Waiting to replace people only after they have struggled with fitting in offers other advantages. It gives management a better understanding of the types of people they have and need. It informs the design of personnel recruitment, performance appraisal, and succession-planning systems, the formal mechanisms for staffing the organization in the long run. Only after management has seen which individuals succeed and which fail can it specify more accurately the personnel who will be needed to work and manage in the new task-aligned structure.

Finally, we come to quadrant 4: modifications in formal organizational systems and structure (part of the consolidating change step). The organization's experience with the new approach to management in the earlier steps on the critical path reveals areas in which more formal mechanisms are needed to sustain revitalization. These modifications can now be precisely tailored to reinforce the patterns of employee attitudes and behavior that are already well on the way toward becoming the norm. Consequently, their introduction at this later stage is less apt to traumatize the organization or demotivate employees. Furthermore, the commitment and competencies needed to implement these systems changes successfully have been developed through employees' experiences with earlier, less permanent changes in roles, responsibilities, and relationships.

Thus the critical path develops the levels of commitment, competency, and coordination needed for renewal in the order most likely to lead to success. The driving force is the commitment developed in earlier stages, which energizes employees to address fundamental problems of coordination (see Figure 4-3). As these are addressed, necessary competencies are learned on the job as well as through supportive training and coaching. If competencies are not learned, they are created through replacement.

Equally important, the pattern of improvements in com-

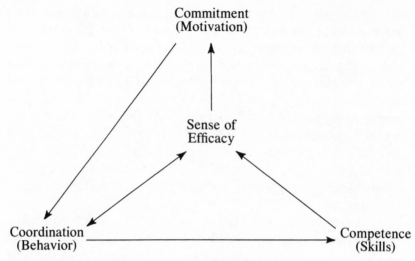

Figure 4-3: A Mutually Reinforcing Renewal Process

mitment, coordination, and competence become mutually reinforcing. In order for attitudes and behavior to change permanently, they must be rewarded. The critical path sequences interventions so that employees feel a greater sense of efficacy. This is a powerful motivator for continued effective coordination or teamwork in the new ad hoc structure.[13] "I certainly see relationships [coordination] improving," said one employee at Navigation Devices. Moreover, as problems are solved through the new means of coordination efficacy is further enhanced.

The act of working in teams also increases the competence of many employees to function in accordance with a new organizational form. "I am a different person," said a supervisor affected by the team organization in Navigation Devices. When employees' competence increases they experience enhanced well-being through a growing sense of efficacy. Their commitment to the organization grows correspondingly.

The idea that changes in personnel, formal structure, and systems should come at the end of the change sequence is, we realize, quite controversial. After all, much change in corporate life begins with such interventions. This may make sense in those cases where the objectives of the interventions do not include revitalization. For example, radical reductions in personnel and restructuring may be used to create a rapid turnaround in profits. And in a new innovative organization, such as a greenfield plant, initial decisions must be made as to personnel, structure, and systems.

However, as our discussion of programmatic change indicated, revitalization led by formal design changes does not typically succeed in older organizational units. Still, it is conceivable that changes in personnel, structure, and systems could be used to initiate revitalization under certain very limited circumstances. If *all* stakeholders agreed that such changes were needed, employee demotivation and resistance would not ensue. Only under such circumstances are people energized to help make adjustments in the structure so that it aligns more effectively with the task and their needs over time.

FORCING BUT NOT IMPOSING RENEWAL

We began this chapter with the story of two engineers contemplating the design of a quadrangle. Should the paths be carefully designed by the engineer and the concrete laid? Or should the laying of concrete be delayed until people choose where to walk and thus clarify the design requirements? These choices, we said, are analogous to the choices typically faced by managers leading revitalization efforts: to lead with top-down changes in "harder" formal organizational elements or with bottom-up changes in "softer" informal elements.

The dilemma is that people do not entertain major changes in their lives unless they are forced to do so. However, imposing structure, systems, training, and staffing changes from the top leads to resistance and rejection. So the central dilemma for a strategy of renewal that seeks to improve coordination and enhance commitment and competence is how to force coordination without imposing it from the top.

Inherent in the critical path sequence, we believe, is an effective resolution of the dilemma. Concrete paths laid immediately impose discipline through authority but do not allow for future adaptation from experience. This is similar to the strategy of starting a transformation effort with harder formal changes. Laying no paths and letting people walk wherever they choose imposes no discipline and results in a quadrangle design that lacks coherence and may not meet the larger needs of the university. This is equivalent to the abdication of managerial authority in a transformation effort.

Ad hoc team structure, arrived at through the vision development process we have outlined, is analogous to laying temporary gravel paths along routes arrived at through an analysis and preliminary consensus of school engineers and student representatives. This solution creates a strong demand that students try to use the paths, but also provides the flexibility for making adjustments in the university's plan as more information is generated about which routes are needed and which are not. At Navigation Devices the first team structure was modified several times as experience showed some teams to be redundant and others inadequately defined to accomplish the task.

The demands for renewal we have described are self-imposed. Developing commitment to a vision causes key stakeholders to impose a new pattern of management on themselves, one that demands they change their behavior. As employees discover that a new approach is more effective—something that happens only if the vision aligns with the core task—they are compelled to grapple with personal and organizational changes they would resist if imposed from the top.

The team structure in Navigation Devices as well as the participative process that created the structure pushed division management and team members toward revitalization. Renewal demands were also furthered by Jerry Simpson's decision to allow departments to go through the critical path process once again, despite the fact that they were reinventing the vision with only minor modifications to suit their circumstances.

Self-discovery gives each department and its individuals freedom of choice within well-understood guidelines. It ensures commitment when departments and individuals do "get on board." The process of reinventing overcame the initial sense of engineers that a new approach was being "jammed down the throat" of their department. The process can unleash a tremendous amount of energy. In turn, that energy and resulting high level of commitment can help overcome initial errors in conception and judgment as people demonstrate flexibility and respond to unanticipated problems.

In summary, we consider the critical path process neither hard nor soft, but "tough." It generates the benefits of starting with soft interventions, which unleash energy but do not threaten, while imposing the discipline of the task and the competitive environment.

The problem of how to force renewal without imposing it from the top is, of course, also the problem facing a top-management team that wants to transform the whole corporation. Imposition of programs led to slow and failed transformations in our corporate revitalization laggards. However, the top management at General Products, the revitalization leader in our sample, successfully orchestrated a strategy for corporate transformation that "forced" renewal in many units without imposing programs. It did so by encouraging plants and business units to follow the critical path.

NOTES

1. See Appendix II for how ratings of change in each of the 26 units were obtained. Questionnaire responses indicated that Navigation Devices had changed the most in the eyes of both informed insiders and the researchers.
2. Profit improved 305 percent in a four-year period, while sales increased 104 percent. Scrap as a percentage of sales declined from 9.2 percent to 2.8 percent. Gross inventory as a percentage of sales declined from 68.2 percent to

THE CRITICAL PATH

37.5 percent. Finally, value-added sales per employee improved from $52,000 to $75,000. Product reliability was higher than that of competitors, 7,000 hours mean time between failures for Navigation Devices versus 2,000 hours for competitors. The business' reputation for customer service had improved substantially.

3. The notion that change is fueled by a dissatisfaction with the status quo is a familiar one. See, for instance, L.E. Greiner, "Patterns of Organization Change," *Harvard Business Review* 45 (May–June 1967), pp. 119–130; and M. Beer, *Organization Change and Development: A Systems View* (Santa Monica, CA: Goodyear, 1980).

4. The idea of developing an attractive ideal for change is discussed in R. Beckhard and R. Harris, *Organizational Transitions: Managing Complex Change* (Reading, MA: Addison-Wesley, 1987).

5. See, for instance, Beer, *Organization Change and Development;* N. Tichy and D. Ulrich, "Revitalizing Organizations: The Leadership Role," in J.R. Kimberly and R.E. Quinn, *Managing Organizational Transitions* (Homewood, IL: Richard Irwin, 1984), pp. 240–264; and G. Barczak, C. Smith, and D. Wilemon, "Managing Large-Scale Organizational Change," *Organizational Dynamics* 16 (Autumn 1987), pp. 22–35.

6. The concept of fit and its contribution to effectiveness has also been discussed by a number of other authors. See, for example, P.R. Lawrence and J.W. Lorsch, *Developing Organizations: Diagnosis and Action* (Reading, MA: Addison-Wesley, 1969); J.P. Kotter, *Organizational Dynamics: Diagnosis and Intervention* (Reading, MA: Addison-Wesley, 1978); Beer, *Organization Change and Development;* R.H. Waterman, T.J. Peters, and J.R. Phillips, "Structure Is Not Organization," *Business Horizons* 23 (June 1980), pp. 14–26.

7. The assumption that people who participate in defining problems and solutions will, as a result of that participation, become committed to the results of that process, is one of the most fundamental of all organizational behavior theories. See, for instance, L. Coch and J.R.P. French, Jr., "Overcoming Resistance to Change," *Human Relations* 1 (1948), pp. 512–532; R. Likert, *New Patterns of Management* (New York: McGraw-Hill, 1961); E.A. Fleishman, "Attitude versus Skill Factors in Work Group Productivity," *Personnel Psychology* 18 (1965), pp. 253–266; and W.W. Burke, *Organization Development: Principles and Practices* (Boston: Little, Brown, 1982).

8. There is a large body of literature on team building and conflict resolution process. See, for example, W.G. Dyer, *Team Building: Issues and Alternatives* (Reading, MA: Addison-Wesley, 1987); R.E. Walton, *Managing Conflict: Interpersonal Dialogue and Third Party Roles* (Reading, MA: Addison-Wesley, 1987).

9. The phenomenon of particular resistance from first-line supervisors has been widely noted. See, for instance, R.E. Walton and L.A. Schlesinger, "Do Supervisors Thrive in Participative Work Systems?" *Organizational Dynamics* 7 (Winter 1979), pp. 24–38; L.A. Schlesinger, *Quality of Work Life and the Supervisor* (New York: Praeger, 1982); J. Klein, "Why Supervisors Resist Employee Involvement," *Harvard Business Review* 62 (September–October 1984), pp. 87–95.

10. The manager cited in this and the subsequent quote was not employed by

108

one of the six companies in our study. He worked for another company undergoing a revitalization process with which the authors have had a long-standing research relationship. For a chronicle of this company's efforts, see Bert Spector and Michael Beer, "Sedalia Engine Plant (A)," in M. Beer, B. Spector, P.R. Lawrence, D.Q. Mills, and R.E. Walton, *Human Resource Management: A General Manager's Perspective* (New York: Free Press, 1985), pp. 607–640.

11. The importance of the task as a source of discipline for groups has been articulated by J.R. Hackman and R.E. Walton, "Leading Groups in Organizations," in P.S. Goodman and Associates, eds., *Designing Effective Work Groups* (San Francisco: Jossey-Bass, 1986).

12. See C. Argyris and D. Schon, *Organizational Learning* (Reading, MA: Addison-Wesley, 1978); C. Argyris and D.A. Schon, *Theory in Practice: Increasing Professional Effectiveness* (San Francisco: Jossey-Bass, 1974) for a useful discussion of organizational learning.

13. We refer here to the basic law of effect, a foundation of virtually every learning theory. The notion that a subjective sense of efficacy can act as reinforcement in the learning process has become part of social learning theory. See A. Bandura and R.H. Walters, *Social Learning and Personality Development* (New York: Holt, Rinehart, and Winston, 1963). Lorsch and Morse postulate that individual needs to feel competent make organizational design and management style contingent on the task. See J.W. Lorsch and J.J. Morse, *Organizations and Their Members: A Contingency Approach* (New York: Harper & Row, 1974). But they do not deal with how the change process itself might influence a sense of competence, a construct originally developed in R. White, "Ego and Reality in Psychoanalytic Theory," *Psychological Issues* 3 (1963), pp. 24–43.

5

Creating a Climate for Critical Path Renewal

If the critical path is the process by which individual plants or divisions of a large corporation successfully revitalize themselves, then corporate renewal can come about only when top management creates a climate encouraging, even demanding, all subunits follow the process. Without explicit efforts by top management to promote conditions for renewal at the unit level, few plants or divisions actually attempt to revitalize. Those that do make an attempt remain isolated, which prevents other units from adopting innovative approaches to management and eventually causes regression in leading-edge units. Thus top management must actively foster a climate that promotes the critical path in an ever-larger number of divisions and plants. That requirement is shown as another ring in the revitalization target (see Figure 5-1).

Five of our six corporations had organizational units that

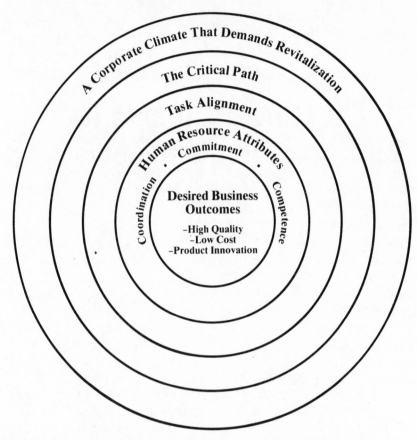

Figure 5-1: The Target of Revitalization: The Role of Corporate Climate

successfully followed the critical path. In many cases these early adopters of innovations in organizing and managing were at the periphery of the corporations. They were plants far from headquarters or divisions in businesses quite different from the corporation's core business. This allowed them to experiment with approaches to management that deviated significantly from the traditional values and operating style of corporate executives.

What distinguished General Products and Fairweather Corporation from our revitalization laggards was top management's ability to recognize the value of these innovations, learn from them, and find ways to spread them. Consequently, the revitalization leaders had many plants and divisions following the critical path. Livingston Electronics and Scranton Steel, companies that changed only moderately, had several innovative units. Not surprisingly, Continental Glass & Container, one of the laggards, had few innovative units and made only modest efforts to learn from them or spread their innovations. For example, Continental's Crawfordsville plant, which we discussed as a model of task alignment earlier, was not generally known within the company to be undergoing renewal. The plant manager single-handedly led revitalization within a division and corporation that gave him no encouragement. U.S. Financial, the other revitalization laggard, had no leading-edge revitalization units from which to learn (see Table 2-2).

What did General Products' top management and that of other corporate revitalization leaders do to create the necessary climate? We found that six strategies were typically employed:

1. Creating a framework for union-management cooperation.
2. Demanding high performance and a significant investment in human resources.
3. Developing innovative organizational models.
4. Investing in learning through conferences, visits, and education.
5. Promoting and developing managers committed to renewal and skilled in leading it.
6. Monitoring revitalization.

The history of the most effective corporatewide revitalization effort in our study, that of General Products, will help the reader understand how these strategies played a part.

113

DRIVING RENEWAL AT GENERAL PRODUCTS

After a long history of worldwide industry leadership, General Products' powerful market position was threatened by increasing foreign competition and escalating union-management conflict. In particular, one European competitor introduced a technologically superior product that increased its worldwide market share substantially at General Products' expense. General Products was forced to compete on both cost and quality. Its president, Tom Watson, described the company's reaction:

> We are a proud and jealous company. We saw our position in danger, and we are pretty good fighters. So all of a sudden, the fighting was on. We started investing more in research and development, and we started investing more in capital [plant and equipment]. We also said we have to invest more in human resources. That was not quite as planned as the other two.

General Products backed into renewal largely as a result of its attempts to address union-management tension and the attendant problems of quality and productivity. After a particularly severe strike, the incumbent CEO directed the establishment of a nonunion plant in North Carolina. He hired Larry Polk, an organizational development specialist, to help with the task. Polk had worked in another company well known for its success in establishing nonunion plants.

"At that point, General Products' top managers had no philosophy," recalled Polk. "They didn't see that anything could be done at union plants; they didn't see organizational renewal as possible." Top management at that time did not share Polk's understanding that "you get to be nonunion, because you do other things right." Thus the call for a nonunion plant was made without any realization that a radically different philosophy of management would be required.

114

Early Experiments and Innovations

Polk began to press for a different philosophy by working with the startup team for the new North Carolina plant. According to Watson, Polk's philosophy of participative management was not accepted initially, both because of its novelty and because Polk was unable at that early stage to translate it into practical implications for organizing and managing a plant with General Products' unique manufacturing technology. Watson, then the manufacturing executive responsible for the North Carolina plant, helped Polk gain the acceptance of the new plant's managers.

The plant was of great importance to General Products, which made the largest initial capital investment in its history to build the most highly automated manufacturing facility of its kind in the world. The startup team for North Carolina spent six months visiting other organizationally innovative plants and meeting with outside consultants. The resulting organizational design was highly participative; management shared more information with employees and gave them more control over their work than in older unionized General Products plants. Plant employees received extensive technical and interpersonal training. "Managers were chosen for their proven 'people orientation' even at the expense of experience or education," according to one corporate document. A member of the startup team explained, "We imagined a dream world of participative management with everyone smiling, and all decisions made by the group."

Early production difficulties led to some modification of the original organizational design and to the replacement of the first plant manager, who was so concerned about employee participation that he neglected the core task: running an efficient and effective operation. The second plant manager, while committed to the overall philosophy of the plant, was more willing than his predecessor to demand high performance and use participation to achieve it.

Despite its early growing pains, North Carolina proved

to be an extraordinarily successful model for General Products. The plant had the lowest costs and the highest quality in the company, a turnover rate of less than 1 percent, and an absenteeism rate of 1 percent.

While the North Carolina plant was the most dramatic example of the new approach to organizing and managing at General Products, it was not the first. The managers at North Carolina were able to draw on the experience of other General Products plants that had quietly begun experimenting with innovative management practices in the 1970s:

- The plant manager at a small Springfield facility achieved impressive results when he greatly increased hourly employees' roles in managing their own work.
- The general manager of a unionized plant in Alabama set out to elevate the level of communication and trust between employees and management and increase employee involvement.
- In Burlington, plant manager Watson, who was later to become the corporation's president, introduced a non-punishment disciplinary system.
- A member of Watson's Burlington management team went on to start up a small plant in Iowa that abolished time clocks, emphasized employee participation, and was built around teams. That individual then became manager of a still larger unionized plant located very near corporate headquarters, where he introduced similar management innovations.
- Some nine months before the North Carolina plant began production, the addition of substantial capacity to manufacture a new product was completed in one of General Products' unionized plants headed by William Bryant, later an executive vice president of worldwide manufacturing. This facility expansion was used as the opportunity to further experiment with changes in organizing and managing in a unionized setting. Changes included the introduction of a gainsharing reward system.

After Watson became president and Bryant was promoted to executive vice president of manufacturing, General Products began to spread the new methods to other locations. North Carolina continued to be used as a laboratory for developing organizational innovations. Several domestic and international subsidiaries as well as the company's Technical Center also undertook revitalization efforts.

The "Perfection Strategy" Drives Renewal

The driving force behind these innovations was what came to be known as the *perfection strategy*. The perfection strategy combined a set of very ambitious product quality standards and other operating objectives with corporate supports to help units achieve those goals. Those supports included the following:

1. Corporate manufacturing staff to advise on production methods and technology.
2. Polk's organizational development department and a network of line and staff managers trained to consult with management about how to follow the critical path to revitalization in their units.
3. Corporate-sponsored conferences at which line managers exchanged experiences with revitalization.
4. Outside consultants who worked with corporate management and Polk's organizational development group to review revitalization progress and advise in developing and implementing strategies for further change.
5. Massive corporate investments in training and education.
6. Frequent morale-boosting trips by Watson and Bryant to innovative units.
7. Periodic audits of innovative plants with results presented to Bryant and/or Watson at headquarters in the presence of the plant manager and human resource manager.

8. Speeches by Watson and Bryant to management groups around the world, extolling the virtues and urgency of renewal.

Bryant, the day-to-day leader of the revitalization effort, frequently talked about the perfection strategy and the North Carolina plant, reeling off statistic after statistic to illustrate the plant's superior performance. As a result, North Carolina became a living symbol of revitalization through the perfection strategy. Bryant made clear that he saw North Carolina as the "lead dog" in the team of General Products' plants. He encouraged others to try to catch up to the relentlessly improving quality and productivity standards of the North Carolina plant by emulating its approaches to manufacturing and management. "There was no resting place," Bryant was often heard to say, as he urged the necessity of continuous improvement. As renewal spread, North Carolina continued to be the pacesetter, the laboratory for innovation.

As efforts were made to spread North Carolina's innovations in organizing and managing to unionized plants, General Products began to run into resistance. Local unions balked at proposed changes in work rules. Top management's response was to insist on certain concessions in work rules before making investments in plant, equipment, and a revitalization effort. Unions and workers quickly learned that to be the beneficiary of further investments, their plant had to be competitive. In exchange for concessions, management made large investments in several older plants. This decision was typically accompanied by a joint union-management effort to change the plant's approach to organizing and managing work.

Revitalization Takes Hold—Mostly

By the time we completed our study of General Products, two-thirds of the corporation's approximately 100 worldwide plants had begun to move down the critical path to revitalization. Promotions to the plant management level were being made on the basis of consistency and fit with the new management approaches. The international division and business units not engaged in the manufacture of the company's main product were also actively engaged in renewal.

The effort was not without its stumbling blocks, however. Reliance on North Carolina had its limitations. North Carolina was an inspiring model, but it was, after all, a manufacturing facility. Managers in other parts of the company sometimes wondered about the relevance the perfection strategy and employee involvement had to marketing and engineering functions, or to the professional employees at General Products' Technical Center. Efforts in nonmanufacturing operations, while occasionally successful, proved more halting than those on the manufacturing side.

Furthermore, complaints began bubbling up from managers at innovative units concerning corporate staff. As unit-level managers moved forward with their revitalization efforts, they chafed at what they considered to be traditional, inflexible constraints imposed by staff groups. Career planning and forced distribution pay systems imposed by the corporate industrial relations department cut against the grain of the innovations taking place at North Carolina, at least according to the plant's management team. Others noted that staff groups had too much power and were overcontrolling.

Neither Watson nor Bryant escaped such complaints. Unit-level managers pointed to the overcontrolling and directive personal style of the two leaders most responsible for shepherding renewal. Some insisted Watson had been heard to say that "participative management is dangerous." Others saw inconsistencies between his day-to-day style of management and the espoused philosophy of employee involvement.

A CORPORATE CLIMATE THAT
DEMANDS RENEWAL

The story of General Products clearly illustrates the six strategies we listed at the beginning of this chapter. Three of them were measured by our questionnaire. When we analyzed the data, they strongly supported our conclusions (see Table 5-1). General Products employed the three strategies more frequently and consistently than did Continental Glass and U.S. Financial; the other companies were usually somewhere in between.[1]

We will discuss the six corporate strategies in the sequence in which we believe they should be emphasized. While there was significant overlap in the implementation of these strategies, we found that when companies substantially deviated from the preferred sequence, the effectiveness of their renewal effort was generally impaired.

Creating a Framework for Union-Management Cooperation

For unionized companies, creating a framework for union-management cooperation is a necessary first step, a foundation on which all other strategies must be built. In general, we found that revitalization was most likely to move forward in individual plants when the corporation and the international union developed a collaborative relationship built on a shared acknowledgment of the demands of the competitive situation.[2] This finding should not be surprising, given that the second and third steps on the critical path call for a shared vision and the development of consensus among all stakeholders. Creating a cooperative context within which local union leaders and plant management could operate made it easier for them to work together.

Given that General Products, Fairweather Corporation, and Livingston Electronics initiated their revitalization efforts in large part out of a desire to open nonunion operations, it may seem ironic to talk about a revitalization partnership between management and union leaders. Nevertheless, top managers quickly came to realize the ultimate competitiveness of their companies also depended on their success in creating renewal in those portions of their business that were already unionized. In accomplishing this task, these managers discovered a cooperative relationship between top manage-

Table 5-1: Corporate Revitalization Strategies Employed in the Six Companies[1]

	Average All Companies	General Products	Fairweather	Livingston Electronics	Scranton Steel	Continental Glass	U.S. Financial
Revitalization Rank		1	2	3	4	5	6
Strategies							
Model organizations	3.96	4.86[a]	4.20	4.17	3.00[b]	3.50[b]	2.67[b]
Investment in learning[2]	3.43	4.82[a]	3.73[b]	3.20[b]	2.78[b]	2.25[b]	2.52[b]
Moving committed managers	3.01	3.71	2.73	2.82	2.77	3.37	2.50
OVERALL USE OF STRATEGIES	3.47	4.46[a]	3.55[b]	3.40[b]	2.85[b]	3.04[b]	2.58[b]

Note: See Appendix II for a complete discussion of these data.
1. Means that are significantly different at the $p<.05$ level have different superscripted numbers. For example, mean x.xx[a] is significantly different from mean x.xx[b].
2. To arrive at a learning strategy score we combined two questionnaire items, one that asked about the use of education and one that asked about the use of conferences and visits to model plants.

ment and international union leaders was indispensable to obtaining the support of local union leaders. The support of local union leaders in turn was crucial in obtaining rank-and-file commitment to renewal.

Typically, union-management cooperation was built around an "enabling clause" in the contract between the international union and corporate management. This clause created mechanisms that allowed plant-level revitalization efforts to move forward. At Scranton Steel, for instance, such a clause called for the establishment of labor-management committees at every level of the company: corporate, plant, and department. Participation by plants was voluntary. The committees, composed of supervisors and workers selected by employees, were cochaired by that unit's manager and a United Steelworkers member. Their objective, according to the document drafted by Scranton and the union, was to improve company performance and provide employees with involvement, adding dignity and worth to their work lives.

Enabling clauses facilitated renewal not only because of the formal joint partnership mechanisms they created, but also by turning the international union officers into active allies. Since plant-level revitalization efforts inevitably called for greater flexibility of work rules, revitalization simply could not proceed without the active support of the union.[3] Plant managers found it difficult to obtain the support of the local union when international officials were skeptical or opposed; but when union leaders became committed to renewal, they were able to move local efforts along in ways that managers could not.

Formal agreements with the union also helped local plant managers in dealing with corporate staff. They signaled top-management's stance to potentially recalcitrant corporate industrial relations staff and thus removed potential barriers to local initiatives. Moreover, these agreements ensured some uniformity in labor relations practice across different parts of the company, thus preventing the distrust we saw arise in some companies when inconsistent policies were applied.

When properly informed about the competitive threat and involved in a dialogue with management, union leaders became partners in the revitalization effort.[4] For example, a three-day retreat at Fairweather involving Teamsters' officials and management developed trust, while highlighting the importance of product quality. That process created the atmosphere that enabled Jerry Simpson at Navigation Devices to develop a cooperative relationship with his local union leaders.

However, alliances between union and management often did not proceed easily, or without at least some hint of pressure and coercion from management. In advising that new capital investments would be made only in plants where local union leadership participated fully in revitalization efforts, General Products' CEO delivered this ultimatum to union leaders:

> [It's up to you] if you want to play hardball in the international league, or softball in the little leagues. . . . Here are the ground rules. We didn't write them, but here's the way the real world is and we're willing to spend our money here or some place else.

At the same time, however, he rebuffed recommendations by a few key executives to replace old unionized plants with new nonunion facilities: "I think it's the height of corporate irresponsibility to just haul off and say, 'Screw you fellows' . . . we have some people down there who owe their livelihood to General Products." In all instances, cooperative efforts would be tried first.

General Products' combination of concern for employees and combativeness toward its union was, in fact, quite typical of the relationship between management and union officials in the other companies as well. Whatever the approach, we observed no cases where the revitalization effort was able to move ahead without at least tacit union support. Active union cooperation typically speeded it up.

123

*Demanding Performance and Investment
in Human Resources*

Lasting changes in organizing and managing human resources come only when they are driven by business demands
and aligned with the organization's core tasks. This is why an
essential step on the critical path is the development of a task-
aligned vision. Top management can play an important role in
helping plant and divisional managers follow the critical path
by focusing unit managers on the task and on performance. In
calls for renewal, the top management of all six companies
paid lip service to the importance of increasing accountability
for performance. It was only in our leading companies that
top management actually supported these words with corresponding actions.

Continental Glass provided an example of the gap between words and deeds. Managers expressed profound skepticism that the CEO was serious in his stated objective of
creating "a new breed of winners" who would be both held
accountable and rewarded for superior performance. They
observed that political connections often proved a better pre-
dictor of career advancement than did individual performance. They also pointed to decisions that gave rise to doubts
about Continental's intention to reward performance—the
abolition of a performance-based bonus plan for middle managers and a corporate decision to reduce headcount through a
voluntary separation plan rather than by merit.

In contrast, a critical component of General Products'
renewal effort was increased accountability for meeting certain product and operating standards at all levels of the organization. President Watson said, "We have to hire fewer
people and hold [them] accountable." He described the new
atmosphere under revitalization as a "pressure cooker." A
number of managers who were not able to adapt to the new
performance demands were replaced or encouraged to take
early retirement. At the level of hourly employees, corporate
management made it clear in plant after plant that the price of

continued corporate investment, and thus of continued employment, was increased productivity and product quality.

Increasing corporate demands for superior performance may be necessary to energize unit managers to begin the process of revitalization, but it is not sufficient to ensure success. Under such pressure, managers may well seek to improve business performance by doing more of what they have always done—overmanagement—rather than by changing their fundamental approach to managing and organizing. More specific direction is needed. Successful corporate revitalization, we learned, depends on holding managers accountable for fundamental change in the way they manage human resources in addition to holding them accountable for business results.

What top managers at General Products did was make clear throughout the organization that improved performance should come through new approaches to organizing and managing people. Watson—and more particularly, Bryant— always saw and emphasized the inherent interconnectedness between the perfection strategy and improvements in the management of the firm's human resources. The perfection strategy, said Bryant, moved managers in two important directions. First, it drove them to a significantly broader understanding of the business aspects of their jobs, including human resources:

> The plant manager never thought about anything else but the technical aspect of the plant. He couldn't tell you what an accident incident rate was, or a loss/time frequency rate was. He didn't know anything about personnel. He didn't care. He didn't know a hell of a lot about the accounting system. Now, this whole concept is forcing the plant manager to get involved in every one of those areas. . . . Now, by forcing him to manage twenty elements of a perfection strategy, and asking him as many questions about the nineteen nontechnical as they do the technical, that's forcing him to

broaden his approach, get the hell off the technical aspect. Nontechnical, safety, in-process inventory, stores' inventory, raw materials inventory, return on investment.

Second, Bryant actively used the perfection strategy to focus managers on renewal. When plant managers complained about the impossibility of meeting perfection standards, he pointed them to Polk's organizational development group and held them accountable for moving down the critical path.

Perfection drives participation. There's no justification for participation if you don't have a goal like perfection. . . . It's essential for getting perfection. It's like organizational development. What the hell is the need for organizational development? That's why it's just a program in many places. It's more than a program here because it's required to obtain the objectives. You can't get the objective any other goddamn way, you just can't. That's what is unique about the strategy. It is goal driven and the goal is perfection.

The rationale in Bryant's scheme was to create a demand system that could be met only by a fundamental change in management: to "create a market for organizational development."

The perfection strategy was effective at General Products at least in part because it specified a broad direction rather than specific solutions. It increased the motivation for revitalization, without precisely specifying the means. It mandated a process for renewal without dictating its content.

While General Products was certainly committed to changing how plant and divisional managers organize and manage their employees, corporate leaders discovered that attempts to mandate specific organizational and management changes directly at the local level do not prove terribly effective. Said Watson:

To be successful in any of these things, you have to have a division calling for it and wanting it, and then it goes. We are very unsuccessful in this company [when we say], "Here's a policy and . . . damn it, do it." . . . Boy, they can sculpture smoke and it will look good. Unless they are willing to take it and embrace it [it won't work].

Such mandates fall into all the traps of programmatic change; most important, they fail to generate the commitment of the line managers who will need to carry out renewal.

In effect, General Products' top management recognized its limited power to mandate renewal. Like other effective corporate revitalization leaders, it saw its role was to create conditions that would encourage each unit to go through a process of self-discovery.

Developing a Growing Circle of Organizational Models

While programmatic changes typically target the corporation as a whole, top management in our more rapidly changing companies was apt to center its initial attention on a few model organizations that exemplified the new management approach. Once convinced that innovative approaches contributed to business performance, it encouraged a growing circle of plants and divisions to follow the critical path.

In almost all cases, the demands of the competitive environment pushed top management to pay attention to plants or divisions in outlying locations that had already begun quietly experimenting with management innovations. Despite a relatively modest use of internal models overall (see Table 5-1), an event in Scranton Steel's history dramatically illustrates how an early model can play a critical role as an initial catalyst for corporate renewal.

In 1980, Scranton was suffering from overcapacity and large losses at the hands of Japanese competitors. The Japanese steel industry converted 90 percent of its rolled steel into finished product, while scrap rates within Scranton Steel reached 25–30 percent. Labor costs were another key variable that helped explain the decline. U.S. steel wages were the highest among all domestic workers as well as the highest in the world, both in absolute dollars and as a percentage of the total cost of finished steel. Scranton suffered particularly because its labor costs—over 40 percent of total operating costs—were among the highest in the industry. At the same time, work rules restricted initiative and flexibility. "We're giving people a hell of a lot of money to produce scrap," noted one plant manager, not entirely facetiously.

In the late summer of 1980, Scranton chairman Don Singer visited a steel mill in Seattle, far from corporate headquarters. Plant manager Ray Baker had been leading his facility in a locally driven revitalization effort:

> I went through a three-year period where that plant changed from autocratic to very participative. It was a lot of hard work: training, communicating, getting rid of the autocratic people. And a lot of positive results: a positive impact on performance, yield, productivity, and people's attitudes.

Baker worked hard to help Singer see the positive changes that had occurred within the plant:

> We designed a visit where each of our department heads told him about their business. But the most impressive thing was that we took Singer around the floor and had the hourlies and foremen talk to him. It was exciting for me to see Singer's reaction to that. It was obvious that he was excited.

If Baker thought Singer was excited by his visit to Seattle, others at corporate headquarters reported that he was "flying." That enthusiasm carried over to the next executive committee meeting over which he presided. His Seattle visit had convinced Singer of both the possibilities for renewal and its bottom-line benefits. "I need a 16 percent increase in productivity," Singer told gathered executives, "and I don't know how else to get it."

As the potential of the new approach to organizing and managing began to be understood, organizational models were explicitly created. These were typically new businesses like Navigation Devices or plants such as North Carolina. In effect these became developmental laboratories for further innovations. Bryant said, "North Carolina is the model that we're putting all of our best thinking into. . . . Anything new comes along, hell, we put it in there."

The importance of identifying or developing successful internal models was strongly supported by our questionnaire data. The lagging companies, U.S. Financial and Continental Glass, had significantly lower scores than General Products on the questionnaire item that read: "There are visible model organizations in this company (plants, branches, or division) that are used to make people aware of the types of changes desired and how to go about these changes." Of all the strategies General Products used, developing models and pointing to them was used most frequently and consistently (see Table 5-1). On the other hand, U.S. Financial employees who filled out our survey gave the use of models a very low rating and were unable to identify any when interviewed.

To serve as effective catalysts for corporate renewal, model organizations need to be perceived as business successes. Bryant went out of his way to make sure the North Carolina plant achieved business credibility. Employing a sophisticated measurement system, he compared North Carolina's performance with traditional plants. That favorable comparison was made frequently and publicly. He emphatically rejected claims by managers that North Carolina's advantages lay solely in its technological superiority:

> We can actually go through North Carolina and say that each piece of equipment in the plant . . . is inherently this much more efficient than yours and we can . . . say, "Okay . . . if you operate exactly like North Carolina does . . . your output per man-hour would . . . improve twenty percent." Now, you notice I didn't say "thirty percent, because North Carolina has an inherent [technological] advantage on you of ten per-

129

cent." . . . We can then come back and show a real difference between North Carolina and [another plant] due to the environment that has been created. That doesn't give any credit for union versus nonunion, saying you ought to be able to do the same thing in a union plant that you can if you're nonunion.

Innovative plants did not necessarily make successful revitalization models. When they failed financially, they were extremely damaging to corporate renewal. Continental Glass & Container stumbled dramatically in its attempt to turn an innovative plant into an organizational model. The facility was a Reidsville, Georgia, box plant that had moved to self-managing work teams. The embodiment of Continental's intention to organize and manage people differently, Reidsville failed over a three-year period to meet profitability goals. Consequently, the teams were systematically dismantled and the plant returned to a traditional management structure.

The reasons for Reidsville's failure were many and complex, having to do in part with poor market conditions, inadequate corporate support, and poor revitalization implementation.[5] What is important to understand here is the interrelationship between the Reidsville effort and corporate renewal.

Within Continental Glass, Reidsville became a symbol of the "folly" of revitalization. Its failure allowed opponents of change to argue that innovative work systems could not succeed within the company. When executives at corporate headquarters began to refer to the innovations at Reidsville as "the Reidsville love-in," it gave even supporters of revitalization in the company ample reason to be cautious about initiating change in their organizations. It did not help that Reidsville's management could not substantiate claims that the team approach had improved quality and productivity. Use of a measurement system at Reidsville that differed radically from the corporate norm made it impossible to compare Reidsville's productivity with that of other Continental plants.

Given the importance of successful models, it becomes incumbent on corporations seeking renewal to keep in mind two key ingredients that our analysis suggests are important to developing a growing circle of organizational models:

1. Support innovations with appropriate resources.
2. Focus those resources on units with the greatest potential for success.

SUPPORTING INNOVATION WITH APPROPRIATE RESOURCES. At General Products it was absolutely clear to everyone that top management supported innovations in management. That point was made through speeches by Bryant and Watson; but more important, it was demonstrated by the enormous amounts of time, money, and people being allocated to support innovative units. When innovative units needed new managers, consultants, or support from staff groups, they got the best the company had to offer.

The situation at Continental Glass was quite different. In the case of Reidsville, corporate leaders paid little attention to involving managers in discussions to develop understanding and obtain support for the new plant. One middle manager reported the following:

> Reidsville was . . . not shared, it was not discussed. We did not use or gather the input of our best managers to ensure its success. . . . At no time was there ever a discussion of us regional managers that this should be a concept that we should try.

Because managers perceived Reidsville to be "force fed," they resented the plant and refused to help when it needed assistance. Said the same middle manager:

> I can remember sitting at a meeting when Smith [the regional general manager responsible for the plant] said I need the following help to fill this kind of a job at Reidsville, and I sat there on my thumbs. I am not going to give him anybody. No one gave him anybody.

And basically the answer that was given to him was you are going to have to get your people the best you can. And so it was doomed.

There was a general sense throughout Continental that even the individual selected to manage Reidsville, Patrick Walsh, was far from the best the corporation had to offer. That manager's previous experiences in sales and planning did not prepare him to handle the rigors of a startup manufacturing operation. Top management's lack of support for the Reidsville innovations was exemplified further by a reluctance to replace the plant manager as soon as it was clear he was having difficulties. He was kept in place until it was far too late to redeem either Reidsville's financial performance or the credibility of the innovations in management.

Competent plant managers are critical, but they are not the only resource required for success. Attention to the exciting aspects of organizational innovation must be matched with care for the operating details that make a plant successful. Continental's director of organizational development believed corporate management failed to do this. He suggested that top management's approach was this:

> Singlemindedly, we were going to make this an experiment that was going to help us prove how to motivate people. But that [should be] only one ingredient in the effort. In the drive for innovation in that area, they [corporate management] drove out more traditionally important things like, "Let's make sure that we get people down there in supervisory capacities [who] know how to make boxes."

Corporate management cannot afford to ignore or downplay the significance of such details as the hiring of employees with adequate technical skills and the development of effective working relationships with managers in other parts of the company.[6]

General Products never viewed the North Carolina plant

as merely a human resource experiment; it was always treated first and foremost as a critical business venture. That approach—treat innovative units as business operations and support them to the fullest extent possible—continued as revitalization moved from site to site and division to division. This was not always easy, however, due to managers' natural skepticism about innovations developed in other functions or parts of the company.

Because of these difficulties, the most effective corporate revitalization leaders focused their resources on one unit that served as a "beachhead" of human resource innovation in each new area of the company. These decisions were seen as crucial by top management and were not left to the human resource function. The metaphor of throwing sufficient troops and equipment into the battle captures the mentality that top management must have. Consider Bryant's plan for spreading General Products' perfection strategy to Europe.

> Somehow or other [we] have to have a roaring success story in an international operation before John Merrow [president of the international division] will buy it totally. He buys it now, but with conditions. . . . We've got the mechanism going to pull this off in Europe. There's a couple of countries over there . . . we are just inundating . . . with high firepower. We've got a top-notch training guy over there now. Steve Johnson [formerly plant manager of North Carolina, and currently director of production for Europe] himself is a damn good OD [organizational development] guy. He knows how to use those facilities. We've beefed up the technical support. We've beefed up the QA support, and I'm personally interceding with them out of the Technical Center in Europe to get them the technical help from that end.

Bryant's discussion suggests the depth of his commitment to providing all resources needed to make new revitalization efforts successful. Bryant recognized that human re-

133

source innovations without effective operations are doomed to the type of failure incurred by Continental Glass at Reidsville.

Focusing Resources on Units That Have the Greatest Potential for Success.   Given the limitations of resources and the high cost of failure, revitalization agents in our leading companies devoted a good deal of time to identifying the most promising locations for pursuing revitalization. The managers relied on a number of implicit rules of thumb in making this determination, and we will look briefly at three of them.

1. Building on Naturally Occurring Change.   One widely used approach was to "piggyback" renewal onto other important changes occurring within an organizational unit's technology, leadership, physical arrangements, product mix, or market strategy. For example, the addition of manufacturing capacity in connection with the introduction of an important new product at General Products provided the opportunity for organizational experimentation in several plants, including North Carolina. Similarly, the beginnings of organizational revitalization in the Technical Center coincided with the movement into a new physical facility. Naturally occurring transitions in management, such as the retirement of an older manager who had previously opposed renewal, often provided the opportunity for the promotion of a manager who supported the new approach.

Such piggybacking was useful in minimizing resistance to the proposed organizational innovations. Some significant change was going to occur; it was simply a question of the form. Commitment comes first from the realization at the plant or divisional level that there is a need for change, noted a human resource specialist at General Products:

> You are always looking for opportunities: . . . new product lines, a new technology, a change in management leadership, poor performance. The poor performance can be from a productivity statistical standpoint, [or] from a human relations standpoint. [It] can be from competitive reasons from within the company. . . . This plant is doing well. This plant is doing poorly.

134

They have the same product line. They ought to be doing the same. Or from a competitive standpoint from outside of the company. It could come from the standpoint that the plant is dissatisfied with where it is. And they call up and say, "We need help. I am getting all kinds of pressure from corporate, and we need help."

The most powerful test of readiness was whether an operation asks for revitalization help. "We want the plants to get into it from a standpoint of them wanting to," noted the human resource specialist, "and not from a standpoint of being forced to. They do a more effective job if it is what they want."

2. Starting with the Easy Units First. Some units are by nature more likely than others to be successful breeding grounds for revitalization. In general, revitalization was more likely to succeed

a) in newer units rather than older units,
b) in small units rather than large units,
c) in organizationally isolated units rather than organizationally central ones,
d) in units that were similar to early models rather than in units dissimilar from those models.

Smaller, newer, and more organizationally peripheral units were easier to revitalize simply because there were fewer barriers to innovation: fewer people to be converted, fewer ingrained norms and traditions to be modified, and fewer corporate constraints to be negotiated. That is why most corporate renewals typically started in new greenfield plants or with new businesses.

3. Avoiding Organizational Units in Poor Markets. A major factor in the failure of Continental Glass's Reidsville plant had to do with its market rather than with its self-managing teams. Crucial to the economic success of a box plant is its location. Box plants typically function as semiautonomous businesses providing boxes for the surrounding region, with their own sales forces. However, one of Reidsville's major local customers never materialized. Whereas the typical box plant sold boxes within a 150-mile radius, Reidsville's two major markets were 350 miles away.

General Products' Mansfield plant was a successful model plant if productivity and quality were the measures. Judged on a standard of profitability, however, it was a failure. The plant's markets were depressed, and it was operating substantially under capacity. According to General Products' Watson, this fact obscured the success of the plant's innovations in management and made it difficult to use as a model. Moreover, managers opposed to revitalization occasionally tried to use it to discredit innovations in management. Only General Products' sophisticated performance measurement system made it possible to disprove this point.

Investing in Learning

Innovative model organizations give corporations experience in new ways of managing from which top management can learn. Model organizations can also be used to persuade and educate others about the effectiveness of innovative management and about the critical path process. However, it is possible for models to serve as catalysts for further corporate renewal only if others are aware of their existence. Ironically, we found in our lagging companies a number of individual plants and divisions that were in fact making substantial changes in their approaches to organizing and managing. These changes were made in isolation, however. Innovative units were not highlighted by corporate management as examples for others to follow. In fact, in a number of cases, other unit managers were unaware that potential models existed within their corporation.

In contrast, General Products—and to a lesser extent Fairweather Corporation and Scranton Steel—went out of their way to expose managers to innovative models and to the critical path process that led to them. A number of strategies to ensure such exposure exist, and General Products used those learning strategies significantly more frequently than any of the other companies (see Table 5-1).

Conferences.   Corporate staff groups found that one effective way of exposing managers to success stories in innovative units was to organize corporatewide conferences. In this setting, top officers could endorse the general direction of change, while line managers could present their own experiences. As one organizational development specialist noted, "There's nothing like some old salt who's been with the company for years standing up in front of his peers and telling them that he's seen the light . . . and that they'd better get on the bandwagon."[7]

Visits to Model Organizations.   Actual site visits to units undergoing revitalization helped managers understand what the new way of managing was all about. General Products institutionalized such an approach by sending managers to North Carolina for as long as several weeks as part of their regularly scheduled training. Managers could learn the practical details of implementing renewal and, equally important, talk to colleagues who could speak to the real performance benefits of these changes.

Training.   All the companies used training programs to increase the understanding and skills of managers. These failed only when they were not embedded in local unit efforts to follow the critical path to renewal. General Products invested millions of dollars in training, far more than any of the other five companies. However, the company ensured that these training programs did not become an expensive false start by insisting that managers attend sessions about revitalization only after their organizational unit had started down the critical path.

Developing and Promoting Revitalization Leaders

Given the skills required to lead an organizational unit down the critical path, it is not surprising that a corporate transformation is dependent on careful development and promotion of plant and division managers who can lead revitalization efforts. In fact, we found successful organizational innovations tended to occur disproportionately often in those plants and divisions managed by certain gifted managers. For example, Watson experimented with changes in managing approaches when he was plant manager of the Burlington facility. As General Products' director of manufacturing, he had oversight responsibility for the North Carolina startup. Following his promotion to president, he began to spread these approaches throughout the corporation. Several of his plant-level subordinates went on to manage successful plant revitalizations. In our other companies as well, we could trace a "family tree" of revitalization efforts that followed the career progression of a few key managers.

Developing Revitalization Leaders. Companies that gave careful attention to developing a cadre of managers who could lead a unit down the critical path had a larger pool of competent managers from which to choose. In fact, broadening the number of organizationally skilled managers available for promotion became a top priority at General Products. Likewise, other companies serious about revitalizing tended to see career progression in developmental rather than hierarchical terms; moves were made not just for the sake of upward mobility but to develop specific skills managers needed to lead renewal.

Lateral transfers occurred at General Products, and moves into staff human resource positions became acceptable. For example, plant managers and others in senior line positions were moved into organizational development roles to enhance and test their revitalization leadership skills.

In addition to lateral moves, corporate leaders consciously used their most innovative plants and divisions as "hothouses" for developing managers, much as gardeners nurture seedlings in ideal growing conditions. Bryant described how he used this process to create a new change agent in General Products' international business:

138

I have a guy over here who I'm personally tutoring.
. . . He was the managing director of Luxembourg. [I]
brought him over here and got him on a three-month
training assignment here, and then he's going to run
one of our big U.S. plants, and then go back to Europe. . . .

[This manager] has spent three weeks in North
Carolina. Before we let him go to North Carolina, we
tutored him for two weeks so he'd know what the hell
to look for when he got to North Carolina. He's due
for a test this week to see if he got what he should have
gotten out of North Carolina. If he didn't . . . he's got
to go back to North Carolina. And he knows that. My
test would be understanding of the concepts and theories and strategies. Those are the same anywhere in
the world. It doesn't make a damn bit of difference
what the race, the nationality, the local government,
the culture, or anything else. The concepts are exactly
the same. How you implement them, what you call
them, how you name your organizational structure,
that's designed to fit the local culture, the local government or whatever . . . .

[This manager] is now comfortable with that . . . .
Buying the system and understanding how good the
system is. Now [he is] thinking in terms of, "Okay,
how can I adapt my local situation to utilize that concept?"

General Products went furthest in using its leading-edge
plants as hothouses for management development. It created
a Manufacturing Leadership Program to "develop plant managers for the 1990s." The program began with a group of plant
managers and production directors working with the corporate human resource staff on a fairly detailed list of characteristics for the ideal plant manager. That list was then used to
recruit high-potential college graduates who were placed in
General Products' most organizationally sophisticated plants

139

such as North Carolina. Those individuals were given a broad exposure not just to revitalization issues, but also to the various technical skills needed to function as effective general managers.

Much of traditional management practice works against taking such a broad view of career progression. There is a natural tendency for managers to view the career development of subordinates in ways that are shaped by the interests of their individual plant, division, or functional area.[8] Managers may protect their best employees in a way that hinders the long-term development of both the employee and the larger organization. Our more successful companies put a great deal of pressure on managers at all levels of the organization to use succession decisions to maximize not just the goals of the local unit, but also the long-term renewal goals of the entire corporation.

The process at General Products described by Bryant is one of the best examples:

> At every plant managers' conference now, one subject that's on the agenda is an evaluation of high-potential people in each plant. Each plant manager comes to that . . . conference . . . and he reels off who his high-potential people are, what their pedigree is, what they're ready for. We've actually got them to the point now where a plant manager will come there and he'll say, "I've got Ralph. Here's Ralph's educational background. Here's the jobs he's been through. Here's the kind of evaluations he's got. Here's what he's damn good at. And here's what he needs. I will not have the next spot for him for at least eighteen months and he's ready to move now. I'm afraid if we don't move him now we're going to be in trouble with this guy. Do any of you guys have a spot for him? And let me tell you something, I'd like to have him back in two years unless you're tracking him faster."

Effective transformations are characterized by top management's realization that corporate renewal depends as much on developing effective revitalization leaders as it does on developing effective organizations. Without highly effective renewal leaders, plants and divisions could not be directed down the critical path. Without highly effective innovative organizational models, however, the company cannot develop effective leaders. This chicken-or-egg dilemma was addressed in leading revitalization companies through careful placement of high-potential persons in innovative units before promoting them to new targets of renewal. Innovative organizations became, in essence, leadership development centers.

Promoting Revitalization Leaders.   At General Products, the movement of revitalization managers into key leadership roles was carefully orchestrated. This spread occurred fortuitously in our lagging companies when it occurred at all. A manager who was technically proficient but without skills in leading revitalization was just as likely to get a key promotion as a technically competent manager who was an effective leader of a revitalization effort.

By leadership skills, we mean a manager's capacity to inspire, share power, involve others, and manage a renewal effort while being tough about performance.[9] These behavioral standards of performance were something that senior managers in our less rapidly changing companies felt were off limits. The top management of the lagging companies seemed to feel in making promotional decisions that it was almost an invasion of privacy to consider a manager's leadership skills. "It doesn't matter how you manage," we were often told, "as long as you get financial results." A manager in one of our lagging companies explained the negative consequences of this attitude:

> What is the philosophy? It is random. I can be a manager in [this company] with absolutely minimum [behavioral] requirements. That [explains why] in any survey we have ever taken we are not number one in anything. We will never be number one until we deal with the quality of management.

141

A result of this laissez-faire approach was insufficient revitalization leadership resources.

Individuals in the corporate human resource departments of all six companies maintained that succession planning was an increasing priority. However, in the more successfully revitalizing companies, high-quality succession planning was not just a priority for human resource personnel; it was equally important for corporate line managers. General Products moved around committed revitalization leaders more systematically and consistently than any of the other companies (see Table 5-1), but top executives at other companies also learned how crucial promotion decisions are. Consider the experience of James Weaver, who ran Fairweather's Defense Group, a revitalization leader in that company:

> We developed a succession planing process after we made half a dozen mistakes [referring to managers who could not lead renewal] in promoting general managers. We didn't really have a succession planning process. Oh, the personnel people thought we did, but all we did was fill out some papers. But it wasn't real. Now we go deeper. We spend a lot of time on it.[10]

To be sure, succession decisions were not always made, even at Fairweather or General Products, with a balanced attention to technical, business, and people skills (see Table 5-1 for the relatively lower score for this strategy compared with the other two). The dilemma was that there simply were not enough qualified individuals with the range of skills needed to serve as leaders of renewal. According to Watson:

> The problem is the candidate list [for management positions]. That's what you've got to work with. It's not the selection process. We select the best we've got, but if you've got two old-liners you're going to select the best of the two old-liners.

A decision to promote someone without the requisite skills to implement revitalization into an important job, or to keep someone without those skills in such a job, may be taken out of necessity. It does not occur without cost, however. That cost can be stated in one word: cynicism. In virtually every company we visited, from the leaders to the laggards, we heard stories about how a particular key manager who seemed to epitomize the old approaches to managing and organizing "proved" that top management "wasn't really serious" about revitalization.

Even General Products, with its careful consideration of succession matters, did not avoid this trap entirely. The authoritarian, intimidating style of an international vice president—more than one person had become ill as a result of his challenges and demands—led overseas managers to question top management's assertions that it wanted to revitalize the company. No renewal could take place, they insisted, until and unless that vice president was replaced.

Monitoring Revitalization

The notion of monitoring the performance of plants and divisions is entirely routine. Traditionally, such monitoring involves sophisticated financial reporting systems for evaluating business outcomes. One of the practices that differentiated the more effective from the less effective renewal companies was the willingness of top management also to devote a substantial portion of its energies to monitoring the quality of the revitalization effort itself.

Much of the monitoring occurred informally. Top corporate management at General Products and Fairweather Corporation simply spent a great deal of time in the field getting a sense for how things were going. General Products' Watson explained how this process worked for him:

> You develop an intuition. You don't know the specifics of what is wrong but you just read the signs. I will get a phone call or somebody will drop in and see me and say, "Hey, I was out in [Plant X]. They have prob-

143

lems." Maybe you push it off for the first time, but maybe you hear something else, and maybe you read their reports. It begins to fit together and all of a sudden I say, "Let's go out there and take a look." You go out and sit with them and say, "What's going on and why isn't this happening?" You probe around into it. The systems have to be monitored. They will not take care of themselves.

In contrast, the executives in our lagging companies spent relatively little time in the field gaining hands-on understanding of the revitalization effort. The isolation of top management at Continental Glass was even mirrored in the physical layout of corporate headquarters, where a separate elevator linked the executive parking level with the executive suites. One respondent described this scenario:

> The top manager can go through a whole day without ever seeing another employee except for his secretary, or his group of peers on the twenty-seventh floor. And in fact, most days probably does. Gets in his company car, drives here, gets in the elevator, goes to the top, stays up there. Lunches up there. Goes back in the garage and goes back home again.

More formal methods were used for monitoring and evaluating renewal as well. Fairweather Corporation relied on employee attitude surveys as a kind of early warning system to alert managers to possible problem locations.

General Products developed a procedure that allowed for a more complex and detailed evaluation of a unit's progress: organizational audits. The members of the audit team—managers from other units and/or external consultants—worked cooperatively with local management in formulating a diagnosis of how far revitalization had progressed. The outsiders interviewed employees and observed operations. After review with local management to gain their perspective and reach consensus on the extent of progress, they reported the results of the audit to upper management. Present in the report-out meeting were key members of the unit under review—for example, the plant manager and the personnel director—and other key executives at headquarters.

The audit process provided a means for top management to increase accountability within the operating units for human resource outcomes and redirect the revitalization effort if necessary. It also served as a major catalyst for organizational learning—by top management, by the managers performing the audit, as well as by those being audited. In one plant audit, the auditing external consultant suggested that workers were still overly dependent on their supervisors for direction. When this issue was raised, a manufacturing executive who had responsibility for another innovative plant was able to share the results of his experiences with a self-managing team that was operating effectively on the night shift without the presence of the supervisor. The audit ended with top management asking the plant manager to investigate the feasibility of increasing the delegation of authority from first-line supervisors to self-managing manufacturing teams.

THE SEQUENCE OF CORPORATE REVITALIZATION

The strategies for revitalization did not unfold in exactly the order we have presented them in any of the companies we studied. In most companies, several strategies were implemented simultaneously. For some, renewal started with emphasis on middle or later strategies in the sequence.

However, given the limited resources of time and money available to top managers, we would like to suggest that the approximate sequence we have presented is preferable. Why?

Companies that began with middle and later strategies in the sequence had to return to earlier strategies to sustain and/ or make further progress in revitalizing. Even when companies implemented these strategies in approximately the order we have suggested, they often had to return to an early point in the sequence when progress in using middle and later strategies was stalled. This occurred when it became apparent that an earlier strategy had been inadequately or incompletely implemented.

General Products skipped the first strategy—developing a framework for union-management relations—when it initially placed emphasis on demanding performance through the perfection strategy (strategy 2) and on the development of a model nonunion manufacturing plant at North Carolina (strategy 3). Despite the apparent success of its efforts, it was unable to make progress in many of the remaining older unionized plants. Returning to strategy 1, it threw resources into developing a framework for union-management cooperation. It then gained union cooperation in managing revitalization in several older and previously resistant plants.

When revitalization efforts led with investments in education (strategy 4), those efforts became perceived as programs and failed. Both Continental Glass and U.S. Financial fell into that trap. At Continental, management education programs inspired the Reidsville experiment. However, without an emphasis on high performance and an understanding of its interconnectedness with human resource innovations (strategy 2), top management viewed Reidsville as an experiment in behavioral science. Operating considerations took a back seat to concern with the human resource innovation, and when the plant failed, the effort became known as weak and ineffective. The performance shortcomings of Reidsville undermined support for human resource innovation throughout Continental. Even if Reidsville had not failed, however, it would probably have remained isolated. Without corporatewide emphasis on high performance standards, it would have been difficult to convince other managers to emulate Reidsville's efforts.

The companies we studied could not avail themselves of strategy 5—the promotion and development of revitalization leaders—at too early a stage in the process. Initially a large pool of revitalization leaders did not exist. Revitalization leaders emerge out of successful model organizational units. Until a cadre of skilled and experienced leaders has developed, strategies relying on moving and replacing managers will not materially increase the number of renewal leaders promoted.

There is another reason why efforts to spread revitalization through better succession planning do not typically work early in the sequence. Managers need to fully understand the characteristics of a good revitalization leader in order to promote one. They cannot know what to look for until they have interacted extensively with such managers. That is not possible until the company has a sufficient number of innovative organizations to supply revitalization leaders. Nowhere was this more clear than in Fairweather's Defense Group. There the succession-planning process described earlier had limited value until Navigation Devices and other innovative units (strategy 3) had gotten under way.

U.S. Financial is the only corporation that led with strategy 6, monitoring renewal. Expensive quarterly attitude surveys were administered by the corporate human resource department, with reports forwarded to the president from the very beginning of the revitalization effort. However, no model organizations were ever established (strategy 3), leaving managers confused about what changes were envisioned. U.S. Financial's culture program demanded an investment in human resources, but did not specify the performance and task demands (strategy 2) required to motivate change in organizing and managing.

Although renewal may begin anywhere in the sequence, it seems prudent for top management not to overemphasize middle or later strategies before examining the extent to which earlier strategies have prepared the way. It is inevitable that a corporate renewal will entail some movement in emphasis forward and backward in the strategy sequence. Understanding the predictable consequences of the movement can help minimize the disillusionment that comes when isolated experiments such as Reidsville at Continental Glass or high-profile training and employee surveys at U.S. Financial fail to move revitalization along.

The basic rationale for the sequence of corporate revitalization strategies lies in the need to create sufficient organizational readiness at each stage of the change effort to allow subsequent stages to unfold.

Successful implementation of each strategy requires certain conditions developed by earlier strategies. Developing commitment to change achieved through strategies 1 and 2 (creating a framework for union-management cooperation and demanding performance and investment in human resources) creates the motivation to construct models of the new patterns of coordination, achieved through strategy 3 (developing a growing circle of model organizations). The model organizations in turn serve as hothouses for the development of leaders with the needed competence to allow strategies 4 and 5 to be enacted—educating, developing, and promoting revitalization leaders to other organizational units targeted for change.

Not coincidentally, this sequence of increased commitment driving changes in coordination that in turn lead to increases in competence is identical to the one we saw unfolding in the critical path at the unit level. That similarity exists because both strategies are built on the same set of assumptions about the dynamics of organizational learning.

CONTRASTING TWO APPROACHES TO CORPORATE REVITALIZATION: A SUMMARY

Effective orchestration of the corporate renewal strategies creates a climate that enables individual units within the company to follow the critical path. These strategies also foster an organic corporate-learning process that spreads revitalization from unit to unit. We believe that process is both different from and more effective than programmatic change.

In contrast to programmatic change, which starts with corporate top managers and human resource executives, the learning process we have described starts with unit managers far removed from the corporate core. This distance allows the unit managers to experiment with new approaches without risk of interference from headquarters. At some point, how-

Table 5-2: Comparison of Two Approaches to Corporate Revitalization

	Programmatic Change Approach	Managing Corporate Climate Approach
Relationship between headquarters and the field	Independent effort to develop changes at headquarters for use in the field that ignores early innovation in outlying locations	Isolated change in field locations Leading to centrally coordinated change in field locations that gradually moves toward the core
Reasons for change	Primarily, example of other companies or personal values of top management Secondarily, perceived link with business results	Perceived link with business results
Major responsibility for developing and implementing change	Delegated to corporate human resource personnel and outside consultants by line management	Retained by line management in headquarters and the field Assisted by HR staff and consultants
Change methods	Training programs, mission statements, changes in corporate-wide systems and procedures (i.e., performance evaluation, succession planning, and compensation)	Successful experiments with new methods of organizing and managing diffused through managerial succession, plant visits, conferences, and corporate OD assistance
Assumed relationship between words, thought, and behavior	Based on observation, reading, and reflection, develop methods to change how people think (through training and mission statements) that will in turn change how they act	Based on trial and error in a variety of field locations, develop methods to get people to act differently. Only then will they begin to think differently, which can then be described in training programs and mission statements
Assumed relationship between corporate procedures and behavioral change	Changed corporate procedures and systems will change how people act	Changed behaviors will guide changes in corporate procedures

ever, top managers begin to learn from the more successful innovations. That learning may come from their own involvement in innovation earlier in their careers and/or from seeing dramatic performance improvements in innovative units. They slowly become convinced that innovations offer an alternative paradigm for organizing and managing that the corporation should adopt in its efforts to become more competitive. As they develop stronger convictions, top managers begin to lead the revitalization effort more aggressively, urging further innovations and diffusing them by means of the strategies described in this chapter.

As Table 5-2 indicates, the underlying reasons for change, the responsibility for implementing change, and the change methods themselves differ markedly in these approaches to corporate revitalization. Equally significant, the approaches differ dramatically in their assumptions about organizational learning. The programmatic approach often falsely assumes that attempts to change how people think through mission statements or training programs will lead to useful changes in how people actually behave at work. In contrast, our findings suggest that people learn new patterns of behavior primarily through their interactions with others on the job. Consequently, an essential way in which successful revitalization efforts promote organizational learning is through the development of model organizations. Working in them exposes people to organizational demands that "force" them to act differently and in turn lead to new thinking. Thinking differently allows managers to produce educational experiences and make promotion decisions that are far more effective than those produced by programmatic change. Changed thinking also leads to revisions in corporate policies and practices that in turn further promote new behavior.

NOTES

1. At the time we administered the questionnaire, we had not identified three of the strategies—demanding performance, monitoring renewal, and creating a

framework for union-management cooperation. Consequently, we do not have quantitative data for them. However, our clinical data suggest that the revitalization leaders tended to employ them more frequently than the revitalization laggards.

2. For confirmation of this general thesis, see R. Walton, *Innovating to Compete* (San Francisco: Jossey-Bass, 1987); and T.A. Kochan, H.C. Katz, and R.B. McKersie, *The Transformation of American Industrial Relations* (New York: Basic Books, 1986).

3. For examples of the union playing a key catalyst role in promoting change, see Bert Spector and Paul Lawrence, "General Motors and the United Auto Workers," in M. Beer, B. Spector, P.R. Lawrence, D.Q. Mills, and R.E. Walton, *Human Resource Management: A General Manager's Perspective* (New York: Free Press, 1985), pp. 683–710; and B. Spector, "Blurring the 'Proper Separation': Quality of Work Life and Contractual Agreements," *Labor Law Journal* 37 (December 1986), pp. 857–863.

4. A number of companies outside our sample of six have established cooperative relations with their unions. See, for example, J. Simmons and W. Mares, *Working Together* (New York: Alfred A. Knopf, 1983); and Kochan, Katz, and McKersie, *The Transformation of American Industrial Relations.*

5. The problems of establishing and maintaining high-commitment work systems have been well documented by R. Walton, "Establishing and Maintaining High-Commitment Work Systems," in J. Kimberly and R. Miles, eds., *Organizational Life Cycle* (San Francisco: Jossey-Bass, 1980), pp. 307–326.

6. The role that inadequate technical skills play in the failure of innovative work systems has also been discussed by Walton, "Establishing and Maintaining High-Commitment Work Systems."

7. Howard Carlson, quoted in Spector and Lawrence, "General Motors and the United Auto Workers," p. 694.

8. See J.P. Kotter, *The Leadership Factor* (New York: Free Press, 1988) for an insightful discussion of this issue.

9. For an extensive discussion of the leadership skills required by corporations in a more competitive environment, see Kotter, *The Leadership Factor.*

10. Weaver's comments about succession planning in the Defense Group do not square with Fairweather's overall questionnaire score on moving committed managers in Table 5-1, which is not much different from that of the other middle and lagging companies. We can speculate that had we analyzed responses in the Defense Group only, the questionnaire score would have been higher.

6

Philosophy and Resources: Conditions that Enable Renewal

Top management can, we found, use six strategies to spread revitalization throughout a company. Why was it, however, that General Products' top management was not only more apt to use these strategies, but also more likely to implement them effectively than revitalization leaders at Continental Glass and U.S. Financial?

As we dug deeper into our survey data and reflected on what we had learned about the six companies, we identified three conditions that facilitated effective top-management leadership of corporate revitalization efforts:

- Balance between ambitious cost reduction and human resource investment goals.
- Balance between concern for task and concern for people.

153

- A network of human resource personnel and external consultants that helped top management facilitate companywide revitalization.

The first two conditions reflect a philosophical stance that top management had or developed as renewal unfolded. The third was a result of top management's philosophy, which in turn further promoted a balanced emphasis between cost reduction and human resource investment and between concern for task and concern for people. Together, the three conditions enabled top management to act on the six strategies that produced a corporate climate for revitalization. They form the next ring in the revitalization target (see Figure 6-1).

BALANCING COST REDUCTION AND HUMAN RESOURCE INVESTMENT

Increased competition is a demanding master, particularly given the pressure for quarterly earnings from U.S. financial markets. All the companies we studied were motivated to renew themselves by intense pressures to reduce cost and improve returns. To accomplish this, they engaged to varying degrees in reducing wages, benefits (particularly health-care costs), and work force at the production and management levels. Their capacity to survive and compete another day was largely dependent on their ability to make reductions quickly. Such pressures make it difficult to sustain a continued investment in human resources.

The task-alignment approach to revitalization succeeds in a performance-oriented environment, where human resource programs fail, because of focus on short-term business demands. However, the performance improvements that come about through aligning the efforts of people with the task do not always affect the organization's bottom line with the same speed as do direct reductions in labor costs or the closing of facilities. The significant improvements in product

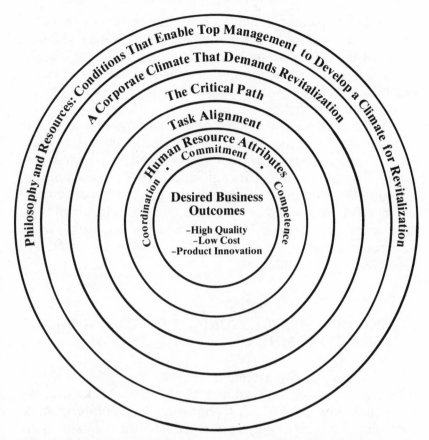

Figure 6-1: The Target of Revitalization: The Role of Philosophy and Resources in Enabling Top Management to Revitalize

quality at Continental's Crawfordsville plant and the quickened pace of new product development at General Products' Technical Center did not improve operating margins as immediately as shorter-term measures would have done.

It takes considerably longer to stimulate critical path renewal in all parts of a company than it does to decree an across-the-board reduction in personnel. The latter demands only compliance; the former requires leadership skills. Moreover, it takes time to develop trust, create innovative model organizations, and nurture the skills of people. Top management must be patient. It must provide the resources needed to support renewal over a time period much longer than the typical quarterly earning cycle by which financial markets often judge the value of the company's shares—certainly much longer than it would take to mount a takeover bid and make a tender offer.

Is revitalization a luxury businesses fighting for short-term survival can ill afford? Perhaps the answer is to make investments in long-term revitalization and at the same time rationalize assets by reducing labor costs and selling off unprofitable facilities? While this approach may encompass the best of two worlds, we found that in practice the two strategies coexist uneasily. The difficulties managers face in undertaking such simultaneous pursuits are well illustrated by the case of Continental Glass.

RESPONDING TO PRESSURE AT CONTINENTAL GLASS & CONTAINER

After some experimentation over a three-year period with human resource development strategies at the management and shop-floor level, Continental's corporate management became increasingly concerned with the company's low overall earnings. Takeover threats and pressure from Wall Street heightened the concerns. An organizational study by external consultants helped convince top management that low earnings were due primarily to excessive manufacturing capacity and bloated operating expenses related to predicted slow growth in the company's markets. Management responded with a number of specific steps:

- A radical reduction in the exempt headcount in general and in the size of corporate staff.
- Reductions in exempt compensation.
- Closure of some glass container plants and the modernization of others.

156

The short-term benefits of Continental's response were impressive; in 1986, the company had its most profitable year. So many competitors in the container business had gone out of business that there was more than enough demand to fill the company's few remaining plants. Since these plants had been modernized, Continental's container division was also in the enviable position of being the low-cost producer in the industry.

While asset rationalization made sense for Continental Glass, at least in terms of short-term earnings, it did not blend easily with Continental's revitalization goals. The chief executive officer's philosophy was to approach the strategies sequentially rather than simultaneously ("Let me straighten out the business first, then we can worry about the people"). That mindset caused the CEO to focus entirely on financial returns as the means for mobilizing energy for change. The response of employees was not positive. The second step the CEO had envisioned—emphasis on people—never seemed to occur. Employees saw no real change in the company's approach to organizing and managing.

While the CEO still expressed support for human resource development activities, he also seemed at a loss as to how to integrate human resource innovations with the company's restructuring efforts. The death of the human resource renewal strategy was exemplified by two facts. First, by the end of 1986, the corporate human resource function had been reduced in size and scope so significantly that it was no longer able to support renewal effectively. Not surprisingly, the vice president who had been hired in the late 1970s to lead change planned to leave, and many other talented employees had already left. Second, the recently appointed chief operating officer did not have much sympathy with revitalization.

A Matter of Balance

Was Continental's CEO wise to prioritize business first and people later? We think not. We do not argue that asset

157

rationalization and cost reduction are inappropriate strategies. We do, however, caution against allowing asset rationalization to become the sole focus for improvement. To do so creates cynicism concerning the organization's commitment to its employees, a cynicism that could well inhibit desired revitalization interventions at a later stage. By postponing renewal until after the business is straightened out, the organization squanders one of its most precious resources—time.

Why did Continental not balance its need to respond to short-term pressures with a longer-term commitment to renewal? Continental Glass was not being liquidated. While some areas of the company were being cut back, other areas were being expanded. Some glass plants were closed, but others were upgraded. After the dust settled, management was still going to have to run a business and make products. The products would eventually compete on more than cost. High quality and perhaps moderate levels of innovation would also be needed as attractive profit margins caused intensified competition. The corporation's ultimate success in remaining profitable would remain dependent on the commitment of the work force, its competencies in developing and implementing creative responses to changing business conditions, and its ability to communicate and coordinate cross-functionally. Given the importance of the pressures of quarterly earnings and the importance, in the long run, of investing in an organizational learning process, it is logical to conclude that successful corporate renewals depend on balancing these goals.

Unfortunately, continual cost reduction pressures can so focus a manager's attention on monthly financial performance that energy is diverted from longer-term investment goals, including innovations in managing people.[1] General Products' William Bryant understood well how short-term pressures can easily undermine commitment to renewal:

> Corporate bureaucracies are hung up on quarterly profit-and-loss statements, six-month profit-and-loss statements. Normally, you forecast financial results

quarterly. But if you're in trouble, you do it every month. Sometimes around here, we do the god damned thing weekly.

Now, the first time those pressures hit, the managers committed to perfection [the "perfection strategy" being General Products' umbrella for corporate renewal] won't be disturbed. But when it keeps happening week after week, you finally wear those poor bastards down. Now those managers say they can't worry about anything but profits and return on investment. And they'll do things that really don't help us in the long run but make their return on investment look good at the end of the year.

In theory, it could be argued that the balance might swing too far the other way, with managers so focused on long-term human resource development issues that they ignore short-term cost pressures. While that particular kind of imbalance did occur in a small number of units, it was far less frequent than overattention to short-term pressures. Financial markets and takeover threats were the explanation.

Short-term cost reduction pressures were high in all six of the companies according to our survey of employees (see Table 6-1). That emphasis was *not,* however, equally high across all the companies. U.S. Financial and Continental Glass, our revitalization laggards, and Scranton Steel, which was only slightly more successful in its revitalization efforts, were substantially above the average in the degree of cost reduction pressure employees perceived. On the other hand, employees in our leading companies, General Products and Fairweather, were below the average for all companies in the cost reduction pressures employees perceived.

More important, General Products and Fairweather were able to achieve a much better balance between cost reduction and investment in human resources than Continental Glass and U.S. Financial. Fairweather had an even better balance than General Products. However, according to employees, Fairweather management was not cutting costs as aggressively as General Products, giving Fairweather's re-

159

Table 6-1: Relative Emphasis on Cost Reduction and Human Resource Investment in Six Companies[1]

	Average for All Companies	Company					
		General Products	Fair-weather	Livingston Electronics	Scranton Steel	Continental Glass	U.S. Financial
		1	2	3	4	5	6
Revitalization Rank							
Cost reduction	4.46	4.36	3.80[b]	4.44	5.00[a]	4.90[a]	4.83[a]
Investment in human resources[2]	3.27	3.71[a]	3.56[a]	3.28	3.25	2.55[b]	2.76[b]
Difference score[3]	1.19	.67[a]	.24[a]	1.16	1.75	2.35[b]	2.07[b]

1. Means that are significantly different at the p<.05 have different superscripted numbers. For example, mean x.xx[a] is significantly different from mean x.xx[b].
2. This score is a composite of several items such as increasing accountability, intergroup coordination, delegation, employee influence, and trust.
3. Smaller difference scores indicate better balance.

newal a "softer" character. Employee self-esteem rather than improvement in performance was the revitalization rallying cry of Fairweather's president.

It is also important to note that according to employees, all six companies emphasized cost reduction more than human resource investment. That is not surprising, given the pressures for short-term performance these companies experienced, but it does raise important questions that this research cannot answer. Would less pressure for cost reduction in our lagged companies have given renewal a better chance? How much emphasis should a company place on investment in human resources compared with other performance improvement strategies? Would General Products have been better served by even more emphasis on corporate renewal, just as Fairweather might have been better served by more emphasis on cost reduction? When does emphasis on cost reduction become perceived as a lack of concern for people and thereby undermine revitalization?

What enabled top management at General Products to balance cost reduction pressures and human resource investment objectives more effectively than others? Top management's conviction about revitalization appears to be an important factor. Watson spoke clearly about how changes in the way people were organized and managed would make the company more competitive, how renewal would improve quality and reduce cost. It was not something the company was doing to be nice to people or to be in vogue. Bryant spoke about how participative management was the only means for achieving "perfection."

The top managers of the remaining companies, on the other hand, were less clear about the role revitalization was to play in their efforts to improve the competitiveness of their companies. Take Fairweather's emphasis on increasing employee self-esteem. That goal appeared to us to be far less well integrated with business goals than the perfection strategy at General Products. When asked to discuss the changes being made at Livingston Electronics, CEO Brad Longstreet mentioned greater emphasis on profitability and returns but neglected to link this to the renewal efforts in his company, even after being pressed for a connection.

At Continental Glass, managers felt that revitalization was initiated because it was in fashion. "We were all into 'buzzword kind of stuff,' " said one manager. The actions of Continental managers, if not their words, suggest that at a more basic level employees were viewed as variable costs rather than as potential human assets. This state of mind is antithetical to effective leadership of corporate renewals.

The External Environment

As our comparison of the leading and lagging companies implies, the balance management struck between cost reduction and revitalization is profoundly affected by the values and assumptions of individual line managers as well as by the organizational culture of which these managers are a part. However, it should also be acknowledged that regardless of these values, the strength of external demands for improvement in financial performance can greatly complicate the task of maintaining balance.

In fact, there seems to be an optimal balance between too little and too much external pressure. Too little external pressure will fail to provide the impetus needed to overcome the inertia and resistance to change that exists on both organizational and individual levels.[2] In such a state, neither the needed cost reduction nor human resource investment activities may be possible. Conversely, too much external pressure can move an organization to abandon a long-term approach, especially when combined with weak resolve on the part of corporate leaders to continue investing in human resources.

Severe external pressures encouraged our three laggard companies (Scranton Steel, U.S. Financial, and Continental Glass) to switch from revitalization to asset rationalization and portfolio management as a way of achieving quick performance improvements:

162

- At Continental Glass, top management began to worry about takeover and turned to rationalization of manufacturing plants and massive voluntary retirement programs to reduce cost. It employed divestiture and acquisition to establish a position in businesses very different from the core businesses.
- At U.S. Financial, large losses undermined the credibility of the CEO with his board. This led to a complete reversal of his revitalization strategy when a successor known to be unsympathetic to revitalization took over.
- Scranton Steel's board likewise responded to large and continued losses by replacing Don Singer with Ed Shields. That change occurred with no explicit intent to either help or hinder the ongoing revitalization effort at Scranton Steel. But hinder the effort it did. Shields's laissez-faire approach to renewal eliminated the focus and persistence so important for success.

Managers Make a Difference

That too much pressure can cause a renewal to derail and too little pressure can prevent one from starting suggests that top management may not be in total control of the cost reduction/human resource investment balance. However, top management can control its destiny to some extent. It can start the revitalization process long before performance problems become so severe that there is insufficient time to pursue a long-term developmental approach. Further, the General Products experience suggests that with sufficient clarity of purpose, it is possible to sustain a steady investment in human resources despite strong external pressures.

BALANCING TASK AND PEOPLE

Managers make choices, either explicitly or implicitly, between emphasizing task and emphasizing people. This is also true in organizational change efforts. Some have as their primary objectives such task-related organizational changes as increasing the delegation of responsibility to employees and holding them more accountable for results. Other change efforts place an emphasis on more people-related objectives such as increasing trust, sharing power, increasing employee influence, and developing people.

It is not surprising that our survey data suggest that, compared with the lagging companies such as Continental, General Products more effectively balanced concern for task and for people in its revitalization efforts (see Table 6-2). Management able to do this is more likely to be able to implement several of the corporate revitalization strategies: for example, creating a framework for union-management cooperation, emphasizing business performance and human resource investment, and developing revitalization leaders. Moreover, a sufficiently high concern for people will cause employees to see innovations in management as aligned with their interests. As we already reported, employees' perceptions that changes in the company were motivated by a concern for people were highly related to perceived support for and amount of change.[3]

We must add an important caveat. Overall, the companies were significantly less likely to emphasize those changes that suggested a concern for people than those that demonstrated a concern for task. In fact, sharing power, equalizing status, and empowering employees received less emphasis in all six companies than any of the other changes made, although General Products and Fairweather were ahead of other companies in this regard (see Appendix II for more detail). That fact presents a potential long-term problem. Levels of commitment to revitalization in our leading companies came from trust, which was based on the belief that new approaches to management were more than an attempt to manipulate employees into making sacrifices. We assumed that employees and unions cooperated because they believed that changes being made would allow them to exercise greater influence in the workplace. These increases in

Table 6-2: Relative Concern for Task and People In Six Companies[1]

	Average for All Companies	Company					
		General Products	Fair-weather	Livingston Electronics	Scranton Steel	Continental Glass	U.S. Financial
		1	2	3	4	5	6
Revitalization rank		1	2	3	4	5	6
Concern for task	3.48	3.77^a	3.68^a	3.54	3.44	3.00^b	2.96^b
Concern for people	3.06	3.64^{a1}	3.43^1	3.01^1	3.05^1	2.10^{b2}	2.57^b
Difference score[2]	.42	$.13^a$	.25	.53	.39	$.90^b$	.39

1. Means that are significantly different at the $p<.05$ have different superscripted numbers. For example, mean $x.xx^a$ is significantly different from mean $x.xx^b$, and mean $x.xx^1$ is significantly different from mean $x.xx^2$.
2. Smaller difference scores indicate better balance.

employee influence undoubtedly occurred, particularly in our leading companies. However, the data suggest that employees believe management wants to hold them accountable for performance far more than it is willing to share power or equalize status.

What effect, if any, will employees' perception that management is more interested in holding them accountable than in sharing power have on the long-term efficacy of revitalization? Will employees sustain their commitment to improved quality and lowered costs if further power sharing does not occur? If commitment fades, what will happen when the next crisis requires further sacrifices and forces management to make difficult trade-offs between profits and employee well-being?

We can only speculate at this stage that if renewal is to sustain itself, management may have to give more consideration to providing mechanisms for employee influence. Further, to sustain long-term employee commitment, this influence may need to extend beyond day-to-day decisions to corporate policies and strategies which have long-run effects on employee well-being.[4]

SUPPORTING REVITALIZATION

On a philosophical level, we have dealt with the importance of emphasizing long-term investment in revitalization as part of the overall corporate response to external competitive pressures. On a more practical level, that emphasis entails providing resources that support the revitalization process on a day-to-day basis. Line managers, we discovered, had to lead revitalization. However, they often found the innumerable complexities of change to be difficult and demanding, and they needed help in following the critical path to revitalization.

Top management at General Products and Fairweather provided such ongoing support in the form of human resource personnel and external consultants. These professionals were more than advisers to line managers in various units; they were agents and partners of top management, encouraging, supporting, and facilitating renewal throughout the company. The closer the partnership, the more effectively these experts in revitalization could help top management learn from experience at lower levels, lower-level managers learn about top-management's intentions, and managers at all levels learn from the experience of others.

We observed that the human resource function and external consultants played a more important role in supporting revitalization in our leading than in our lagging companies. General Products maintained an extensive network of internal renewal agents and external consultants, whereas Continental Glass and U.S. Financial had underdeveloped networks or none at all.

Human Resource Personnel as Catalysts

In effective revitalizations, corporate human resource professionals played a vital role in guiding field units through the critical path. In particular, they did the following:

- Aided corporate managers in planning and monitoring the revitalization.
- Facilitated the sharing of learning from one unit to another and served as knowledgeable resources on revitalization.
- Served as coaches for line managers who had not fully mastered the necessary interpersonal and leadership skills to negotiate revitalization successfully.

General Products took some important steps early in its revitalization effort to develop a corporate human resource function capable of providing such support. A group of internal organizational development consultants was assembled and headed by Larry Polk. One of Polk's employees explained the group's role:

[We are a resource] to the organizational development activities going on out in our plants and in our subsidiaries. We are really internal consultants . . . . We go in and help plants analyze themselves: their strengths and weaknesses, and opportunities . . . . Let them develop the future model. Then work with them to put in the processes to change from where they are to where they want to be.

Our strategy is to . . . help them learn lessons from each other, understanding that each of our locations has uniquenesses. They are not carbon copies . . . . We have a lot of educational sessions, conferences, seminars and we are also the group that puts them in contact with the right kind of outside consultants . . . the right kind of public seminars, the right kind of reading material, the right kind of plant visits.

A vital reason for the success of Polk's group was that top management never expected it to take primary ownership of the revitalization effort. At General Products, renewal was led by top management. Corporate staff was never allowed to become the main driver. In Watson's view:

Larry Polk is kind of our preacher man. He is really not our implementer per se. His group of people provides resources. Once a person decides [they want] to do this, they say, "We need help. I hear what Bryant is telling me to do . . . [but] I don't know how to do that." [We respond] "Well, go talk to Larry." So Larry is the preacher man. He preaches at them and he gives them ideas and direction, and he comes out and helps them analyze and he helps them shape a program, but the program has to come out of the people who want it.

The principal agents of renewal remained line managers who, through their requirements for superior business and human resource outcomes, created a demand for the staff group's services.

Polk's group did far more, however, than passively provide support when asked. As "preacher man," Polk traveled the corporation with his disciples, spreading the gospel and adding focus and momentum to the change effort. Polk and his colleagues actively scanned the organization for places where they could catalyze change. If managers at what looked like promising sites did not immediately understand that they needed help, Polk and his group gently persuaded them. That persuasion, according to one of Polk's staff, involved making the case for the interconnections between performance and human resources:

> From a business viewpoint we try to help them see human resource management is a bottom line strategy, and businesses that are the most effective at the bottom line in most cases are businesses that have the most effective people involvement processes, the most effective training, the most effective communications, the most effective feedback systems, etc. . . . We will send people from one of our plants that is not doing so well to one of [our more successful] plants and help them see what is . . . happening. We also do the same things with plants outside of the company . . . . The main way is through exposure to experiences and information.

Polk's group managed to combine two roles: it proactively served the needs of upper management for centrally orchestrated revitalization, and it remained responsive to the diverse needs of plants and divisions in the field. Polk worked constantly on balancing the two roles. Many of the other corporate human resource functions had neither the skills nor the credibility to maintain this difficult balance.

Limitations of the Function.   Historically, human resource executives in our six companies were most often asked to be police officers. According to one human resource professional at Fairweather, "Top management always asked us to keep them out of trouble and out of jail." One of their major responsibilities was ensuring that corporate exposures to violations of the law in labor, equal employment, and health and safety were minimized. In monitoring field units for possible violations, human resource personnel became quite good at saying "no." As one corporate human resource executive told us, "We say no, and then ask what the question is."

Therefore many traditionally trained human resource executives were cautious about supporting innovations in organizing and managing. Resistance to renewal was often particularly severe in labor relations departments responsible for union relations and contract negotiation. When Donald Singer, as Scranton Steel chairman, began talking about the need for human resource revitalization to regain competitiveness, one of the first executives to voice doubts was his director of Industrial Relations (IR). In fact, some Scranton Steel executives began referring to IR as the "Internal Resistance" function.

The fact that revitalization-oriented groups like Polk's organizational development team typically reported to traditional-minded vice presidents of industrial relations created many problems. Under such reporting, the constraints of a labor contract or of personnel policies—rather than the imperatives of revitalization—dominate decisions. Personnel managers whose careers were subject to the decisions of traditional industrial relations executives avoided contact and cooperation with revitalization-oriented departments.

Watson recognized the existence of those problems at General Products:

> Our personnel division [had as] its number one objective . . . get us the best contract possible every three years. . . . They worked about half the time in between getting ready to do that. Polk used to stop by [my office] in total frustration, wondering what the hell he had done. His number one problem was his boss, the manager of industrial [relations] or human resources for the company. . . . While [the industrial relations manager] believed he needed Larry Polk, his number one priority [was the contract]. "Don't bother me, I

have a contract coming up, and as soon as I get that over, maybe I will have some time to talk to you."

General Products ultimately dealt with the conservatism and risk-averse behavior of personnel managers with structural changes: Polk's reporting relationship changed from the manager of industrial relations to a new vice president of industrial relations with a much broader mandate and all personnel managers in innovative plants reported directly to Polk.

The one area where human resource executives were traditionally asked to be proactive was in "maintaining employee morale." In nonunion locations at companies such as Livingston Electronics, this activity was seen as important in protecting against possible organizing drives. For the most part, however, the view of human resource staff as "social directors" persisted. A human resource executive at Continental Glass explained:

> Personnel were always the people who brought the watermelon to the picnic. They went to funerals and they screwed you at increase time. Because the supervisor would always say, "I put you in for more than that, but those damn people in personnel."

Consequently, line managers saw the human resource function as engaged in activities either peripheral or even antithetical to the primary task of running the business. Given the function's low status, many felt that human resources was a dumping ground for those who had failed elsewhere. We were generally quite impressed by the intelligence and commitment of those in human resources, although we did find that years of worrying about keeping their bosses "out of trouble and out of jail" did not serve as useful preparation for their new role as proactive renewal agents.

Even those in the corporate organizational development groups, who presumably had the most relevant experience as corporate revitalization agents, were sometimes viewed with suspicion by line managers. That suspicion grew out of an association between the label "organizational development" and a whole range of interpersonally oriented programs such as T-groups (sensitivity training) and transactional analysis, which organizational development experts promulgated in the 1960s and 1970s. Organizational development experts were often seen as being more concerned with "humanizing" the corporation than with addressing real business issues.

Developing a Change-oriented Human Resource Function. Because of perceived, as well as real, weaknesses, it was sometimes necessary for corporate top management to oversee a revitalization effort within the human resource function before moving it out into the company. Without this preliminary step, the function could not effectively provide top management with support for the wider change effort. Revitalization of the human resource function usually involved three common components:

- Creating a new department within the function to provide support for revitalization.
- Bringing new personnel into corporate human resources.
- Developing training programs to upgrade the skills of existing human resource professionals.

These strategies develop a different set of skills and predispositions than those typically found in traditional personnel departments. Individuals who excel at contract negotiations or compensation and benefits administration are not necessarily able to serve as "preachers" and strategists for corporate renewal.

Typically, one of the first signs of a shift in direction for the corporate human resource function was creation of a separate group that could focus on supporting revitalization, such as the organizational development department at General Products. Similar groups were established at Fairweather, Scranton Steel, and Continental Glass. Interestingly, however, Continental Glass gradually abolished this group as top management enacted its cost-cutting measures and lost interest in revitalization. U.S. Financial, our other

172

laggard, never established such a group. Scranton Steel, under severe pressures to cut costs, substantially reduced its commitment to maintaining a group of internal consultants.

Effectively staffing internal consulting groups was not always easy. As we have seen, traditional human resource activities did not often develop professionals who had either well-developed revitalization management skills or credibility with line managers in the business. The major strategy our companies used for rapidly increasing this skill base was to recruit top-level human resource staff from a variety of sources outside the function. Some of the new recruits were successful line managers from the corporation. Others, such as Polk at General Products, were brought in from other companies.

To increase credibility with operating units, newly recruited human resource staff members were provided extensive training as internal consultants and catalysts. The development of a pool of internal consultants occurred most systematically at General Products and Scranton Steel. Early in its revitalization efforts, Scranton established a "shadow organization" of special assistants in each plant and division undergoing renewal. Sometimes referred to as "guerrilla warriors," they reported directly to the general manager. An external consultant who helped design the selection process for special assistants described it this way:

> We said the special assistant should be an operations person and a volunteer. He would have an open style and be respected by other operation types. And he should be considered a comer, a person with a real future in the company. That would make the job— which involved moving off the line for a period of years—something of a risk. To make sure we got good people, we had to offer a verbal guarantee: such an assignment would be appreciated, would be for a fixed duration, and would be rewarded in some unspecified yet important way when they returned to the line. . . .

173

This was the process, and it resulted in some very good people, and some others who used the job to kill time.

Choosing support personnel from the line organization did not guarantee effectiveness, but it tended to increase the credibility of human resource revitalization agents among line managers. Yet the very differences in orientation and skills that made these revitalization agents more credible with line managers often led to their being viewed with suspicion within the human resource function.

Human resource personnel acting as internal consultants for revitalization were often described to us by their more traditional colleagues as reckless, overly interested in self-promotion, and lacking a solid personnel management grounding. These characterizations were the flip side of statements we heard from members of organizational development groups and other human resource staff engaged in revitalization work. They saw traditional human resource people as overly cautious and unskilled in organizational diagnosis and revitalization techniques. At Fairweather, where the organizational development group worked closely with top management, tensions grew to the point where the vice president of human resources and his key subordinates undertook team building to improve coordination and teamwork.

One of the most effective strategies for dealing with these interdepartmental tensions was through training programs that developed a broader set of shared skills in the human resource function. At Continental Glass, an educational program was put together for traditional human resource managers by the head of the organizational development function. Program participants learned about everything from business strategy and innovative approaches for organizing and managing, to the details of intervention techniques. The program was taught in multiple segments, between which participants were required to apply what they had learned in a consulting project back on the job.

174

External Consultants as Catalysts

The corporate human resource function was typically not able to support the revitalization effort on its own. All six companies made extensive use of external consultants. These consultants served a variety of roles.

Too frequently, external consultants helped companies implement programmatic change. They designed and staffed corporate training programs, drafted corporate mission statements, designed gainsharing programs, and implemented quality circles. Such programs are ideally suited to the role of external consultants. They are easy to describe to potential customers. Precisely because they are programmatic, they can be replicated from one company to the next. Because customers are buying a known product, they can accurately estimate the time and cost of implementing the new program. Programs that do not require lasting changes in ongoing employee behavior are not usually threatening. But while such programs are easy to sell to the companies, they do not promote revitalization.

Not all external consultants sold programs. Some were highly skilled in supporting revitalization by helping managers diagnose problems, frame solutions, and implement various changes. These consultants were generalists in organizational effectiveness rather than specialists in a particular organizational problem or technique.

Perhaps because of the human resource function's traditionally low status and/or its inadequate skills in organizational diagnosis and revitalization, outside consultants often had more credibility with the line organization than did internal staff members. This credibility was particularly helpful where a high level of distrust existed between union and management or within a top management team. Here, consultants acted as facilitators whose views and interventions were seen as more reliable precisely because of their experience and neutrality.[5] On these occasions, employees felt more comfortable talking to a disinterested third party who did not control

175

their future than they felt talking directly to their bosses or even to internal human resource staff. When levels of trust were not high enough to allow managers to discuss difficult issues among themselves, consultants could assume the useful role of "saying the unsayable." Unlike internal human resource staff, these consultants were not risking their careers.

Human resource personnel often recognized the difficulty and the risk of being a "prophet in their own land," persuading top management to invite external consultants to advise about new forms of organizing and managing. Effective use of consultants occurred when a long-term relationship between the consultant and top managers was established and then integrated into the process of planning and strategizing corporate renewal. This relationship provided the consultant with a deeper understanding of the corporation's culture and the barriers to revitalization. Effective utilization of consultants by line managers was dependent on management's understanding of their role and potential contribution.

The availability of such consultants did not reduce the need for a company to develop the same set of skills among its internal human resource staff. The best internal consultants developed the same effective relationship with key executives and union leaders and had the skills to deal with difficult, emotional, and risky issues.

We have emphasized the ways in which external consultants helped an organization learn about both the revitalization process and itself. Self-understanding was critical because corporate renewals do not come "one size fits all." They must respond to the individual circumstances and needs of a given organization. Nevertheless, there are certain common features in successful revitalizations. Because consultants work in a range of companies, one extremely valuable function they serve is in simply helping clients learn what other organizations are doing. Many consultants originally establish their credentials as internal revitalization agents at other companies. As they work with new clients, they are able to draw on past experience to guide them past difficulties in implementation. It is also common, especially during the early stages of renewal, for consultants to arrange visits to leading-edge units at other companies.

LINE MANAGERS AS ORCHESTRATORS

While the human resource function plays an important support role in revitalization efforts, line management is the key. Line managers must have the vision to stay the course of renewal despite pressures for cost reduction. They have to balance concern for task with concern for people. They are the ones who make it possible for the human resource function and external consultants to be effective in supporting revitalization. The ability and skill of leaders in managing change make a difference.[6]

The top management of General Products had a much better understanding of all aspects of the revitalization process than did managers at the other companies. When we spoke with them, they articulated more clearly than others a vision of the new approach to organizing and managing as well as the strategy for change that they were employing.

Livingston Electronics' most ardent top-management change agent, an executive vice president of its largest business, was an example of less effective leadership. He talked passionately about the need for renewal and particularly about the Japanese model. It was well known to everyone in the company that he was pushing for renewal. However, he was unable to articulate a change strategy for revitalizing the company. His implicit strategy was to create revitalization through urging it.

At Continental Glass, top management had simply stopped actively pursuing revitalization. The CEO admitted his own confusion on the subject of revitalization. "I haven't really known how to push it," he said, "and I haven't been very [well] advised by others as to how it might work."

What are the differences in commitment and skill between revitalization leaders? How did these differences actually manifest themselves in behavior? These are some of the questions we will address in Chapter 7.

NOTES

1. The impact of short-term goals on long-term investment in R&D, plant, and equipment has been addressed by many other scholars. See for example, R.H. Hayes and W. Abernathy, "Managing Our Way to Economic Decline," *Harvard Business Review* 58 (July–August 1980), pp. 67–77; R.H. Hayes and D.A. Garvin, "Managing As If Tomorrow Mattered," *Harvard Business Review* 60 (May–June 1982), pp. 70–79; R.H. Hayes, Steven C. Wheelwright, and Kim Clark, *Dynamic Manufacturing: Creating the Learning Organization* (New York: Free Press, 1988).

2. The impact of too much and too little pressure on industrial renewal has been well documented by P.R. Lawrence and D. Dyer, *Renewing American Industry* (New York: Free Press, 1983).

3. The idea of balance between task orientation and concern for people has a long history in leadership research. Many scholars have suggested that such a balance is important to both supervisory and organizational effectiveness. See, for example, R.R. Blake and J.S. Mouton, *The New Managerial Grid* (Houston, TX: Gulf Publishing, 1978); R.R. Blake and J.S. Mouton, *Corporate Excellence Through Grid Organization Development: A Systems Approach* (Houston, TX: Gulf Publishing, 1968).

4. In their recent study of the evolving industrial relations patterns in U.S. industry, Kochan, Katz, and McKersie come to similar conclusions. Management has allowed unions—and through them, employees—a greater level of influence over shop-floor decisions regarding how work is done, even decisions regarding the shaping of some industrial relations policies. They have been considerably more reluctant to take the next important step: allowing influence over corporate strategy and policies. See T.A. Kochan, H.C. Katz, and R.B. McKersie, *The Transformation of American Industrial Relations* (New York: Basic Books, 1986).

5. R.E. Walton, *Managing Conflict: Interpersonal Dialogue and Third-Party Roles* (Reading, MA: Addison-Wesley, 1987).

6. Walton reaches a similar conclusion about the importance of the skills of top management in moving transformation along. See R.E. Walton, *Innovating to Compete: Lessons for Diffusing and Managing Change in the Workplace* (San Francisco: Jossey-Bass, 1987).

7

Revitalization Leaders— The Scarce Resource

Corporate renewal is not an impersonal process unfolding of its own accord. It is possible only when individual managers at the unit and corporate level have sufficient commitment and skill.

We found that leaders at the unit level had to be willing to break traditions of management and labor relations that may have existed for many years. To do this they raised dissatisfaction with the status quo by articulating with some urgency the core tasks—improving quality, decreasing cost, and/or increasing product innovation—their organizations had to perform to compete successfully. They then managed a participative change effort that aligned the organization and management process with the business's core task. All this required commitment to renewal as well as conceptual and consensus building skills.

At the corporate level, top management had to develop a

climate that encouraged revitalization in all units of the company. It did this by enabling innovative approaches to organizing and managing to take root in a few model organizations, then spreading those innovations by means of education and the transfer and promotion of managers committed to revitalization. Top management had to persist in this effort for a long time. In our leading companies, it was able to do so by maintaining the delicate balances of emphasis between cost reduction and human resource investment, and between concern for task and concern for people.

It is because leaders were so important in every aspect of the revitalization process that we depict leadership as the

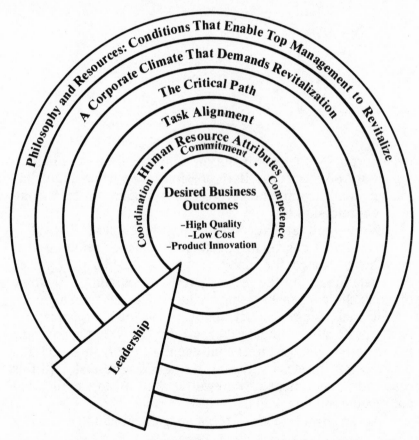

Figure 7-1: The Target of Revitalization: The Role of Leaders

factor that cuts across all rings of our revitalization target (see Figure 7-1). And for this reason we now pay detailed attention to revitalization leaders. Who were they? What attributes did they possess? How might companies go about developing them?

These questions are key when one considers that such leaders are in short supply. General Products' Tom Watson was well aware that skilled revitalization leaders were a scarce and valuable resource:

> It's easy for us to sit here and say all these things we are saying and let our eyes sparkle . . . . But when you pass the baton [and tell someone] to go out and do it, that's a small group that are capable, believe me.

This scarcity led to failures in revitalization and made it difficult for companies to spread revitalization at the rate they would have liked.

WHO WERE THE REVITALIZATION LEADERS?

Who were the members of the small group capable of running with the baton of revitalization? In all six companies, employees saw top management as the most powerful driving force behind revitalization, but there were no significant differences among companies in the extent to which top management was perceived to play this role (see Table 7-1).

To our surprise, we found that even in cases of successful revitalization, this group of corporate leaders did not necessarily include the very top executive. The CEOs at General Products and Fairweather were not active partners in managing revitalization, although neither CEO opposed it. However, the key leaders were at high levels: an executive vice president of a major business group, a vice president of manufacturing, the chief operating officer. They had responsibility for sufficiently large company segments to get revitalization started, and they typically exerted influence over other parts of their companies by their persuasive powers and, often, through their transfer from one segment to another.

In General Products, the key revitalization leader became the CEO. In the laggard revitalization company, U.S. Financial, revitalization leader Henry Lester served as the top executive throughout the change effort. Thus, while having the top corporate officer on board the revitalization effort is certainly useful, our evidence indicates that having renewal emanate from the very top of the company does not guarantee success.

The support of top corporate management was helpful to unit-level managers pushing their own revitalization efforts. However, for revitalization to succeed at the unit level it was essential that the general manager be actively engaged as its leader. Perhaps because of their smaller size and relative homogeneity, we saw no examples of successful unit-level revitalization that were not led by the general manager. Conversely, we saw many failures where general management leadership was lacking.

For this reason, successful corporate renewal required numerous committed division- and plant-level managers. It is not surprising that the rankings of the relative extent to which middle managers—division and plant managers, for example—served as initiators for change exactly paralleled those for the extent of revitalization (see Table 7-1). This suggests that the difference between success and failure may lie in the ability of a firm to develop revitalization leaders.

The corporate human resource function was not seen as playing a strong leadership role in moving revitalization in any of the six companies (see Table 7-1). That finding even held at U.S. Financial, where the vice president for human resources worked in close partnership with Lester.

In none of the six companies did union officials become revitalization leaders (see Table 7-1). That is not to say that union leaders cannot or do not play a leadership role. United Auto Workers' Irving Bluestone and Don Ephlin were revitalization leaders at General Motors and Ford Motors, respectively, two companies we studied less intensively. The leadership of the two men allowed management to develop a partnership with the union in revitalizing their companies.

Table 7-1: Sources of Corporate Leadership for Revitalization in Six Companies

	Average for All Companies	General Products	Fair-weather	Livingston Electronics	Scranton Steel	Continental Glass	U.S. Financial
Revitalization Rank		1	2	3	4	5	6
Source of Leadership							
Top management	4.13	4.42	3.93	3.62	4.55	4.25	4.50
Middle management	3.39	3.92	3.86	3.35	2.88	2.75	2.67
Human resources	2.62	3.00	3.20	2.05	2.88	1.88	2.5
Unions[1]	1.82	1.75	2.33	1.47	2.33	1.5	N/A

[1]U.S. Financial did not have a union; therefore this dimension does not apply to it.

However, this type of leadership did not generally characterize union leaders in the companies we studied.[1] To the extent that this finding holds more generally, it raises many questions about the future of labor unions in an environment of rapid change; it implies that the relationship between corporations and their employees may be getting redefined without active union leadership.

CHARACTERISTICS OF REVITALIZATION LEADERS

Although revitalization leaders functioned at all levels of the organization, we found they generally shared a common set of attributes.

At the unit level, we found three attributes that distinguished those managers who were most successful in leading revitalization:

1. A persistent belief that revitalization is key to competitiveness.
2. The capacity to articulate this conviction in the form of a credible and compelling vision.
3. The ability to implement this vision through a consistent pattern of words and behaviors.

The attributes of effective revitalization leaders at the corporate level overlapped, with one important exception. Consistency between words and actions was much less important for corporate managers leading successful revitalizations than it was for corresponding unit managers. Our discussion of leadership attributes will note both the overlap and the differences because of organizational level.

Persistence of Belief

Effective revitalization leaders shared a common conviction. They believed that fundamental changes in organizing and managing people would have a significant impact on the bottom line of their organizations. Lacking that belief, the long-term commitment necessary to oversee the complex process of systemwide renewal was missing.

Conviction.   What was it about the nature of their conviction that distinguished successful revitalization leaders from those who failed? General Products' Watson and Bryant demonstrated conviction by their understanding of the interconnectedness between revitalization and ultimate success in an increasingly competitive environment.

Compare their response to that of CEO Jim Taylor at Continental Glass & Container, one of our lagging companies. His business-first, people-later philosophy indicated that despite espousing the need for renewal, he was not convinced developing the human side of enterprise would contribute to an improvement in Continental's performance.

Lack of conviction was occasionally exhibited in our leading companies by top managers who were less involved in renewal. Joseph Brown, CEO at Fairweather Corporation, was not the company's revitalization leader. Although he supported it, he did not believe wholeheartedly that changing the way people were managed would inevitably lead to improved bottom-line performance. When asked to explain his company's pursuit of renewal, he talked of demographic shifts, of changes in the attitudes and values of "young people," but never of how the renewal would directly improve the performance of his company.

Brown's lack of faith surfaced when he addressed a Fairweather quality-of-work-life conference. "These kinds of changes are fine," Brown stated, "as long as they improve our profitability. And if they don't, we'll simply drop them and try something else." Commented one frustrated manager, "I thought we had gone beyond the point of wondering if these changes would improve our performance."

Persistence.   A short-term perspective like Brown's, a belief in renewal as long as profits stay up, will not sustain a leader's commitment through the inevitable variability in profits likely to occur during the long revitalization process.

While effective revitalization leaders understood the importance of strengthening their companies' short-term financial results, they believed it was equally important to create the foundation for sustained long-term profitability. Revitalization efforts will show up as bottom-line improvements over time rather than immediately.

The high level of these leaders' conviction allowed them to maintain their commitment to renewal in the face of many pressures. It sustained the efforts at General Products as the company sought a balance between ambitious cost-reduction goals and human resource investment goals.

General Products' Bryant devoted an enormous amount of energy over the better part of a decade to moving the revitalization effort forward through an ongoing series of speeches, seminars, group meetings, and off-site retreats. He paid constant attention to the succession process. Which managers in the organization represented the managerial model consistent with the revitalization effort? Were they being properly trained and developed? If a plant is undergoing a revitalization process, "I live there," he said. "I'm in the plant every damn day."

Bryant further emphasized pushing a sense of restlessness and persistence down through the organization in order to "get them all—the designers, the compounders, the chemists, the production people, the union, the quality assurance people, the purchasing people, and the suppliers—dreaming, thinking, pushing, shoving, and intellectually working every aspect of achieving perfection."

Contrast Bryant's focus and persistence with the revitalization leadership at Scranton Steel. By late 1986, the corporate revitalization process in that company had ground to a halt. We believe a major reason for the regression was the lack of a persistent willingness to drive revitalization by the new CEO, Edward Shields.

Shields, formerly head of Steel Operations, replaced Don Singer, a leader of the revitalization, as chairman. While Singer drove renewal from the chairman's office, Shields adopted a laissez-faire attitude. Shields explained this approach:

> We set out to promote greater teamwork and more openness, and we succeeded. We've now reached the point where we don't need to tell plant managers what to do. If they want to promote teams, fine. If they don't want to promote teams, that's fine too. What's important is tonnage per man-hour.

Ultimately, the willingness of leaders to persist in revitalization depends on the nature and strength of their beliefs. Was the leader satisfied and complacent about the changes that had already taken place in the organization? Or was he or she restless, dissatisfied, seeking greater improvement?

Shields's opening words in the preceding quote offer an excellent example of complacency. "You can't back down on any of this," concluded Bryant, reflecting persistence. "There is no resting place."

Capacity to Envision and Articulate Vision

Effective revitalization at any level cannot occur without a vision of the future state of the organization, a vision that aligns new patterns of management with the performance of the organization's core task. It is not surprising, then, that effective unit and corporate revitalization leaders had conceptualizing skills that allowed them to envision this future state.

Conceptualizing skills alone are not sufficient, however. Effective leaders also had the capacity to present their vision in a way that appealed to their constituents. That appeal allowed employees to commit to change emotionally, not just intellectually.

Conceptualizing Skills. In developing a task-aligned organization, leaders typically go beyond traditional hierarchy, rules, and procedures to find more effective ways to enhance organizational coordination. Consequently, revitalization leaders must be able to envision the consequences of proposed changes in organizational mechanisms and management processes.

We found that a surprisingly large number of the managers we observed were relatively weak in conceptualizing the organization as a total system. This shortcoming made it quite difficult for them to imagine how the organizational and management process might be redesigned to fit the core task more effectively. Bryant described the difficulties faced by one such manager at General Products:

> He just has a hell of a time conceptualizing, taking the concept and putting some meat and bones on that concept and then [repeatedly] coming back to the various levels [of the organization] and trying to visualize how the concept would fit at each of these levels. What problems might there be with it? How might you man it? What might the policies be at each one of these levels? . . . And it isn't that he is not smart enough . . . . He just never thought that way.

At the corporate level, not surprisingly, Watson and Bryant provided us with the most articulate and persuasive vision of how proposed changes in organizing and managing would lead to improved organizational effectiveness. In our interview with Bryant, he described the complex considerations involved in transforming a large manufacturing facility. That description demonstrated an ability to see the complex relationships between putting information in the hands of production workers via new information technology and his objectives of modifying the plant's authority structure, reducing hierarchical levels, and changing the role of plant management from directors and controllers to supporters and facilitators.

> If I put enough [information] down there, the questioning from the floor is going to be persistent enough to penetrate a large organization. . . . Now, the decisions are going to be made here [factory floor], and the data

is all going to be down here so that the [plant manager and staff] become the support group. They [plant manager and staff] are not driving the wagon. . . . They're the facilitators. . . . [Shop-floor employees become] the perfection teachers and . . . prophets. That's the big revolution that occurs, and it occurs because you put the information down there [on the factory floor].

Although the executives at Fairweather Corporation and Scranton Steel had a sense of where they were trying to move their organizations, few articulated their visions as clearly and as comprehensively as Bryant.

An Appealing Vision.   People in organizations want to feel they are contributing to meaningful goals and that their institutions contribute to a better world. When that perception exists, a moral basis for motivation can be stimulated to supplement control and incentives.[2] Effective leaders had the capacity to present revitalization in a way that provided such a perception. They did so by bonding goals like quality products and quality of work life with business objectives. They also articulated how these goals were an extension of the organization's history, its original purpose, and manner of doing things. These are goals that all constituents can agree are worthy. Management understands that striving for quality products leads to higher market share and lower costs. Since quality appeals to employees far more than reduction in costs or improvement in profits, it was a theme used by many leaders to develop commitment for revitalization.

To illustrate what we mean by making the vision of revitalization more appealing, we turn to the United Auto Workers' Irving Bluestone. As one of the leaders in General Motors' revitalization effort, he had to convince the rank and file that the Quality of Work Life program General Motors and the union were jointly sponsoring was something to which they should become committed. Quality of Work Life represented a new, and to many within the union a dangerous, direction in labor-management relations.[3] On a philosophical level, many union leaders wondered whether QWL represented an abandonment of the union's traditional role as militant defender of the particular interests of workers. On a more operational level, local leaders, stewards, and committee members questioned the possible impact on their own roles and positions as workers entered into a newly defined and vaguely understood relationship with management.

In his attempt to move the UAW into a new partnership with auto industry management, Bluestone sought to articulate a vision for his union's future that included QWL as a centerpiece. He asserted that the union had been concerned with the quality of its members' work life since the 1930s. Unlike his management counterparts at General Motors, Bluestone placed the matter of job satisfaction in the context of a push for industrial democracy. He meant not only the right to bargain collectively, but also the extent of influence and responsibilities workers have in the management of their work and the decisions of the enterprise. Collective bargaining that resulted in material advantages and a level of job security was the first necessary step toward industrial democracy. Challenging management's sole responsibility for decisions and their prerogatives, Bluestone believed, was the second.

That vision represented a key element of Bluestone's ability to "sell" the QWL idea to union leadership. Instead of seeing Quality of Work Life as a break with the union's past, he placed its thrust in the context of a natural extension of its historical efforts.

While the vision of Bluestone and other successful revitalization leaders was aligned with the central task of the organization—bringing about better working conditions for a union or remaining economically competitive for a corporation—it was stated in broader terms than just bottom-line performance.

Bluestone's vision for the United Auto Workers seemed to work on two levels simultaneously: it related to the key success factors of the organization and went beyond them to a higher level of expression. He asserted that Quality of Work Life would help the union represent workers better—the core task of the union—while stressing the higher values of industrial democracy.

Not surprisingly, our leading revitalization company, General Products, also found a vision that was effective at two levels. Bryant's vision for "the big revolution" at General Products included three elements:

1. Participative management driven by perfect quality.
2. Increased span of control that would force decision making down through the organization.
3. Information in the hands of shop-floor workers so that they could express ideas and opinions and make decisions.

"Perfection," "participation," information sharing, and shop-floor-level decision making—these concepts fused neatly into a task-aligned vision that also appealed to employees' desire for a more central role in producing a product of "perfect quality."

Implementing the Vision

A seemingly endless round of speeches, conferences, meetings, and other methods allowed revitalization leaders to articulate the vision and spread the word about the need for change. These forums helped individuals in the organization understand what revitalization was all about and where it was heading. They kept up pressure for continued forward movement. Leaders at General Products were perceived by those who completed our questionnaire as espousing the need for revitalization slightly more than those in the other companies, although this strategy was quite commonly used in all six cases (see Table 7-2).

The speeches and public statements of corporate revitalization leaders apparently had far more than a public-relations impact on their organizations. They also granted permission for revitalization throughout the organization. In explaining

Table 7-2: Top-Management's Espousal of Revitalization and the Consistency Between Words and Action in Six Companies

	Average for All Companies	General Products	Fair-weather	Livingston Electronics	Scranton Steel	Continental Glass	U.S. Financial
Researcher's Rank of Extent of Revitalization		1	2	3	4	5	6
Management Consistency							
Top management espoused revitalization	3.78	4.14	3.77	3.41	3.94	3.88	3.58
Top management consistent in words and actions	2.68	2.61	2.71	2.84	2.29	3.00	2.39

one of the most successful unit-level revitalizations in our study, Fairweather Corporation's ship operations, that division's general manager pointed to the permission granting contained in the public statements of his superiors, particularly those of vice chairman Hugh Dorsey:

> Hugh Dorsey provided a sanction to do things differently. Nobody was telling me exactly what to do, but I was getting the word from top management, often through their speeches. We could now question the traditional ways of managing.

Often the notion of top-management sanction could overpower the skepticism of immediate supervisors and peers toward renewal. The manager of one Fairweather factory was brought in specifically to determine why there were so many labor-related problems in the plant and to correct them. His diagnosis and the actions he took to address the problems surprised some of the other managers in his division: "I decided what we had here was poor teamwork, no communication, and no ownership of quality within the plant."

The concrete steps he took to rectify those shortcomings—quality circles, replacement of traditional first-line supervisors with people-oriented supervisors, joint efforts with the union to develop job flexibility and skill-based pay, and sharing information with the hourly work force on finances and quality control—all met with less than unanimous support. "I felt alone in this," recalled that plant manager. "A number of the other guys thought I was crazy." So why did he feel secure in continuing to push such innovations? "If you believe what Hugh Dorsey says," the manager explained, "the people at the top of this organization support this kind of change."

Time and time again, unit-level managers and supervisors pointed to the speeches of corporate revitalization leaders as their rationale for promoting revitalization in their own units. Local managers even engaged in innovations that their peers and immediate supervisors were less than enthusiastic about.

Consistency.   Revitalization leaders communicated values and intentions not only through words, but also through actions. At Navigation Devices, Jerry Simpson's strongest asset in the eyes of some of that unit's managers was his ability to manage in a way consistent with his espoused philosophy. The most important aspects of that philosophy were the ability to confront problems and the willingness to be confronted. Noted one of Simpson's managers:

> An important part of the culture change is that the privilege of rank—of being able to go around unchallenged—go away. The hard questions are now directed up to Jerry Simpson. And he is ready to handle this kind of thing himself. He works well with it.

There was considerable support throughout Navigation Devices for the conclusion that Simpson "practices what he preaches" about open behavior.

Just how important is practicing what you preach when leading a renewal effort? In a study of leadership, *The Leader: A New Face for American Management,* Michael Maccoby finds consistency of behavior to be of critical importance. Among the key attributes of successful managerial leaders, asserts Maccoby, is their ability and willingness to behave in ways consistent with the changes they are trying to bring about in their organizations. These leaders are personally "participative," "they don't try to control everyone," they "share the functions of leadership without becoming insecure," while at the same time they "are able to assert authority on matters of principle." And when these attributes do not come naturally or easily, the new leaders are willing and able to "develop themselves," to struggle "with his or her character defects," and "to demand much from themselves and use consultation and participation to compensate for their weaknesses and to stimulate internal growth."[4]

Our own evidence suggests a somewhat more complex conclusion. While Simpson is certainly an example of Maccoby's "new" leader, none of our most successful top management revitalization leaders would fit even roughly into that profile. The questionnaire results summarized in Table 7-2 suggest that in all six companies, top managers preached about renewal with great strength and conviction, but the consistency with which they practiced what they preached was not high. Top management at General Products showed no more consistency than top managers at Continental Glass and U.S. Financial.

Watson, who stated his belief that "in this day and age I don't think you can manage that way any more," offered no evidence that he had changed his personal management style from the self-described top-down, hard-core approach. He displayed not even a slight inclination toward the self-appraisal and willingness to struggle with his character defects that would lead to the individual development and internal growth alluded to by Maccoby.

Yet Watson moved his organization well beyond that of Brad Longstreet of Livingston Electronics or Henry Lester of U.S. Financial—both of whose managerial behaviors were, according to our observations, more consistent with the core values of revitalization. Consistency of beliefs, personal introspection, and willingness to change and develop are all traits that our most successful corporate-level revitalization leaders did not possess.

The same cannot be said of unit-level revitalization leaders, however. In fact, one of the strongest relationships we found in our questionnaire data was between the extent of change perceived by employees in their unit and the capacity of the leader and his or her immediate subordinates to act consistently and/or struggle to become consistent with the philosophy espoused (see Table 7-3). Furthermore, while overall there was a gap between unit managers' verbal support for revitalization and the consistency of their actions, the difference was less than for corporate top management. Not surprisingly, then, the two most successful unit-level revitalizations in our sample were led by managers whose own behaviors were in fact consistent with the direction in which they were attempting to move their organizations.

To understand what appears to be a contradiction, we need to focus more explicitly on the issue of consistency between words and actions at different organizational levels.
Inconsistency at the Top.   There could be little doubt that

Table 7-3: The Effect of Unit-Leader Espousal and Consistency of Words and Actions on the Extent of Revitalization

Unit Manager Words and Actions	Mean	Extent of Revitalization
Unit top management espouses change	3.83	.43*
Unit top management's consistency in words and actions	3.23	.63**

N = 26 plants and divisions
*p<.05
**p<.001

Scranton Steel's chairman, Don Singer, failed to practice what he preached.

"From what we've seen and heard," reported a manager with direct personal experience, "we don't believe there is any collaborative decision making when Singer is involved. He's a dictator." That reading of Singer's behavior was not contradicted by any other manager. Consider the following example.

When Bud Boyson was placed in charge of the quality-of-work-life effort in Scranton's construction division, he found the greatest roadblock to revitalization was the skepticism of the division's vice president. That skepticism emanated from the personal behavior of the vice president's boss, Singer. Early in the revitalization effort, Boyson reported a particular incident that he believed reinforced the view among the chairman's direct reports that Singer's desire for collaboration and participation were not real and thus could be ignored:

> Singer asked all his vice presidents to go back to their groups and find out what the reaction would be from their people if we took away a week of their vacation. So at the next meeting, my boss [the divisional vice president] reported that it would be a disaster. That's what the feedback was. Well, Singer immediately took my boss on. "You lousy sons-of-bitches from Con-

struction! No wonder you're all screwed up.'' And all the other vice presidents at that meeting went silent.

Boyson believed that Singer's actions in this case spoke louder than any call for a change in managerial behavior. Those actions convinced the vice presidents at the meeting—who may have been skeptical to begin with—that there was no real mandate to change their own autocratic, nonparticipative management style.

Inconsistency between the top manager's words and actions clearly slowed any possibility for revitalization at the top of the companies we studied, in what we have come to call the ''top manager's unit'' (CEOs and the key line and staff executives reporting to them). It did not, however, stop substantial progress from occurring in the rest of Scranton Steel and our leading companies. How was that possible?

In fact, most managers in Scranton Steel, particularly those in plants where most of the revitalization effort was focused, lacked immediate access to Singer. Many more managers pointed to his speeches and statements rather than to his individual behavior. ''Singer tends to be more participative [than past chairmen], and his support for participative management permeates the organization,'' insisted one typical manager. For evidence, that manager pointed to a speech Singer frequently gave on the ''New Golden Rules of Management'' at Scranton Steel. ''Singer makes no bones about it,'' the manager continued. ''We're going to change our style. Every one of those Golden Rules is different from what had been our philosophy in the past. Now, that's where I get my direction from, and the same for everybody else.''

Top management in its role as revitalization leader is removed from the day-to-day operations of the enterprise. Many more people hear what they say than see how they behave. Even when inconsistencies on the part of corporate leaders such as Singer or Watson were recognized by managers further down the organization, they tended to be tolerated. ''Given all the pressures he is under from the stockholders and the board, he's got to act that way'' was a frequently heard rationale for reported inconsistent behavior on the part of a corporate leader. As one Scranton Steel manager put it most succinctly, "I'm willing to put up with an awful lot of crap as long as Don keeps moving us in the right direction." **Consistency at the Unit Level.** Unwillingness to examine inconsistencies on the part of divisional and plant managers was far less tolerated and far more detrimental. None of the units in our study achieved much progress in its revitalization effort when the unit's head managed in ways inconsistent with the precepts of involvement, participation, and teamwork. One unit held back by the behaviors of its leader was Specialized Products of Fairweather.

In the early 1980s, Fairweather's Defense Group, of which Specialized Products was a part, attempted to promote revitalization by emphasizing collaborative, problem-solving behaviors with open, frank communication both horizontally and vertically. This was coupled with a business plan that emphasized managing assets, controlling costs, and improving return on investment. In Specialized Products, however, the unit's general manager, Herbert Folk, stifled innovation and revitalization despite his public support for change. Noted one Specialized Products engineer, "When I got to the engineering department, I found so much fear, so much paranoia, that no one was willing to take risks, to express ideas. It was a dead organization, an organization without a future." Said another engineer, "Our costs were sky high and we couldn't meet a single schedule. It was a nightmare."

Despite pressures to comply, Folk's management style clashed directly with the new style being espoused from above. "Directive," "autocratic," "punishing," "insensitive," and "arrogant" were adjectives used by managers in describing that style. "He was a hard-hitting, fist-pounding goddamnit personality," said a Specialized Products manager. "Everytime I saw him," remembered another, "he would greet me by saying, 'Well, Bob, what have you screwed up today?' That was sort of demoralizing." Still another reported that the atmosphere under Folk was such that

198

nearly everybody avoided open, honest communication, keeping news—especially bad news—to themselves. "We had a couple of 'leakers' [cost overruns] because we were afraid to talk about our problems until it was too late to do anything about them."

Folk himself acknowledged that as general manager of Specialized Products, he remained the roadblock to revitalization. The managers above and below Folk also agreed that no real change occurred in the operation until Folk was replaced by a general manager whose personal operating style matched more closely the model being promoted from above.

It is not hard to understand how inconsistencies in an operating unit can be far more detrimental to the revitalization process than inconsistencies in top managers leading corporatewide renewal. Inconsistent behavior in units is simply more visible. How a unit-level leader behaves is part of the everyday life of that unit and will thus either reinforce or undermine the revitalization effort.

Mixing Hard and Soft in Management.   While the interpersonal behavior of some corporate leaders may have been inconsistent with their espoused ideals, there was one area of management practice where successful revitalization leaders at all levels acted both consistently and skillfully. This was their ability to make management decisions that maintained a delicate balance between achieving "hard" task and "soft" human resource development objectives.

Effective revitalization leaders at all levels were task-oriented and impatient; they set high performance standards. However, that so-called hard orientation was mixed with a soft orientation that caused them to be concerned with developing the human resources of their organizations.[5] This ability enabled them to maintain a proper balance between cost reduction and human resource investment, as well.

Gene Bonner, vice chairman of Scranton Steel, was a good example of a top manager who was unable to implement a well-developed revitalization vision because of his exclusively soft approach. Throughout the 1970s, Bonner

199

churned out ideas for transforming his company: joint union-management productivity efforts, quality circles, quality-of-work-life initiatives. To many staffers in the human resource function, Bonner became something of a hero. His plethora of ideas won him the titles of "company humanist" and "the visionary." But he made virtually no organizational change. Noted one manager:

> He would read an article on quality circles and then send a memo asking why we weren't doing this. Then he would read another article on quality of work life and send another memo asking why we weren't doing that. It was always this goddamn off-the-wall stuff.

The merit of Bonner's ideas cannot be questioned. A number, in fact, later became incorporated into Scranton Steel's revitalization effort. Bonner was unable, however, to promote real revitalization with a hard rationale for his ideas. Excessive softness undermined his ability to express a task-aligned vision. He promoted revitalization as quality circles and quality-of-work-life programs rather than as ways of improving his company's ability to meet the competitive crisis. When many of those same ideas were later promoted by chairman Singer as ways of cutting labor costs, improving productivity and quality, and responding to Japanese competitors, they were implemented.

Managers who wanted to mix hard and soft often struggled with how to make their concern for people harder, how to translate it into something more than simply being nice. The most effective, like Simpson and Bryant, were hard on the process by which their subordinates managed people, while continuing to hold them accountable for business results. Those who effectively mixed hard and soft were also more likely to replace ineffective managers. Consider Al Parker, who headed U.S. Financial's middle-markets operation, one of the few successful revitalization leaders in the institution. His mixture of hard and soft was reflected in his statement concerning managerial effectiveness:

One thing all my managers have to understand is that there is no "product" in this business; it's only a people business. And you can be damn sure I use attitude survey data. I hold my managers absolutely accountable for survey results. If there are problems in communications or whatever, I expect my managers to fix them. If they can't, I'll move them. I just removed my middle manager. I was hearing from people that he wasn't communicating, and the survey data confirmed it. Now you understand I don't want everybody to be perfectly happy. I'm not looking for one hundred percent scores. I want this place to be tough. That regional manager wasn't just communicating poorly; he wasn't getting his job done right.

Parker effectively mixed a soft emphasis on treating employees differently with a hard insistence that the job be done right. To Parker, those hard and soft characteristics did not represent a dichotomy. They were two sides of the same coin.

Balancing hard and soft does not come easily; it takes creative new ways that many of our most successful revitalization leaders recognized as an ongoing struggle. Bryant revealed that struggle when he said, "Now I don't know how in the hell you can be nonconfrontational at every place else but at the bargaining table. There may be some way to do that, but we haven't figured that out yet."

HOW LEADERS DEVELOP

We have seen that effective revitalization leaders had developed a deep conviction in a vision of a revitalized organization, as well as the verbal and action-taking skills needed to implement that vision. Such a combination was rare.

Yet these attributes can be developed. We were not able to distinguish effective revitalization leaders from their colleagues by their superior intelligence, by their charisma, or by their unchangeable personal characteristics. Rather, we found that these leaders developed as a result of a unique set of organizational experiences.

Operating Experience

Only those leaders with a depth of operating management experience seemed able to successfully implement their vision of a revitalized organization.[6] Some of the most glaring failures occurred when the leader did not have that experience. Explained Watson:

> You have to know the business. You have to know how to make the product. You have to know what it takes to make good products. You have to know the equipment. And you have to know what it takes to make the business run better.

Lack of operating knowledge fatally undermines the ability to bring about organizational renewal for several reasons: it inhibits the leader's ability to visualize and articulate a business rationale for the revitalization, it precludes enacting innovations in management that align with running an efficient and effective operation, and it limits the leader's credibility among line managers. These are the skills and characteristics needed to implement a task alignment approach to revitalization.

The lack of operational experience plagued revitalization leaders at all levels of the organization. The reader will recall that when Ed Carline, head of Continental Glass's container division, set out to create a model participative plant in Reidsville, he hired Patrick Walsh to be the startup plant manager. He knew Walsh to be an intelligent and risk-taking manager, traits that he hoped would outweigh Walsh's almost total lack of manufacturing experience.

Despite Carline's optimism, Walsh's background in planning and sales did not prepare him to deal with the demands of starting a new manufacturing operation. That lack of operational experience led him to create a management team that some considered naive and others denounced as incompetent. Walsh was described as "detached" from the operations of the plant, and the same adjective applied to his director of manufacturing. Waste problems plagued Reidsville's operations. In three years, the corporation replaced Walsh and systematically dismantled every innovation put into place. Walsh's lack of operational skills had undermined his good intentions.

General Products' successful leading-edge North Carolina plant was an example of effective integration of innovative ideas with operating experience. The company's director of organizational development, Larry Polk, found that line managers had trouble accepting his ideas until they were shaped by an experienced operational manager. That operational experience came from the director of manufacturing, Watson, who noted:

> They [line managers] started deviating from his [Polk's] recommendations. . . . So several times I had to get the two groups together. . . . These guys were "on the street," and Larry was preaching from the Bible. There had to be some middle ground.

Company chairmen, no less than plant managers or vice presidents, could find their own efforts undermined by lack of operational expertise. A number of critics of Henry Lester's efforts to promote renewal in U.S. Financial noted his lack of operating experience. Lester failed to make running the business more effectively and profitably the cornerstone for innovation and change at the bank. Certainly the culture program was not that cornerstone, and his renewal effort eventually floundered badly.

Leaders with recognized operating management experience and skill seemed better able to ask more of organizational members. Because of their recognized track record, others in the organization seemed more willing to follow their direction. That depth of credibility certainly helps explain Watson's success in gaining acceptance for Polk's ideas.

Operating experience also provided skills and perspective that directly enhanced the leadership of revitalization. That experience often developed in leaders many of the competencies necessary for successful revitalization. Experience taught the leaders such critical revitalization skills as how to work through other people, how to gain commitment, and how to build competence on the part of subordinates.

In addition, leaders with a depth of operating experience were more apt to be a part of the organization they were trying to change. That connection allowed them to articulate a vision and act in ways that did not seem overly revolutionary to organizational members. It is impossible to imagine an outsider or even an insider with little or no line experience gaining the credibility that a Watson or a Bryant was able to command.

Developing Conviction and Skill

General operating experience was necessary, but not in itself a sufficient condition for effective revitalization leadership. Leaders also needed to develop conviction about the importance of revitalization and the skill to act on that conviction. We found that leaders developed conviction and skill in the same way they had developed their technical expertise—not through training programs or as a result of listening to speeches—but through experience on the job.

Self-revealing Experiences. A number of revitalization leaders, all at middle-management levels, developed their convictions from on-the-job experiences that forced them to confront their own limitations. For these managers, a belief in the efficacy of revitalization was learned on a personal level as they were forced to confront how their behaviors influenced the effectiveness of their work units.

Charles Post, manager of Scranton Steel's accounts-payable division, became a supporter of revitalization when an attitude survey revealed that his employees found him cold and aloof, overly directive, unwilling to stand behind his people, and blatantly sexist. "I was surprised," he confessed. Given the company's emphasis on revitalization, his new-found awareness led Post to examine his behavior and make adjustments with some success.

Post's experience is similar to that of many other managers in revitalizing organizations. As their units began to revitalize, demands for teamwork together with a more open environment caused them to consider changes in their approach to management. Attitude surveys, feedback from human resource facilitators, and direct feedback from empowered employees led to that open environment. It enabled revelations about management style and a reexamination of assumptions about management not possible in traditional hierarchical organizations. To survive in the new environment, managers could not ignore the feedback.

A Personal Role Model. Occasionally, managers developed convictions, if not new behaviors, from observing the behavior of other managers. Positive and negative role models helped clarify in James Weaver's mind where he wanted to take his organization. When he became senior vice president of Fairweather's Defense Group, Weaver decided that the division's management style "wasn't keeping up with the times." He was especially concerned with what he called the "repressive style of management" that permeated the organization. "We were highly autocratic, very orderly, very demanding, very disciplined."

"We really didn't know what to replace the old style with," Weaver admitted. As he wrestled with the question of management style, Weaver focused on two individuals who came to represent, in his mind at least, models of where his organization had been and where it was headed. First he pointed to a "villain": his old boss. "I had a cold, negative, unfeeling boss, and I didn't like it," recalled Weaver. However, he also found a "hero" in Bob Lee, a senior vice president. "He got results, great loyalty from his people. He became our role model for how to manage."

Negative and positive role models were also cited by a number of middle-level revitalization leaders as having played an important part in the development of conviction and vision.

An Operational Model. For most corporate leaders and

many middle managers, the belief that corporate performance and the development of human resources were interconnected came from far less personalized experiences. Observing innovative operations directly and seeing them perform effectively over time was an important breeding ground for the beliefs of these managers.

Singer, Scranton Steel's CEO, developed his conviction, the reader will recall, after visiting a West Coast plant and seeing what labor-management cooperation could produce. For the first time he understood the potential inherent in employee involvement. Jerry Simpson and his planning team found their conviction and vision following a visit to an innovative plant organized around teams.

DEVELOPING THE SCARCE RESOURCE

If organizational revitalization occurs in large part because of the presence of effective revitalization leaders, then organizations need to think more proactively about how they can ensure an adequate supply of these leaders. The evidence from our study suggests that effective revitalization leaders are "made" rather than "born."[7] Furthermore, the process of "making" an effective revitalization leader appears to grow out of relatively consistent experiences.

Two possible conclusions can be drawn. One is that organizations can hope that a large number of managers will have these experiences serendipitously, and so develop into effective revitalization leaders. Our experience as well as common sense suggests that this wait-and-hope approach is dangerously flawed. Effective revitalization leaders were seen by top managers in our leading companies as their scarcest resource. Their scarcity continuously threatens progress in making companies more competitive.

We favor the second conclusion: Organizations can systematically and consciously expose managers to experiences that approximate those we have found associated with the development of conviction, vision, and skill. Operational experience, self-revealing experience, positive role models, and experience with successful models of the new way are most easily obtained by embedding prospective revitalization leaders in innovative leading-edge organizations. That is how the probability of exposing managers to developmental experiences, which occurred serendipitously for the managers we described, can be increased substantially. This is exactly the role played by General Products' North Carolina plant in developing that company's growing number of revitalization leaders.

Simply stated, in order for effective organizations to be developed, organizations need to develop effective leaders. That is best done, as we have said, by creating an organizational context that encourages the development of leadership skills in its members. However, since current leaders are very much part of the context that must be altered in order to develop revitalization leaders, corporations face a dilemma. How can a new corporate context be developed by leaders who have not yet learned new attitudes and behaviors themselves?

The answer lies in the revitalization strategy we have presented, which in our view is not only an effective organizational development strategy, but also a highly effective management development strategy. By encouraging innovative organizational units, top managers who may themselves not be capable of modeling the behaviors they know are needed for successful revitalization can get the process started. If the most promising leaders from these units are promoted, they will shape the wider context of the corporation. Once started, the process can become self-perpetuating.

This ongoing and mutually reinforcing process of leadership and organizational development suggests, once again, that corporate renewal must be thought of as a long-term process. However, for the corporation to sustain the process and develop a capacity for ongoing renewal, top management itself will ultimately have to develop renewal leadership skills.

Our understanding of this final phase of revitalization was limited by the relatively short time frame of our research—three to five years, depending on the company. Nevertheless, based on how revitalization unfolded in the time frame we observed, we were able to extrapolate how top management and corporate groups must become involved in revitalization if a corporation is to institutionalize a capacity for readaptation and renewal.

NOTES

1. The lack of union leadership in work innovations, despite ample opportunity, has been noted elsewhere. See, for example, M. Beer and J. Driscol, "Strategies for Change," in J.R. Hackman and J.L. Suttle, eds., *Improving Life at Work: Behavioral Science Approaches to Organizational Change* (Santa Monica, CA: Goodyear Publishing, 1977), pp. 364–453.

2. The notion of moving from bureaucratic control to a moral basis for commitment was set out by A. Etzioni, *Comparative Analysis of Complex Organizations: On Power, Involvement, and Their Correlates* (New York: Free Press, 1961).

3. Details on the quality-of-work effort in General Motors can be found in B. Spector and P.R. Lawrence, "General Motors and the United Auto Workers," in M. Beer et al., *Human Resource Management: A General Manager's Perspective* (New York: Free Press, 1985).

4. M. Maccoby, *The Leader: A New Face for American Management* (New York: Simon & Schuster, 1981), pp. 223–225.

5. A considerable body of research has dealt with the hard and soft dimensions of leadership, although the terms used to describe the two dimensions differ. Much of the research on what has also been called task-oriented and relationship-oriented leadership has been summarized in B.M. Bass, *Stogdill's Handbook of Leadership: A Survey of Theory and Research* (New York: Free Press, 1981). See also R.R. Blake and J.S. Mouton, *The New Managerial Grid* (Houston, TX: Gulf Publishing, 1978).

6. This finding is quite consistent with other research that has shown the importance of knowing the business to effective general management. See, for example, J.P. Kotter, *The General Managers* (New York: Free Press, 1982).

7. The same argument about the scarcity of leaders and the need to develop them in the face of an increasingly competitive environment has been made by J.P. Kotter, *The Leadership Factor* (New York: Free Press, 1988).

8

Sustaining Revitalization

What will it take for the leading companies in our sample
to sustain the hard-won progress in revitalization? Continuous
renewal is necessary if they are not to falter as strong global
competition continues unabated into the twenty-first century.

Both General Products and Fairweather Corporation
were beginning to run into new issues that, if not resolved,
could stall renewal. As plants and divisions pushed forward
with innovations, managers in those units began to view corporate policies and staff as significant barriers to further revitalization. Change at the top, they insisted, was needed.

At the same time, pressures from financial markets and
takeover threats forced top management to reexamine its
portfolio of businesses. While the sale of some businesses
was being considered, top management also began to focus on
ways that potential synergies between businesses might be
exploited more effectively. Thus the question of how to

improve coordination around common markets, customers, technology, and physical and human assets became an issue companies increasingly had to confront.

The inconsistency between top management's words and actions now posed a barrier. To improve teamwork at the corporate level and reexamine corporate policies and staff practices that innovative units perceived as hindering further progress, top management had to apply the process of revitalization to itself. The top-management unit had to become the focus of revitalization.

As we saw early signs of strains between the top and bottom of the company triggered by the corporate revitalization process, we realized that the conclusions about corporate renewal we have presented so far apply only for the early years of a corporate transformation. In this phase, top management enabled and orchestrated revitalization in various units in the company. It did not attempt to transform its own management practices or those that governed the decision-making process at the top.

How long does the first phase of change take? Within our revitalization leader, General Products, a company with approximately $10 billion in revenues and over 100 plants worldwide, upper management took ten years to successfully move through this phase. That is not to suggest that this phase is over for General Products. After a decade of effort, there were still some plants, mostly overseas, that had not yet made significant progress in revitalization. Nevertheless, top management clearly understood how to manage this phase of the revitalization process and was well prepared to complete it.

It is impossible to know exactly how long it will take to complete the first phase of renewal, if indeed there is ever a completion point, given continued change in the external environment. What is clear is that 10 or more years is not an unrealistic period of time. Our emphasis in Chapter 7 on the need for leaders to demonstrate persistence takes on more meaning when this time frame is considered.

The distinction between the phase of change we have described in this book—innovation at the unit level orches-

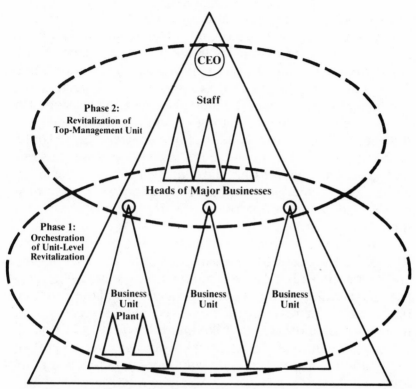

Figure 8-1: Phases of Revitalization: Moving from Lower-Level Units to the Top-Management Unit

trated by top management—and what we see as a necessary next phase—change in top management's own behavior—is depicted in Figure 8-1. We hasten to emphasize, however, that these phases overlap in time.

THE SECOND PHASE: REVITALIZATION AT THE TOP

Throughout the early years, pressures first from the competitive environment and later from top management energize

211

change. While these sources of pressure obviously continue, a new source is added as more and more units undergo transformation. As inconsistencies in the behavior and policies of corporate staff groups begin to interfere with revitalization in units, these units begin to exert pressure for change at the top. Performance evaluation, compensation, succession planning, budgeting, and goal-setting systems, unless aligned with the needs of innovative units, become an ever greater source of frustration. Further, as capital markets impose demands for higher financial returns, these pressures can cause an examination of synergies and interdependencies between businesses and reinforce internal pressures for revitalization at the top.

The CEO can no longer limit his or her role in the corporate-change process to espousing, encouraging, supporting, and resourcing revitalization efforts at the unit level. He or she has to target the top-management group and the corporate organization for revitalization and become an effective unit-level revitalization leader. Like any other unit-level revitalization, the failure of the CEO and his or her direct reports to model the team-oriented style will undermine renewal at the top.

The CEO must lead the top-management unit down the steps of the critical path. Those steps include energizing immediate subordinates to embrace fundamental change; clarifying and, if necessary, changing corporate strategy; and developing a strategically aligned vision of how business units, line and staff, union and management, and domestic and international operations are to be coordinated into a team effort producing maximum possible synergy. Like the successful unit-level leaders, the CEO must develop consensus that change is needed, support the personal development of top-level executives who lack the values or skills to manage in the new way, and, through team building and replacement, create a cohesive team committed to change in the corporate culture.

While neither General Products nor Fairweather Corporation had completed this stage in the period of our field work,

212

both began to grapple with "back pressure" from innovative units. After about six years of unfolding revitalization effort, General Products' manufacturing function—where most of the revitalization had occurred—complained about various corporate line and staff functions. It was time, they insisted, for revitalization to take place in the marketing, finance, sales, and distribution departments, functions with which they interacted regularly. Little was done in response to these concerns, in part because Tom Watson, the company's revitalization leader, had not yet been promoted to CEO.

At Fairweather, back pressure began to build in two business groups where the behavior of the top executive was increasingly seen as a barrier by division managers revitalizing their units. One of these was the Defense Group, where James Weaver's efforts to revitalize his top-management unit provides an illustration of how a CEO might apply the critical-path change process at the very top of the corporation.

Weaver was a senior vice president in charge of a cluster of 11 business units whose aggregate revenues were $1.5 billion. The divisions operated in a highly decentralized mode. Many of the business units, including Jerry Simpson's Navigation Devices unit, had been managing a revitalization effort for some time. Within Fairweather, Weaver's Defense Group was on the leading edge of change.

Over time, Weaver's general managers began to question his management style: his top-down decision-making approach and his use of staff groups to maintain tight control over the divisions. The gap between the more participative style these general managers were encouraging in their own divisions and the more directive style they were experiencing from Weaver caused increasing demands for change.

At the same time, Weaver himself began to be concerned about the performance of his group. For ten years, the group's rate of growth had been in the top quartile of the industry, but its return on assets was in the lowest. Weaver reasoned that part of the problem lay in the unwillingness of autonomous and growth-oriented general managers to work cooperatively in identifying the best capital investment opportunities in the group and in sharing assets such as plant and highly expensive equipment.

His desire to develop a more integrated strategic-planning and capital allocation process was in direct conflict with his general managers' desire to retain their independence. An external consultant was brought in to lecture at a management meeting on how a decentralized organization might manage the balance between "loose" and "tight" control. In addition to delivering the lecture, the consultant chose to involve Weaver and his general managers in a diagnosis of their unit and its management process. The operative question: How well did the group's structure, systems, Weaver's management style, the backgrounds, predispositions, and skills of the general managers, and the top group's shared values fit the strategy the group had to pursue in order to improve return on assets?[1]

The general managers and staff heads were divided into small teams and each reported back their observations. The consensus: Weaver's style, the group's planning and decision-making process, the culture, and the reward system at the top all mitigated against managing common customers and assets (both physical and human) more synergistically.

Two separate task forces were commissioned to further study the problems raised in the preliminary diagnosis and make recommendations for change. While the general managers on the task forces acknowledged their own predisposition to go after contracts and make capital expenditures without regard to potential synergies was part of the problem, they pointed to another: Weaver's management style and that of his staff. That style, they felt, stood in direct contrast to the pattern of management they and Weaver had agreed was needed—more teamwork and coordination between the traditionally independent divisions. The adjectives they used— "directive," "punishing," "watch-dog like"—expressed their sense that Weaver's style would not allow them to implement what they believed to be the management solution to duplicate assets and unexplored opportunities with common customers. That solution was a general management board, composed of all divisional general managers with responsibility for managing issues that cut across divisions.

Despite their conviction that Weaver's style needed to change if the board was to function effectively, they were reluctant to raise the issue of Weaver's style in their report to him. Such trepidation was common at all levels, but seemed to be particularly intense the closer revitalization got to the top of the companies we studied. In the end, Weaver's subordinates did give him feedback, but only at the urging of the consultant, and then in a watered-down manner.

Nevertheless, Weaver got the message. He hired another consultant to help him gain insights and control over his operating style; with that help, he met with the general management board on several occasions to redefine respective roles, responsibilities, and relationships. As the process of revitalization at the top unfolded, Weaver expressed genuine surprise that the revitalization effort he had been urging on his division managers for the past several years could be applied to the work of the top-management team. The insight that motivated him to proceed further represented to us an illustration of what revitalization at the top might encompass.

The fact that corporate revitalization at General Products or Fairweather Corporation is still in process makes it difficult to project what will happen to revitalized business units and plants if this phase is not completed successfully. We speculate, however, that if top management fails to revitalize the corporate core, there is a risk that gains made in plants and business units will not be sustained in the long run.

The most immediate difficulty is likely to be the development of top-level successors whose approach to management is consistent with revitalization goals. Unless a CEO develops a top-management unit where the expectations for coordination, commitment, and competence are the same as those in lower-level units undergoing revitalization, group heads and key staff vice presidents in the company will not develop the values and management skills demanded by revitalization.

215

Without these values and skills, the candidate pool for CEO and COO positions will lack key executives who could lead revitalization.

Lacking leaders who can succeed to the top jobs, sustaining renewal becomes virtually impossible. Standing still means moving backward. Continental Glass's CEO bemoaned the fact that he had just promoted a key executive to the presidency who shared none of the aspirations for renewal that spurred his original call for change. How could he regain lost momentum? In our view, the new president made that impossible. On the other hand, if a company passes successfully through the top-management phase of revitalization we have described, the result should provide a number of key executives competent in and committed to the revitalization.

WHY CORPORATE REVITALIZATION RARELY STARTS AT THE TOP

Top managers are in their positions, in part at least, because of their desire for power and their skill in managing it. They rose to their positions in an era in which maintaining strong control was an effective means of managing. Watson was quite candid when he described his early years in the company, a time when it operated very hierarchically. "In those days," he said, "we built organizations and ruled them with an iron hand." It is not surprising, therefore, that those who rose to the top in all the companies we studied had developed strong needs for control. Their positions also insulated them from bad news, and they became accustomed to operating in an environment free from challenge, especially on matters of their own behavior.

Another barrier to revitalization at the top was the difficulty top managers found in challenging their subordinates, many of whom had successfully run their operations over the years in a style very different from what was now demanded. For these reasons, managing change at the top was difficult to contemplate, let alone implement, unless momentum for revitalization had already developed at lower levels in the company.

Even if top management was philosophically ready to start a corporate transformation from the top, such an effort might not succeed. The CEO is unlikely to have available model units and leading-edge managers from which to learn. Lacking knowledge about the new approach to management and skills in implementing it, top managers would not be able to involve line and staff headquarters personnel, the organizational unit of which they are the leader, in a renewal process. Moreover, staff groups and powerful managers at headquarters would offer massive resistance early on, making change from the top difficult even for the most committed and skilled top manager.

There is another reason why change typically does not start at the top. The barriers to competitiveness presented by traditional practices are often first recognized at lower levels and in organizational units far away from headquarters, not at the corporate core. That is because outlying units are where the struggle to implement goes on daily. It is also where operating results of past hierarchical management practices are most evident. Managers at this level have the best capacity to kick sacred cows, which those in power have a stake in preserving. Unlike corporate managers who were probably selected because they represent the core values of the company and are beholden to the CEO, managers at the periphery have not yet been completely socialized into the current management culture, nor do they all aspire to the top.

Does this mean that revitalization cannot start at the top with a focus on the corporate core? It is possible, but not probable. It is possible, of course, that the corporation could bring in an outsider from a corporation already involved in renewal. That outsider might have the attributes necessary to lead a revitalization of the top-management unit. Outsiders come with other problems, however. Most important, they may lack enough credibility in the new organization to develop support and commitment.

Even if revitalization got a start at the top, the company

would still have to implement the first phase of change. Model organizations would still have to be developed and diffused across the company. Without such model organizations it is more difficult for lower-level executives to learn new behaviors. Even a committed top manager who models the new approach to management cannot make programmatic change work.

Though we have seen no successful efforts that have begun at the top, it is possible this will happen more frequently as the labor market for top executives includes more people whose behaviors and management philosophy align with the new paradigm for organizing and managing.

THE EFFECT OF CAPITAL MARKETS

Management's attempts to lead a revitalization for the top unit of the corporation do not take place in a vacuum. Corporate executives in the United States are subject to severe pressure from capital markets. They must maintain attractive financial returns, often on a quarter-to-quarter basis. If returns fall substantially below the breakup value of the company, it is subject to takeover. The top management of all six companies lived in fear of that possibility. Capital markets were the context that often shaped decisions about many business matters, including revitalization. Thus we can add capital markets as the outer ring in the revitalization target (see Figure 8-2).

Capital markets were not, however, the only source of pressure. It was the challenge of global competition and deregulation that started our six companies on the path to renewal. Thus top managers were caught between two demanding and sometimes conflicting masters, the competitive environment and capital markets. What role did each play in top management's decisions regarding revitalization?

The competitive environment clearly was the stimulus that propelled our companies to revitalize. The need to develop innovative, high-quality products at relatively low cost

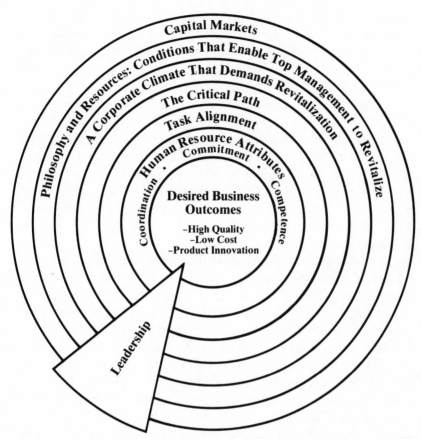

Figure 8-2: The Target of Revitalization: The Role of Capital Markets

made them search for a new way to organize and manage. The Japanese model and early innovations in their own corporation showed them that superior quality at lower cost than had ever been contemplated was achievable through radical innovations in organizing and managing. The effectiveness of new approaches to management reinforced top management's growing commitment to revitalization.

Capital markets, on the other hand, played a more complicated role. There is some reason to believe, although we saw only a few examples, that capital markets have the potential to stimulate the changes at the top that are essential for

219

sustained corporate renewal. Weaver's efforts to increase return on assets through more effective teamwork between independent but potentially synergistic businesses is a good example. We believe such a step may be forced on many multibusiness corporations undergoing revitalization.

Capital markets demand that corporations identify and exploit potential synergies between related businesses and find ways to divest those that do not fit. Shareholder equity in corporations that do not do this is likely to be undervalued by capital markets, particularly when compared to the potential value of equity in each of the business units were they to sell equity as independent units.[2] In effect, the corporate whole must add up to more than the sum of its parts. While that is a strategic problem, it is also a problem of organizing to maximize coordination. Neither of these problems can be solved effectively without revitalizing the organization and management process at the very top.

Unfortunately, capital markets also have the definite potential to weaken top management's resolve to revitalize. While managers in companies such as General Products have sustained revitalization over a longer period than others, they have had to do it in the face of enormous pressures for short-term performance. Several lagging companies, most notably Continental Glass and U.S. Financial, were unable to sustain an investment in human resources when short-term performance pressures became too persistent. In the end, these pressures overwhelmed their human resource development strategy. Instead of enhancing organizational vitality, executives at Continental and U.S. Financial turned exclusively to acquiring businesses and/or reducing overhead. Slowly, top management came to focus on finance to the exclusion of people and organizational renewal.

While we believe pressures from capital markets may have some positive outcomes for shareholders and society, we also note their negative consequences. We are not the first to identify the negative effects of pressure for quarterly earnings, nor are we the first to raise questions about their role in the difficulties of American corporations in remaining internationally competitive.[3] We were, however, in a position to observe the effects of these pressures on managers' capacity to sustain an investment in human resources.

Although we noted in Chapter 6 that managers can make a difference in the struggle to balance long-term human resource investments and short-term financial goals, we also wish to emphasize that a redesign of capital markets may be in order. Short-term financial pressures and threat of takeovers strengthen the hand of financially oriented managers, not the operating managers who were more successful in leading renewal. Even managers who started out wanting to invest in human resources lost their focus. It is not a coincidence that Japanese companies, less subject to pressures from financial markets and able to manage toward longer-term objectives, have already learned to organize and manage in the ways American companies are trying to adopt.[4]

To sustain the competitive advantage of revitalization, an organization must continue its investment in human resources. This may require a more favorable context than capital markets in the United States now offer. Identifying necessary reforms for capital markets is well beyond the scope of this book, but innovative equity arrangements, broad employee ownership, and/or tax legislation that limits the gains from short-term transactions are possibilities.[5] The trend toward leveraged management buyouts will also have to be reversed as LBOs place severe pressures on management to cut costs. Less short-term pressure from financial markets is essential if top management is to set and follow the long-term renewal agenda we have presented.

NOTES

1. For a complete discussion of the "7S" framework used by the consultant, see R.H. Waterman, Jr., T.S. Peters, and J.R. Phillips, "Structure Is Not Organization," *Business Horizons* 23 (June 1980), pp. 14–26.
2. Considerable research has demonstrated that conglomerates are not as profitable as single-product companies or companies in related businesses. See

R.H. Hayes and S.C. Wheelright, *Restoring our Competitive Edge: Competing Through Manufacturing* (New York: Wiley, 1984), pp. 13–14. Moreover, acquisitions of unrelated business do not generally lead to better financial performance. See M. Porter, "From Competitive Advantage to Corporate Strategy," *Harvard Business Review* 65 (May–June 1987), pp. 43–59.

3. R. Hayes and W. Abernathy, "Managing Our Way to Economic Decline," *Harvard Business Review* 58 (July–August 1980), pp. 66–77; M.L. Dertouzos, R.K. Lester, and R.M. Solow, *Made in America* (Cambridge, MA: MIT Press, 1989).

4. S. Marsland and M. Beer, "Note on Japanese Management and Employment Systems," No. 481–009 (Boston: Harvard Business School, 1980).

5. The emergence of white knights who own large blocks of preferred stock may be one answer. See R. Lenzer, "White Knights Are the Wave of the Future," *Boston Globe,* December 22, 1989, p. 63.

9

Where and How to Start

Corporate revitalization rests on the capacity of leaders to develop an organizational context that will influence people—managers, workers, and union leaders alike—to change behavior and attitudes. However, each change leader's capacity to begin and sustain revitalization is also a function of the environment within which he or she operates. The unit manager's ability to manage change is affected by the many policies and practices handed down from headquarters and the support for revitalization provided by top management. Top management's ability to manage and sustain renewal is in turn affected not only by business conditions and capital markets that shape the economic environment of the corporation, but also by the response of its board to external factors.

Thus corporate revitalization is a play within a play within a play. Each manager's effort to revitalize, while a function of his or her own conviction and skills, is also a function of a corporate environment he or she may be able to influence, but cannot control. Given this reality, it is easy for a manager to conclude there is nothing he or she can do to start revitalizing the organization. Until changes occur at the next level, we have heard some managers say, "nothing can be done." We believe this is far too pessimistic an attitude and is self-defeating.

American corporations will become more competitive only when individuals at every level—unit managers, human resource executives, union leaders, top managers, or public policymakers—take the initiative to create a favorable environment for renewal in the domain over which they have some control. A good-faith effort to work cooperatively with the next level up to shape the environment so that it supports revitalization initiatives is also called for. Not knowing how to get started, well-intentioned managers too often do nothing. Just as often, managers who start revitalization fail. Lacking some of the insights discussed in this book, they make false starts that lead to disillusionment and loss of energy.

Our research has pointed to what prospective revitalization leaders at each level can do to get started.

THE UNIT GENERAL MANAGER

Revitalization in every company we studied began with unit leaders who were willing to risk being pioneers. When they took those risks carefully and with skill, they succeeded in becoming change leaders in their companies. Such a course is not without its dangers, but given increasing competition and heightened awareness of the management innovations that companies can adopt, those dangers are not unreasonable. The task-alignment approach can ensure the revitalization effort will remain focused on improving business results, making it more apt to be both credible and successful.

Unit managers can identify the pressures for improved performance on their units. They can find ways to start down the critical path by using those pressures to energize the organization. Visits to suppliers and customers and information about competitors can help raise the level of readiness for change, even if competitive pressures are not at crisis proportions. Staff unit managers can identify internal customers and put people in touch with customer perceptions of the quality of the service their units are providing.

Unit managers need to stay focused on the core task of the organization. They can involve line managers, workers, and union leaders in diagnosing how the organization is currently failing to achieve that core task and how functions and levels can coordinate more effectively. They can design ad hoc teams to achieve improved coordination.

Unit leaders need to remember they are not alone. It is likely that within the company there are innovative managers from whom they can learn. Leaders and key employees can visit those operations. If there are none in the company, they can find other companies that are engaged in renewal and visit those innovative organizational models.

If unit leaders are uncertain about what to expect or how to proceed, they can find a human resource professional at corporate headquarters and/or an external consultant who can offer advice and perhaps work with the leader and his or her staff in getting started. Those consultants should be skilled generalists in organizational diagnosis and change who can help manage a critical path process, not specialists in a particular programmatic solution. And unit leaders should remember that the credibility of their efforts rests on a good-faith endeavor to examine their own functioning and that of their top-management team.

Unit leaders need to keep their bosses informed about plans to improve business performance. When sharing the new philosophy of organizing and managing that underlies the revitalization process, they should be sure to explain how and why new patterns will improve commitment, skills, and ultimately teamwork and financial performance. Unless they make these explicit connections, their efforts may appear to be naive human relations initiatives that make people feel better but do not contribute to the business. If the connection between new patterns of management and improvements in quality, cost, or products/services cannot be articulated, the revitalization effort is probably flawed.

Keeping higher-level managers informed will help condition the environment for support. Unit leaders can invite corporate executives to visit their units. They can put those executives in touch with employees, groups, and union leaders whose attitudes and behaviors have changed dramatically as a result of revitalization initiatives. They can shape the future of revitalization by helping corporate management learn from their unit's experience.

THE CORPORATE HUMAN RESOURCE MANAGER

Corporate human resource functions cannot drive the change effort, but they can play a significant role. To make an important contribution, they will have to change their traditional role and behavior.

A good start is to back away from human resource programs. This can be done by avoiding sponsorship of such programs and countering top management's requests for them.

The human resource function can assume an important consulting and facilitating role in those divisions, plants, and branches that are ripest for revitalization. These are the units under the most competitive pressure. The first step is to select one or two units, preferably ones led by effective managers willing to embark on revitalization rather than by managers who are weak and already in trouble. Good candidates are new managers who have taken over a business that requires revitalization. After establishing a consulting relationship with these managers, the human resource function should focus resources on their units and provide intensive consulting and coaching support.

What does the consulting role entail? Through conferences and visits, human resource managers can put unit managers in touch with other innovative managers both inside and outside the company. Through a better understanding of the business and its competitive strategy, they can play a leadership role by pointing to ways in which the business unit can realign its approach to organizing and managing with its core task. Through confronting line managers with the gap between their words and actions concerning renewal, they can help revitalization leaders develop the consistency we have found so important for successful unit-level change.

Top management needs to be aware of the revitalization efforts the human resource function is supporting. Exposure to the most successful of these efforts will serve both to educate top managers and to persuade them of the value of renewal. The human resource manager should focus on how changes in organizing and managing are intended to help the unit achieve its core task and performance objectives.

The human resource manager can be a voice for change and an adviser to top management on how revitalization can be spread and encouraged. In particular, he or she can assist management in aligning replacement and promotion decisions with the needs of units undergoing revitalization. When top-management actions threaten the balance between cost reduction and revitalization efforts, the human resource manager should be prepared to argue for that balance. However, he or she should remember that it will usually be more persuasive to point to the effects of balance on the company's ability to implement its business strategy rather than on employee morale.

Our findings suggest that confronting top management with inconsistencies in its own management is not essential, is perhaps even counterproductive, early in the corporate revitalization process. Revitalization of the top-management unit is probably essential, however, in the second phase. The human resource manager must judge when pushing for change at the top will be productive and act appropriately.

The need to support field units with consulting resources should cause reexamination of roles, responsibilities, and skills within the human resource function. It will be necessary to develop an internal consulting group that can work with the expanding circle of managers who will begin to revitalize their units. Human resource professionals must be trained in innovative approaches to organizing and managing and should develop an understanding of how these might fit the business and its competitive strategy. They must develop skills in confronting difficult problems and people. An education and training function capable of supporting revitalization efforts with tailor-made rather than corporatewide programs will be needed. Finally, human resource managers can develop various means by which top management can monitor revitalization and hold managers accountable for progress.

THE UNION LEADER

Although union leaders were not perceived as a driving force for change in the six companies, they played an important role in several other companies we studied. We described Irving Bluestone's leadership role in General Motors' revitalization efforts. He and others like him worked with management in planning and implementing revitalization. Union leaders played a major role in helping rank-and-file members understand the benefits of revitalization to them as well as to the company. They also served as a check on management's action, ensuring that employee well-being was taken into consideration.

The union leader can begin by shaping a different role. He or she needs to become just as active in revitalization as in the traditional role of representing workers at the bargaining table and in grievance meetings. This will make it possible for the union leader to shape the revitalization agenda in a way that protects the interests of the union while ensuring acceptance by union members. The revitalization leader role will, however, challenge the union leader's capacity to balance cooperation with the traditional adversarial role expected by militant rank-and-file members.

The union leader can find natural allies in managers who support revitalization. He or she can become involved in strategic and policy decisions that affect the welfare of the union and the course of revitalization in the unit or company. By finding creative solutions that improve effectiveness and contribute to members' well-being, the union leader can become a revitalization leader. In short, union leaders should be tough on management, demanding that it recognize the union's role as a full partner in revitalization.

The union leader also needs to articulate to membership how revitalization efforts can enhance job security and provide an opportunity for a more challenging role in the enterprise. Peers from innovative units inside and outside the company can help communicate that message to members. Conferences about—and visits to—innovative units can be effective mechanisms. Finally, the union leader must become informed about the business and about innovative management methods.

THE TOP MANAGER

Corporate leaders of our most successfully revitalizing companies recognized the limitations of programmatic change and the opportunities inherent in a less dramatic but more fundamental process of corporate revitalization. They learned from innovations, and as their convictions grew, they began to orchestrate the transformation.

After identifying a company's innovative units and leaders, the top manager can visit the organizations and investigate the efforts. The manager can focus training, managerial, and consulting resources on these units to help make them successful. He or she can keep in touch periodically by returning to monitor progress and learn more about the innovations.

The top manager can develop a network of line managers and human resource specialists committed to revitalization, meeting with them regularly to assess progress and strategize about further initiatives. The corporation should recognize their efforts publicly through speeches and by giving them opportunities to make presentations at management meetings. From this group, the top manager can identify those who are ready to lead efforts elsewhere in the company and promote them. Managers who are most visibly failing to revitalize their organizations or are struggling with the leadership tasks that revitalizing requires should be replaced.

The top manager can use external consultants and senior human resource executives to learn, monitor, and strategize. After becoming confident that management innovations can lead to a more effective corporation, the manager can begin to articulate his or her vision and expectations for change.

Business strategy and financial policies must be carefully examined. To prevent pressures for short-term improvements in financial performance from overwhelming the revitalization effort, decisions about acquisitions and debt structure are important. Too much financial risk may push the manager into short-term decisions. Similarly, strategic decisions can affect the predictability and cyclic aspects of the business, making continuous investment in human resources more or less difficult.

The top manager can inform and educate the board about the human resource investment strategy and the need to sustain it over a long period of time, connecting both to strategic concerns. Board members will need to be involved in the development of a management philosophy and vision for the corporation. Revitalization does not preclude cost reduction. Balance between the two is the key.

Early identification of potential successors whose management philosophy is consistent with organizational renewal must be addressed with the board of directors. The second phase of revitalization—revitalization of the top-management unit—will help develop several candidates. With the leadership of the CEO, the top corporate team will need to examine their management process. Directing a critical path change at the top requires nothing less.

A PARTNERSHIP OF CHANGE LEADERS

Any one of the actors we have listed can begin the process of revitalization so long as he or she recognizes the unique role each plays and what each can or cannot do. Thus simply beginning the process is the most important step.

However, revitalization of a large corporation requires that all actors in the drama eventually become involved and take the initiatives we have suggested. In effect, the transformation of a large corporation requires that change leaders work as a team. Each has a different and valuable perspective. Each commands the respect and loyalty of a different constituency. Each is able to influence some, but not all, of the many conditions for companywide learning. Each requires help and support from the others. Together they can succeed in creating the task-driven corporate organization that can survive and prosper in the hotly contested global markets of the 1990s and beyond.

Appendix I

Overview of Companies

CONTINENTAL GLASS & CONTAINER

Continental Glass & Container began its operations as a producer of glass bottles and diversified into other glass products, including laboratory glassware and television tubes. Later, other types of containers such as plastic bottles and cardboard boxes were added to its product line. In the late 1970s, an education program for high-potential middle managers and the top 100 executives was launched. Outsiders were brought into the human resource function to stimulate innovation and change; an innovative, high-involvement plant was brought on line.

Organizational Units Discussed

Crawfordsville—Glass container plant that successfully achieved task alignment around quality improvement efforts.
Reidsville—New box plant that failed in its efforts to develop a high-involvement, team-based work system.

Key Players

Jim Taylor	Chief executive officer
Richard Vanaria	Manager, Crawfordsville glass plant
Ed Carline	Head of container division
Patrick Walsh	Manager of Reidsville plant during startup

FAIRWEATHER CORPORATION

Fairweather Corporation is a large, highly decentralized multibusiness firm, mainly in the defense, controls, and computer businesses. Historically, its culture had been autocratic and its performance lackluster. The revitalization effort was sparked by the deep belief of one of its key executives, Hugh Dorsey, in the importance of self-esteem for all employees. With the help of a highly professional human resource function, that belief was transformed into culture change initiatives predominantly spearheaded by Dorsey as he moved from one part of the company to another, ultimately becoming its chairman. Under James Weaver, who succeeded Dorsey as its head, Fairweather's Defense Group became the leader in revitalization within the company.

Organizational Units Discussed

Navigation Devices—Business unit that successfully followed the critical path to revitalization as an integral part of its move into the commercial and business aviation markets.

Key Players

Joseph Brown	Fairweather chairman
Hugh Dorsey	Head of Fairweather's computer operations, then corporate chairman replacing Brown
James Weaver	Head of the Defense Group
Jerry Simpson	General manager, Navigation Devices
Herbert Folk	General manager, Specialized Products

GENERAL PRODUCTS

General Products is primarily a single-product company servicing worldwide markets, but it also has a presence in other businesses, including defense. In its primary product it enjoyed the highest share of the worldwide market. In the late 1970s, it began to transform itself in response to increasing foreign competition. Corporate leaders pointed to a new plant as a model of both new technology and innovative management practices. By the early 1980s, these executives had devised a corporate strategy for spreading the highly successful innovations to other General Products plants and divisions.

Organizational Units Discussed

North Carolina Plant—New organizationally innovative plant, used as a model for future General Products revitalization activities in other units.
Technical Center—Corporate R&D center that successfully developed task alignment around the new product development process, after initially undertaking programmatic false starts.

Key Players

Tom Watson	President and chief operating officer at the time of the study. Later became chief executive officer
William Bryant	Vice president of manufacturing, author of "perfection strategy"
John Merrow	Vice president of international operations
Larry Polk	Corporate manager of organizational development

LIVINGSTON ELECTRONICS

Livingston Electronics is a basic power-generation, defense, and consumer electronics business that undertook a major diversification effort in the mid-1970s. Two successive CEOs sold off less promising businesses in the 1980s and focused business-unit managers on new, tough financial goals. The company began a major, corporately driven quality and productivity improvement effort in the early 1980s. At the same time, the executive vice president of the defense business encouraged innovations in management practice in various plants and divisions, and a number of these practices began to spread through the company.

Key Players

Brad Longstreet   Chief executive officer

SCRANTON STEEL

Scranton Steel, long a leading domestic steel producer, suffered in the 1970s from poor union-management relationships and performance. In 1982, the CEO launched its revitalization effort after he visited one of the company's steel mills and found that employee involvement had dramatically changed motivation and union-management relations. Soon many other plants and business units were experimenting with innovative approaches to organizing and managing.

Organizational Units Discussed

>   *Seattle Mill*—Steel mill at which successful organizational changes convinced Scranton chairman Don Singer of the possibility for successful corporate revitalization.

Key Players

Donald Singer	Became Scranton Steel chairman and CEO in 1980
Ed Shields	Head of steel operations under Singer, promoted to replace Singer as chairman
Gene Bonner	Vice chairman
Ray Baker	Manager of innovative Seattle plant
Bud Boyson	Quality-of-work-life manager for construction division

U.S. FINANCIAL

U.S. Financial is a large international bank that grew steadily during the 1970s. The company faltered, however, under the highly competitive environment of deregulation. In the early 1980s, the bank hired a new vice president of human resources from a large corporation well known for its excellence in HR management. Working closely with his newly hired vice president, the chairman initiated a massive intervention designed to change the culture of the organization.

Key Players

Henry Lester	Named president in 1981
Ben Tutt	Hired by Lester as vice president of human resources to lead the culture change effort
Al Parker	General manager of middle-markets operation

Appendix II

Quantitative Analysis of Clinical and Questionnaire Data

RESEARCH METHODOLOGY

Data Collection

The data that form the basis for the observations and conclusions in this book come from a variety of sources. First and most significant were personal interviews with employees in the six corporations that constituted the focus of our study.

Because revitalization is an unfolding process, we needed to do more than take a single snapshot of each company at a particular point in time. Therefore we maintained contact with them and returned at least two or three years after our initial exchange, sometimes for further interviewing and sometimes to feed back the results of our research. All in all, our research relationship extended between three and four years beyond each initial entry.

In addition to the six primary research sites, we visited half a dozen or so other companies undergoing renewal efforts. These secondary sites, while studied in less detail, were used to both test and extend the theory of corporate revitalization we developed through our primary sites.

Interviews were conducted in each of the six companies from late 1983 until the end of 1985. We talked with employees at all levels of the organizations, including shop-floor workers, union leaders, middle- and upper-level managers, support staff, personnel in the corporate human resource function, and corporate top management. This broad range of interviews was critical because it was imperative that we keep opinions (even propaganda) concerning a company's progress or lack of progress separate from real revitalization. Our multifaceted, multilevel approach allowed us to view the revitalization effort from every possible perspective. We were able to isolate individual opinions, whether expressed by a machine worker or the company CEO, from the consensus view of how the renewal process was really unfolding.

As important as these many interviews were, they were not the only source of data. When they were available, we used primary source documents relating to the renewal effort. The companies generously shared their memos, reports, and videotapes. Of special value were several internal attitude surveys. The research also benefited from one of the authors' observations as a consultant to three of the companies: Continental Glass & Container, Fairweather, and General Products. That relationship sometimes preceded the initial phases of research and sometimes followed. In no case did the author/consultant play a central role in helping top management plan and manage the corporate transformation. However, in some cases, the consulting relationship did allow unique access to the internal workings of management as the revitalization process unfolded.

As with the interviews, we took no single source of data at face value. Rather, we triangulated each bit of information against other sources in order to arrive more closely at something that might be called "the truth."

As the first phase of our research came to a conclusion, several preliminary findings became apparent and shaped the next phase of data collection and analysis. First, the six companies differed significantly in the extent of their revitalization. Second, it became clear that corporate transformations depend on successfully innovating in the organization and management of a few plants or divisions and then spreading these changes to other units. Thus one had to understand how organizational units revitalize in order to understand corporate renewal. Finally, we began to formulate ideas about how successful change in an expanding circle of subunits was related to the corporate context in which they were taking place, a crucial aspect of our revitalization theory.

Clinical Data

Our initial observations were captured in case reports. As hypotheses about the transformation process began to emerge, we developed a set of behaviorally anchored rating scales, each measuring an element of our emerging theory of revitalization. The purpose of the scales was to provide a means for systematically comparing various sites along a set of theoretically important dimensions. The statistical analysis of data also helped ensure that we would not unwittingly overemphasize the results of a few dramatic change efforts in developing our theory of revitalization.

Rating scales were developed to assess three areas:

- Extent and nature of revitalization.
- The revitalization strategies utilized.
- The leadership of the revitalization effort.

These scales were filled out for each plant and division visited. Where two field researchers had knowledge of the same organization, both rated the unit visited and their ratings were averaged. The set of scales are reproduced in Appendix III.

To measure the overall success of the revitalization effort in a given plant or division, we evaluated the amount of improvement in the four substantive areas—interfunctional coordination, decision making, work organization, and concern for people—that managers in our six companies most typically cited as objectives for their revitalization efforts. Improvement in these areas was measured using a set of items adapted from the Survey of Organizations, a standardized survey of organizational climate developed at University of Michigan's Institute for Social Research. These items were also chosen because they have been found in previous research to predict long-term economic performance.[1] Again, behavioral anchors were created for each item on the scale.

Questionnaire Data

As an additional check on our clinical observations, questionnaires were sent to all the individuals we had interviewed in each of the six companies on various aspects of the revitalization process. Corporate executives were asked to rate the companywide revitalization process, while those at divisions and plants were asked to assess the revitalization efforts in their particular units.

Again the major outcome measure was the scale assessing improvement in organizational functioning adapted from the Survey of Organizations. To simplify the questionnaire, we did not use behavioral anchors. Respondents were asked to rate the extent to which the behaviors described in each item occurred on a one-to-five scale that ranged from "to a much lesser extent than before the change began" (1) to "to a much greater extent than before the change efforts began" (5).

Additional outcome variables were created to evaluate the extent of support for revitalization, the overall effects of revitalization on employees' actual behaviors on the job, as well as respondents' perceptions of the impact of revitalization on organizational financial performance and on the "individual well-being" of employees. The complete set of questionnaire scales, as well as their component items, are provided in Appendix IV.

THE RELATIONSHIP BETWEEN UNIT-LEVEL
REVITALIZATION STRATEGIES AND OUTCOMES:
QUANTITATIVE RESULTS

The quantitative results are presented in three sections
that parallel the developing argument in the main body of this
book.

- Revitalization strategies at the unit level, as presented
  in Chapters 3 and 4.
- Differences in corporate outcomes, revitalization
  strategies, and focus of change, as discussed in Chapters 5 and 6.
- Revitalization leadership at both the corporate and
  unit levels, as described in Chapter 7.

An important caveat is in order. The statistical significance levels used in the following tables need to be inter-
preted with some caution, as we are measuring the same
sample used to develop our theory of organizational revitalization. This is a hypothesis-generating, rather than a controlled hypothesis-testing study. These statistical analyses do
not offer definitive proof of the theories proposed in the book.
Rather, they are presented to allow the reader to follow and
evaluate the logic of inference that leads us from raw data to
our proposed theory.

Revitalization Strategies at the Unit Level

Clinical Data. In Table 1, researcher ratings of the use of
various revitalization strategies, as well as of the external
economic and business pressures for each organizational unit,
are correlated with researcher ratings of the extent of overall
revitalization. In addition, the third of the units that had improved the most on the organizational revitalization measure
was compared to the third that had changed the least; the
percentage of the revitalization leaders exhibiting each characteristic was compared with the percentage of revitalization
laggards.

**Table 1: Correlations of Researchers' Ratings of Unit-Change
Strategies and Organizational Revitalization**

Variables	Extent of Organizational Revitalization	Ratio of Leaders to Laggards[1]
Change Strategies		
[*Mobilized energy*]		
Pressure from top management	.09	100% : 100%
Pressure for financial performance	.35	100% : 75%
Pressure from competitive environment	.13	89% : 78%
Change influenced by model	.13	88% : 56%
Model was external	−.24	14% : 44%
Model was internal	−.08	75% : 44%
[*Developed a task-aligned vision*]		
Alignment with business issues	.47**	100% : 56%[2]
Roles, relationships, and responsibilities redefined	.45*	100% : 66%
New information channels	.69***	100% : 29%
Participative process to create vision	.43*	66% : 25%
Vision/articulation of end state	.25	63% : 25%
[*Fosters consensus, competence, and cohesion*]		
Goals for behavior	.45*	89% : 33%
Goals for results	.26	89% : 86%
Key managers replaced	.21	50% : 17%
[*Use of training, mission statements, and so forth*]		
Use of programs	.15	66% : 86%
N = 26 units		
*p<.05		
**p<.01		
***p<.001		

1. The nine units with the highest scores on the extent of organizational revitalization measure are compared to the nine units with the lowest scores.
   When the researchers did not have enough information to make an accurate
   rating of a variable, a missing value was assigned. Consequently, in some
   instances percentages may be based on less than nine responses.
2. For those measures rated on five-point scales, scores greater than three are
   coded as representing the use of a strategy, while those three and below are
   coded as representing the nonuse of that strategy.

The rated variables have been ordered roughly according to the sequence in which they occur on the critical path. However, it should be noted that the data presented in Table 1 were collected at one point in time. Thus, although the results do show the extent of use of various strategies as well as their bivariate correlation with organizational revitalization, they do not allow us to determine whether the strategies were used in the particular order implied by the critical path.

We suggested that in the mobilizing energy step of the critical path, more successful revitalization processes occur in units facing pressures for improved performance and in units influenced by another model organization. Both hypotheses were supported by positive—although not significant—correlations between the extent of organizational revitalization and measures of both pressure and of the use of a model. Perhaps one reason why there was relatively little difference between leading and lagging units on the three ratings of pressure for performance was that almost all units, whether successfully revitalizing or not, were under pressure.

Measured against the lagging units, our leading units were more apt to use internal models and less apt to use external models. This is not surprising, since we have suggested that internal models tend to be seen as more relevant than external models. We found a weak correlation for the use of models, though leading units tended to use the model more frequently than lagging units.

We argued in Chapter 4 that during the next step on the critical path, developing a task-aligned vision, organizational units need to do several things:

- Establish a clear and broadly understood link between business problems and revitalization (measured by the variable—alignment with business issues).
- Change organizational roles, responsibilities, and relationships to improve financial performance (roles, relationships, and responsibilities redefined).
- Create new channels of information in the organization, either between functions or between the top and

245

the bottom of the organization. These changes typically occur as a by-product of the new ad hoc organization (new information channels).

- Develop a participative revitalization process (diagnosis and action planning) that leads to a shared vision
of the desired future organizational state (participative
process).

There were significant positive correlations between the
use of each of these strategies and the extent of organizational
revitalization.

In fact, the first three of the revitalization strategies were
used in every one of the nine units exhibiting the most
change. The final strategy that we hypothesized was important to the successful completion of this step—articulating a
vision of the end state of revitalization—did characterize a
substantially higher percentage of the leading revitalization
units than of the lagging ones. However, this relationship was
not statistically significant.

We maintained in Chapter 4 that as revitalization leaders
move to the point on the critical path where they seek to
foster consensus, competence, and cohesion, it is important
that employees be held accountable for behaving in ways that
are consistent with the revitalized organization. This is supported by the data. The leadership of successfully revitalizing
organizational units was significantly more likely to articulate
for its employees specific behavioral requirements that were
integrated into performance evaluations. There was also a
nonsignificant positive correlation between revitalization and
two other strategies we suggested tended to characterize
more successful renewal efforts—the replacement of key
managers who did not fit the behavioral goals of the revitalization effort, and the provision by a general manager of clear
overall performance goals for his or her unit.

We have argued that while programs such as training and
quality circles that emerge out of a participative critical-path
change process may play a valuable supporting role, these

programs do not lead to successful transformation when they constitute the main vehicle for revitalization. Successful revitalization is less related to whether programs are used than it is to *how* they are used. Consistent with these contentions, the use of programmatic revitalization efforts did not distinguish between our leading and our lagging plants and divisions. Interestingly, however, there was a somewhat higher percentage of lagging units (86 percent) than of leading units (66 percent) that used programs.

Questionnaire Data.   In Table 2, correlations are shown between the questionnaire variables measuring the use of various change strategies that we have hypothesized contribute to successful revitalization, and the set of outcome measures. In addition, means are given for each change strategy. Because we were interested in analyzing organizational transformations, all of the statistics in Table 2 are based on the unit averages for each of the 26 plants and divisions examined.

The results are generally consistent with our revitalization model. A composite variable made up of items measuring the seven change strategies listed in Table 1 is consistently and significantly positively correlated with the set of dependent variables. Successful revitalization was most likely in those cases where unit managers had become part of a larger network supportive of change, where education in the new methods of management was provided, and where individuals felt that their possibilities for promotion would be positively affected if they supported the revitalization effort.

Surprisingly, the existence of model organizations in the company and the spreading of change through the movement of committed managers or through conferences and visits were not significantly positively associated with the dependent measures. In fact, moving committed managers was negatively, although not significantly, correlated with a number of the outcome measures.

It might also be argued that given their local perspective,

247

Table 2: Effects of Change Strategies on Outcomes for 26 Plants and Divisions

	Mean[1]	Employee Questionnaire Responses				
		Extent of Organizational Revitalization	Support for Change	Business Improvement	"People" Improvement	Behavioral Change
Change Strategies Used						
Model organizations in company	2.94 (.18)	.20	.28	.12	.38	−.17
Change spread through moving committed managers	2.38 (.14)	−.07	−.27	−.23	−.25	−.34
Conferences and visits spread change	3.31 (.17)	.15	.30	.23	.40*	.07
Network of change agents	2.98 (.18)	.59***	.62***	.41*	.50**	.47**
Education in new methods	3.84 (.19)	.62***	.63***	.58**	.48**	.31
Succession used	3.35 (.18)	.31*	.40*	.36	.29	.69***
Evaluation used	3.58 (.12)	.24	.42*	.30	.33	.45*

	Mean					
Overall Use of Change Strategies	3.09 (.09)	.47*	.58***	.39*	.55***	.38*
Reasons for Change						
Improve employee welfare	2.42 (.19)	.72***	.72***	.44*	.68***	.47**
Improve business results	3.95 (.14)	−.23	−.06	.08	−.27	.12
Support for Change						
Support for change	3.44 (.13)	.80***		.71***	.81***	.77***
Cost Reduction Emphasis						
Lower cost through wage or people cuts	4.02 (.17)	−.35	−.35	−.20	−.69***	−.15

N = 26 plants and divisions

*p<.05
**p<.01
***p<.001

1. Standard errors are given in ( ) beneath each mean.

unit managers may not have been able to judge accurately the extent to which corporate models, the flow of managers in and out of their unit, and conferences and visits played a role in moving renewal along within their organization. This argument gains some support when we consider that data from corporate managers (presented in Table 3) support the conclusion that model organizations and conferences and visits, two of the strategies, are significant contributors to corporate revitalization.

A related explanation for these equivocal results is that all three of these questions suggest that the major ideas for change came from outside—from the example of other units, from managers transferred in from other units, or from ideas learned at conferences. Yet we have suggested that for an organizational transformation to be successful, those in the unit must feel a sense of personal ownership. They must believe that an organizational solution has been created that is tailored to their particular needs. When respondents read these three questions, they may have perceived that we were asking them whether their new approach to management had been adopted by their units off the shelf, rather than being customized to their organization.

Table 2 provides other insights into the revitalization process. A comparison of variable means suggests that respondents felt change efforts were most apt to occur primarily as a result of their unit management's attempts to improve business results rather than to improve employee welfare ($t = 5.90$ $p < .0001$). However, despite these mean differences, the correlational results strongly imply that it was only where respondents felt that top management also had a commitment to their interests that revitalization occurred.

The explanation for this finding presumably lies in the strong relationship between attempts to improve employee welfare and support for change, a variable that in turn has an extremely high association with our outcome measures. Task alignment is an effective strategy only when there is a shared commitment to change, and this commitment is likely only when the change is perceived to be in the best interests of a broad range of the organization's members. We have seen that it is difficult to achieve this commonalty of interests when the primary objective of the change strategy is to lower costs by cutting wages or employees. Thus it is not surprising that there is a strong negative association between the use of a cost reduction strategy and a perception that individuals in the organization are better off, and there are negative, although not significant, correlations between the use of this strategy and both support for change and revitalization success.

Differences in Corporate Outcomes, Revitalization Strategies, and Focus of Change

Outcome Measures. Table 3 presents a statistical comparison of the six companies in our sample based on questionnaires administered to both the line and human resource executives interviewed at the corporate level. Researcher rating scales were not developed for comparing the six companies at this level.

Table 3 provides support for our assessment of General Products as the most successfully revitalizing company, as well as for viewing Continental Glass and U.S. Financial as the revitalization laggards. General Products has a significantly higher score on the organizational improvement measure than the latter two firms. In fact, respondents' ratings at both Continental and U.S. Financial suggest that these companies are slightly worse off organizationally now than they were before the change process began.

Change Strategies. General Products was also more apt to use a number of the corporate change strategies measured by the questionnaire. Table 3 shows that the company was rated significantly higher than Continental or U.S. Financial on the use of model organizations, education, and conferences and plant visits to spread revitalization. Finally, respondents at General Products gave it the highest rating in our sample on having a network of management change agents, although this

Table 3: Corporate Revitalization Outcomes and Strategies[1]

	Overall Means	General Products	Fairweather	Livingston Electronics	Scranton Steel	Continental Glass	U.S. Financial
Extent of Original Revitalization							
Interfunctional coordination	3.46	3.85[a]	3.70[a]	3.50	3.50	2.72[b]	2.92
	(.10)	(.12)	(.14)	(.23)	(.31)	(.21)	(.43)
Organizational decision making	3.56	4.03[a]	3.70	3.61	3.61	2.88[b]	2.83[b]
	(.10)	(.10)	(.19)	(.18)	(.23)	(.33)	(.56)
Work organization	3.52	4.05[a]	3.31	3.75[a]	3.36	3.31	2.62[b]
	(.10)	(.12)	(.16)	(.19)	(.22)	(.31)	(.47)
Concern for people	3.43	4.14[a]	3.76	3.45	2.85[b]	2.70[b]	2.86[b]
	(.11)	(.13)	(.15)	(.22)	(.22)	(.29)	(.42)
Extent of Organizational Revitalization (Average)	3.49	4.04[a]	3.58	3.61	3.3	2.96[b]	2.78[b]
	(.09)	(.09)	(.12)	(.18)	(.22)	(.28)	(.44)
Change Strategies							
Model organizations in company	3.96	4.86[a]	4.20	4.17	3.00[b]	3.50[b]	2.67[b]
	(.13)	(.10)	(.17)	(.13)	(.44)	(.57)	(.42)

Conferences and visits spread change	3.48 (.15)	4.78[a] (.11)	3.60[b] (.25)	3.65[b] (.23)	2.89[b] (.39)	2.33[b] (.35)	2.12[b] (.56)
Network of change agents	3.01 (.14)	3.86[a] (.21)	3.20 (.26)	2.88 (.28)	2.33[b] (.33)	2.63 (.42)	2.50 (.50)
Education in new methods	3.38 (.16)	4.86[a] (.10)	3.87[1] (.22)	2.76[b] (.29)	2.66[b2] (.41)	2.37[b2] (.38)	2.83[b] (.54)
Change spread through moving committed managers	3.01 (.14)	3.71 (.29)	2.73 (.23)	2.82 (.29)	2.77 (.40)	3.37 (.46)	2.50 (.43)
Succession used	3.50 (.11)	3.14 (.27)	3.50 (.21)	3.29 (.15)	3.61 (.31)	4.25 (.30)	3.75 (.46)
Evaluation used	3.33 (.11)	3.57 (.20)	3.13 (.20)	3.11 (.26)	3.05 (.35)	3.81 (.19)	3 67 (.40)
Use of Corporate Revitalization Strategies (Average)	3.38 (.09)	4.11[a] (.10)	3.46[b] (.15)	3.24[b] (.15)	2.90[b] (.27)	3.15[b] (.25)	2.89[b] (.23)

1. Means that are significantly different at the $p < .05$ level have different superscripted numbers. For example, mean x.xx[a] is significantly different from mean x.xx[b] and mean x.xx[1] is significantly different from mean x.xx[2]. Significance levels were calculated using the Tukey' studentized range test. Standard errors are given in ( ) beneath each mean.

score was not significantly greater than that achieved at any of the other companies except for Scranton Steel. When all of the corporate change strategies measured on the questionnaire were averaged into a single composite variable, again General Products scored significantly higher than any of the other companies we examined.

The Character of the Corporate Revitalization Effort. Table 4 summarizes respondents' ratings of a series of items characterizing the nature of the changes occurring within each of the six companies. These items have been divided to show the relative emphasis in each company on cost reduction as opposed to human resource investment. The latter changes have themselves been divided into two groups. The first consists of changes that are clearly and directly linked to task performance: increasing accountability for profitability, quality, and customer service, or developing better organizational mechanisms for cooperation and coordination between interdependent organizational units. The second consists of people-oriented changes such as developing employees' interpersonal skills, increasing employee influence, or increasing trust between groups. These changes are critical in enabling a successful corporate revitalization, particularly in gaining employee acceptance, but they might be expected to have more of an indirect and perhaps longer-term impact on economic outcomes.

The overall corporate means suggest that the transformations taking place in our companies are most focused on those changes that will have the greatest immediate impact on the bottom line—personnel reductions and/or wage and benefit reductions—rather than on those that represent more of an investment in developing human resource capabilities ($t = 8.89$, $p < .0001$). Furthermore, even within the human resource investment category there was a greater emphasis on those changes that were more directly linked to task performance than on the more people-oriented changes ($t = 5.97$, $p < .0001$). These same relative emphases were present in all six of our companies.

However, the results also suggest substantially better balance in emphasis at our leading companies than at our lagging ones. The differences between cost reduction and human resource investment priorities were significantly smaller for General Products and Fairweather than they were for Continental Glass and U.S. Financial. Further, General Products and Fairweather were seen as emphasizing HR investment changes significantly more than U.S. Financial and Continental Glass. Conversely, the emphasis on cost reduction was significantly higher at Scranton Steel, Continental Glass, and U.S. Financial than it was at Fairweather. Finally, the differences between concern for task and concern for people were significantly smaller at General Products than at Continental.

These results suggest that our leading companies, General Products and Fairweather, were better able to maintain the delicate balances—between cost reduction and human resource investment, between concern for task and concern for people—that we suggested in Chapter 6 are essential to successful renewal efforts. Moreover, the data suggest but do not demonstrate unequivocally that the greater balances between cost reduction and investment at General Products and Fairweather were achieved in part because those companies did not place quite as high an emphasis on cost reduction as the lagging companies did.

Revitalization Leadership

The Role of Unit Leadership in Managing Change.   Table 5 shows the correlation of researcher ratings assessing the extent to which change leaders model the management style they are espousing. The ratio of change leaders to change laggards on this item is also given. In Table 6, correlations are shown between the questionnaire measures assessing unit revitalization leadership and various outcome variables.

255

Table 4: Character of Corporate Change[1]

	Overall Mean	General Products 1	Fairweather 2	Livingston Electronics 3	Scranton Steel 4	Continental Glass 5	U.S. Financial 6
Researcher's Rank of Extent of Revitalization							
Cost Reduction Strategy							
Lower cost through wage or people cuts	4.46 (.10)	4.36 (.20)	3.80[b] (.31)	4.44 (.17)	5.00[a] (.00)	4.90[a] (.10)	4.83[a] (.17)
HR Investment Strategy							
Emphasis on Task							
Increased accountability for results	3.86 (.11)	4.14 (.25)	3.47 (.24)	4.00 (.21)	4.00 (.29)	3.70 (.30)	3.83 (.48)
Increased employee task input	3.39 (.11)	3.86[a] (.21)	3.80[a] (.20)	3.39 (.23)	3.22 (.30)	2.70[b] (.33)	2.66 (.33)
Improve intergroup coordination	3.18 (.15)	3.64[a] (.25)	4.20[a] (.17)	3.00 (.29)	2.78 (.43)	2.40[b] (.34)	2.00[b] (.52)
Increased delegation of authority	3.49 (.11)	3.42 (.20)	3.27 (.28)	3.77 (.21)	3.77 (.32)	3.20 (.25)	3.33 (.49)
Overall Task Emphasis (Average)	3.48 (.08)	3.77[a] (.17)	3.68[a] (.11)	3.54 (.18)	3.44 (.22)	3.00[b] (.22)	2.96[b] (.36)
Emphasis on People							
Sharing power and equalizing status	2.67 (.11)	2.85[a] (.25)	3.13[a] (.17)	2.56 (.20)	3.22[a] (.28)	1.90[b] (.31)	1.83[b] (.40)

Increased employee influence over how treated	3.11 (.12)	3.50[a] (.20)	3.73[a] (.18)	3.22[a] (.24)	2.78 (.22)	2.10[b] (.38)	2.40 (.24)
Developing people skills	3.31 (.12)	4.23[a] (.15)	3.33[b] (.23)	3.22[b] (.22)	2.88[b] (.26)	2.40[b] (.27)	3.50 (.56)
Increased trust between groups	3.18 (.12)	4.00[a][1] (.15)	3.53[a] (.17)	3.05[a][2] (.24)	3.33[a] (.29)	2.00[b][2] (.26)	2.50[2] (.34)
Overall People Emphasis (Average)	3.06 (.09)	3.64[a][1] (.15)	3.43[1] (.12)	3.01[1] (.18)	3.05[1] (.18)	2.10[b][2] (.24)	2.57[b] (.28)
Overall HR Investment (Task Emphasis + People Emphasis)	3.27 (.08)	3.71[a] (.15)	3.56[a] (.09)	3.28 (.16)	3.25 (.19)	2.55[b] (.20)	2.76[b] (.29)
Difference Scores That Show Balance							
Difference between Cost Reduction and HR Investment	1.19 (.13)	.67[b] (.25)	.24[b][2] (.30)	1.16[1] (.21)	1.75[1] (.19)	2.35[a][1] (.20)	2.13[a][1] (.30)
Difference between Concern for Task and People	.42 (.07)	.13[b] (.12)	.25 (.15)	.53 (.13)	.39 (.14)	.90[a] (.22)	.39 (.32)

1. Means that are significantly different at the p<.05 level have different superscripted numbers. For example, mean x.xx[a] and mean x.xx[b] and mean x.xx[1] is significantly different than mean x.xx[2]. Significance levels were calculated using the Tukey' studentized range test. Standard errors are given in ( ) beneath each mean.

Appendix II

Table 5: Unit Leadership of Change (Researcher Ratings)

Variable	Extent of Organizational Revitalization	Ratio of Leaders to Laggards
Leadership of Change		
Leader models new style	.44*	88% : 50%

N = 26 plants and divisions
*p<.05
**p<.01
***p<.001

Both tables provide evidence for the importance of the actions of unit top management in successful revitalization efforts. The researcher ratings in Table 5 show a significant correlation between unit general managers who model the new style of management and the extent of revitalization. In 88 percent of the units that changed the most, the formal leader was seen by those we spoke with as acting consistently with the espoused direction for renewal and acting as a model for the rest of the organization. This was true in only half the lagging units. These results are also supported by the questionnaire results presented in Table 6. These suggest that while there is some value in a unit's top-management team publicly espousing support for renewal, change outcomes are even stronger when the top-management team actually applies the change process to itself.[2] However, despite the importance of practicing what you preach, a comparison of the means for these two scales shows that it is more common for top-management teams at the unit level to espouse the importance of change than to actually examine and modify their own behavior (t = 3.93, p<.001).

Corporate Leadership of Change. There were no significant differences among the six companies on the variables assessing the leadership of change summarized in Table 7. There is, however, a one-to-one correspondence between the extent to which change is driven by the initiatives of innovative plant and divisional managers and the extent of

258

Table 6: Effects of Revitalization Leadership on Outcomes for 26 Units

			Employee Questionnaire Responses			
	Mean	Extent of Revitalization	Change Support	Business Improvement	"People" Improvement	Behavioral Change
Nature of Revitalization Leadership						
Unit top management espouses revitalization	3.83 (.15)	.43*	.33	.38*	.33	.14
Unit top management consistent in words and actions	3.23 (.15)	.63***	.84***	.70***	.69***	.63***

N = 26 plants and divisions

* p < .05
** p < .01
*** p < .001

Table 7: Corporate (Means) Change Leadership

	Overall Mean	General Products 1	Fairweather 2	Livingston Electric 3	Scranton Steel 4	Continental Glass 5	U.S. Financial 6
Researcher's Rank of Extent of Revitalization							
Management Consistency							
Top management espoused revitalization	3.78 (.12)	4.14 (.22)	3.77 (.18)	3.41 (.31)	3.94 (.21)	3.88 (.32)	3.58 (.49)
Top management consistent in words and actions	2.68 (.12)	2.61 (.28)	2.71 (.26)	2.84 (.27)	2.29 (.31)	3.00 (.38)	2.39 (.34)
Source of Leadership							
Top management	4.13 (.14)	4.42 (.23)	3.93 (.21)	3.62 (.41)	4.55 (.18)	4.25 (.41)	4.50 (.50)
Middle management	3.39 (.15)	3.92 (.30)	3.86 (.31)	3.35 (.36)	2.88 (.35)	2.75 (.31)	2.67 (.49)
Human resources	2.62 (.15)	3.00 (.35)	3.20 (.31)	2.05 (.29)	2.88 (.31)	1.88 (.23)	2.5 (.56)
Unions[1]	1.82 (.13)	1.75 (.30)	2.33 (.25)	1.47 (.24)	2.33 (.33)	1.5 (.27)	NA (.00)
Sufficiently skilled HR staff	2.58 (.15)	2.86 (.29)	2.60 (.25)	2.65 (.36)	2.67 (.37)	2.38 (.50)	2.33 (.71)

1. U.S. Financial did not have a union; therefore, this dimension does not apply to it.

overall revitalization. These results provide some support for our conclusion that unit leaders and unit-level renewal are the key to corporate renewal, particularly in the early years.

A number of other not significant trends in the data are also consistent with our clinical observations. For example, the top management at General Products was seen espousing revitalization more than the management of any of the other companies; however, it had a lower rating on management consistency than Fairweather, Livingston, or Continental. Since General Products was also our most successfully transforming company, the data provide support for our argument that management consistency is less important at the corporate than at the unit level, at least in the early years of the corporate renewal effort. General Products also had the highest rating on having a sufficiently skilled number of HR staff—an attribute we suggest is an important support for successful corporate renewal. Not surprisingly, the two companies that were ranked the highest on union leadership of the change effort, Fairweather and Scranton, were also the two where corporate agreements with union officials created an overall framework for change.

Finally, an analysis of the overall means for the leadership variables reveals two interesting patterns. First, as was true for the leaders of plants and divisions, it was more common for top corporate leaders to espouse change than to apply it to themselves ($t = 8.96$, $p < .0001$). Second, there appears to be a hierarchy of change leadership, with the corporate revitalization effort most likely to be led by line managers at the corporate, divisional, and plant levels, somewhat less likely to be led by the corporate human resource function, and least likely to be led by unions.

NOTES

1. D.R. Dennison, "Bringing Corporate Culture to the Bottom Line," *Organizational Dynamics* 13 (Autumn 1984), pp. 4–22.
2. C. Argyris and D.A. Schon, *Organizational Learning* (Reading, MA: Addison-Wesley, 1978).

Appendix III

Definition of Variables Used for Researcher Ratings

EXTENT OF ORGANIZATIONAL REVITALIZATION

All ratings are made from a baseline that assumes an organization that has few mechanisms for interfunctional coordination, poor upward communication, traditionally organized jobs, and so forth. If the baseline is substantially better or worse than this, then all ratings should be adjusted accordingly. In general, the anchors are built on the following premise:

1.0 = Organizational characteristic exists to a much lesser extent than before the change.
2.0 = Occurs to a somewhat lesser extent than before.
3.0 = No change.
3.5 = Minor positive change.

4.0 = Substantial positive change, but only in some areas of unit or at some levels.

4.5 = Fairly broad-based substantive change.

5.0 = Complete transformation, state of the art.

Interfunctional Coordination

To what extent do different parts of the organization plan together and coordinate their efforts?

3.5 = Some attempts at improving interfunctional or interarea planning, but little evidence in interviews of substantive improvement.

4.0 = Some improvement in quality of interfunctional or interarea planning reported in interviews.

4.5 =

5.0 = Extensive improvement in quality of interfunctional or interarea *planning* reported in interviews.

N = Not enough information to make a rating.

To what extent does your part of the organization receive cooperation and assistance from other parts of the organization?

3.5 = Some attempts at improving interfunctional or interarea coordination, but little evidence in interviews of substantive improvement.

4.0 = Some improvement in quality of interfunctional, or interarea coordination reported in interviews. Increased and reported successful use of task forces or interfunctional meetings in some parts of the unit.

4.5 =

5.0 = Extensive improvement in quality of interfunctional, or interarea coordination reported in interviews. Top management team is reported to work well together. Routine and effective use of temporary decision-making groups such as task forces in all areas of the business.

N   =   Not enough information to make rating.

Organizational Decision Making

When decisions are made, to what extent are the persons affected asked for their ideas?

3.5 =   Increased worker input on relatively minor business issues, or not taken seriously.

4.0 =   Increased worker input on important business issues but not systematically, with not all employees involved, or not on all major issues.

4.5 =

5.0 =   Institutionalization of new systems that systematically gain input from all levels of the organization.

N   =   Not enough information to make rating.

People at all levels of an organization usually have know-how that could be of use to decision makers. To what extent is information widely shared in this organization so that those who make decisions have access to such knowledge?

3.5 =   Institutionalization of meetings or newsletters to share general nonsensitive information about the competitive environment.

4.0 =   Regular meetings that share substantive financial information.

4.5 =

5.0 =   Creation of new channels for sharing information. For example, creation of new relationship between factory workers and customers or providing access to a new information system.

N   =   Not enough information to make a rating.

To what extent is this plant generally quick to use improved work methods?

3.5 = Unit allows change only in limited and fairly peripheral areas such as quality circles, information-sharing meetings. Little change in more substantive areas.

4.0 = Unit adopts major changes that have been debugged at other company locations.

4.5 = The unit is at the corporate state of the art in its approach to organizing and managing. Actively working to adopt changes occurring at other leading-edge locations. Willing to allow internally generated innovations in some areas. However, changes are not as extensive and innovative as in 5.0.

5.0 = The unit is *pushing forward* the state of the art in its approach to organizing and managing. Takes the lead in initiating these changes in work design, with or without support from the rest of the corporation. Serves as a model for the rest of the corporation.

N   = Not enough information to make a rating.

To what extent does this plant have goals and objectives that are both clear-cut and reasonable?

3.5 =

4.0 = Goals are communicated. Employees receive some information on how are they doing against goals. But not nearly as extensive or as integrated into the rest of work as in 5.0, not much employee involvement in setting goals.

4.5 =

5.0 = Broad-based involvement in the goal-setting process. Everyone interviewed throughout the unit clear on strategy. Clear information and mea-

sures that allow individuals to know whether they
have achieved these goals.

N = Not enough information to make a rating.

To what extent are work activities sensibly organized in
this organization?

3.5 = Minor changes in work design, or changes made
not seen as having improved things very much.
4.0 = Changes in work design in a few parts of the unit
that interviews report have improved things.
4.5 =
5.0 = Total system redesign that is seen as quite successful.
N = Not enough information to make a rating.

Work Organization

In this organization, to what extent are decisions made at
those levels where the most adequate and accurate information is available?

3.5 =
4.0 = In interviews employees report that they have increased and regular input to their superiors concerning decisions that concern them. In interviews few reports of "dumb" decisions getting
made because key parties were not involved;
however, few reports of effective initiatives being
developed from any groups other than top management.
4.5 =
5.0 = Extensive delegation of decision making for
work-related matters to lower organizational
levels. Role of first-line supervisor changes to
that of adviser. System approaches that of self-

managing work teams. In interviews reports of effective and substantive change initiatives being developed by groups other than top management.

N = Not enough information to make a rating.

Concern for People

To what extent does this organization have a real interest in the welfare and overall satisfaction of those who work here?

3.5 =
4.0 = Some evidence of improvement, but interview comments less consistent, not an ideological commitment.
4.5 =
5.0 = Ideological commitment by top management, consistent comments in interviews from all levels of the organization.
N = Not enough information to make a rating.

How much does this organization try to improve working conditions? This item refers to improvements in hygiene conditions.

3.5 = Isolated improvements, mostly cosmetic.
4.0 = Some substantive improvements but in isolated areas.
4.5 =
5.0 = Fundamental redesign of facility or creation of new facility with one of major purposes being improvement in use of hygiene variables.
N = Not enough information to make a rating.

To what extent are there things about working here (such as policies, practices, or conditions) that encourage you to work hard?

3.5 = Use of programmatic activities such as employee recognition programs. No strong interview evidence of increase in motivation.

4.0 = Some evidence in interviews that employees are working harder. Also some discussion by superiors and subordinates of increased use of goal setting, and rewards for effective performance, or could be other structural change (such as cutting levels) that has result of making employees work harder.

4.5 = Clear evidence in interviews that employees are working harder, also clear and consistent evidence of change in performance management (goal setting and reward system) system.

5.0 = All of the above, plus increased peer pressure to do quality job—a high-commitment work system.

N = Not enough information to make a rating.

PERFORMANCE PRESSURE

Was there increased pressure to perform? Did the pressure come from top management, from the financial performance of the unit, or from the unit's competitive environment?

Pressure from Top Management

Yes/No/Not enough information

Pressure for Financial Performance

Yes/No/Not enough information

Pressure from Competitive Environment

Yes/No/Not enough information

CHANGE INFLUENCED BY MODEL

Was the change influenced by a model?

Yes/No/Not enough information

MODEL WAS EXTERNAL

Was the model external?

Yes/No/Not enough information

MODEL WAS INTERNAL

Was the model internal?

Yes/No/Not enough information

ALIGNMENT WITH BUSINESS ISSUES

Was the change led by articulating a business problem?

1 = Human resource values are the driving element.
2 = General belief that human resource changes are good for performance, but no clarity around specific links.
3 = A general link is established between business outcomes required and HR changes attempted.
4 = A diagnosis is made, a link established between results desired and organizational rearrangements attempted, but not clearly/widely understood.
5 = A clear link is established between business problem and change and this is consistently understood in the organization.

ROLES, RELATIONSHIPS, AND RESPONSIBILITIES REDEFINED

Were roles and responsibilities and relationships changed to improve performance? In other words, were people organized around the key problem?

Yes/No/Not enough information

NEW INFORMATION CHANNELS

New information channels have been established within the organization above and beyond the information that emerges from the new interactions that are generated by the change in roles, relationships, and responsibilities. (For example: placing competitors' glassware on the shop floor at Reidsville.)

Yes/No/Not enough information

PARTICIPATIVE PROCESS TO CREATE VISION

Did the change involve a participative process (diagnosis and action planning) that led to a vision of the future state?

Yes/No/Not enough information

VISION/ARTICULATION OF END STATE

1 = No vision exists and no articulation of end state.
2 = A general reference to other organizations or words as exemplars (i.e., perfection, participation).
3 = A statement of philosophy and general direction.
4 = A statement of philosophy and direction combined with pointing to specific exemplars. "We want to be like them."
5 = A statement of philosophy and detailed operating picture of the future state.
N = Not enough information to make a rating.

GOALS FOR BEHAVIOR

1 = Required behavior is neither understood nor articulated by the leader.

2 =
3 = Generalized behavioral change requirements are understood but not articulated.
4 =
5 = Specific behavioral requirements are understood, articulated, and integrated with performance appraisal.
N = Not enough information to make a rating.

GOALS FOR RESULTS

1 = Performance goals are not emphasized and people goals are emphasized.
2 =
3 = Goals are generally known but not used explicitly to manage change.
4 =
5 = Goals are used actively to manage the organization, and people have information and feedback about them.
N = Not enough information to make a rating.

KEY MANAGERS REPLACED

Have key management people been replaced because they don't fit the behavioral goals of the change effort?

Yes = one or two key people of a smaller set at the top or several of a larger set lower in the organization.

No/Not enough information

USE OF PROGRAMS

Did the organization institute programs to implement change?

Yes/No/Not enough information

LEADER MODELS NEW STYLE

Leaders model the problem-solving style as indicated by interviews with subordinates or research observation. People describe the leaders' behavior as exemplars of what they are trying to do. They do not mention the leader as a counter-example.

1 = Completely inconsistent with espoused direction.
2 = People make comments about inconsistency and it is not discussable with leader.
3 = Inconsistent but aware of inconsistency and willing to talk about it.
4 = Inconsistent, discussable, and trying to change.
5 = Completely consistent and seen as a model.
N = Not enough information to make a rating.

Appendix IV

Definition of Variables for Revitalization Questionnaires

DEPENDENT VARIABLES

SUPPORT FOR CHANGE

These items are rated in response to the following instructions:

Please indicate whether each statement is an *accurate* or *inaccurate* description of the change process in this plant [division/corporation].*

1	2	3	4	5
Very inaccurate	Mostly inaccurate	Uncertain	Mostly accurate	Very accurate

---

*Words in brackets describe changes made to make items suitable for plant, divisional, or corporate respondents.

Most people in this plant [division/corporation] believe the new approaches to managing and organizing people will improve our financial performance.

Most people believe when the transformation in our approach to managing is complete they will be personally better off.

A consensus has been reached among the key managers in this plant [division/corporation] about the need for the new methods of management.

Overall, how much resistance is there to the new ways of managing and organizing employees?

[This item is reverse coded and rated on a scale that ranges from 1—"Most levels and parts of the plant [division/corporation] are not committed to change" to 5—"Almost all . . . are committed to change."]

EXTENT OF ORGANIZATIONAL REVITALIZATION

Sum of items in Interfunctional Coordination, Organizational Decision Making, Work Organization, and Concern for People scales below. These items are rated on the following scale:

1	2	3	4	5
To a much lesser extent than before the change began	To a somewhat lesser extent than before	No change	To a somewhat greater extent than before	To a much greater extent than before the change began

Interfunctional Coordination

To what extent do different parts of the plant [division/corporation] plan together and coordinate their efforts?

To what extent does your part of the plant [division/corporation] receive cooperation and assistance from other parts of the plant [division/corporation]?

Organizational Decision Making

When decisions are made, to what extent are the persons affected asked for their ideas?

People at all levels of an organization usually have know-how that could be of use to decision makers. To what extent is information widely shared in this plant [division/corporation] so that those who make decisions have access to such knowledge?

Work Organization

To what extent is this plant [division/corporation] generally quick to use improved work methods?

To what extent does this plant [division/corporation] have goals and objectives that are both clear-cut and reasonable?

To what extent are work activities sensibly organized in this plant [division/corporation]?

In this plant [division/corporation] to what extent are decisions made at those levels where the most adequate and accurate information is available?

Concern for People

To what extent does this plant [division/corporation] have a real interest in the welfare and overall satisfaction of those who work here?

How much does this plant [division/corporation] try to improve working conditions?

To what extent are there things about working here (such as policies, practices, or conditions) that encourage you to work hard?

BUSINESS IMPROVEMENT

Overall, what impact have the efforts to develop and implement new ways to organize and manage employees had on the plant's [division's/corporation's] financial performance?

[This item is rated on a scale that ranges from 1—
"Extremely negative impact" to 5—"Extremely positive
impact."]

"PEOPLE" IMPROVEMENT

Overall, what impact have the efforts to develop new
ways of organizing and managing employees had on the
individual well-being of the employees in this plant
[division/corporation]?

[This item is rated on a scale that ranges from 1—
"Extremely negative impact" to 5—"Extremely positive
impact."]

BEHAVIORAL CHANGE

Overall, how much impact have the plant's [division's/
corporation's] change efforts had on how managers and
other employees in this plant [division/corporation] actually go about doing their jobs?

[This item is rated on a scale that ranges from 1—"Few
changes" to 5—"Extensive changes."]

The attempts to introduce new methods of organizing and
managing have had few effects on how the individuals in
this organization relate to one another on a day-to-day
basis.

[This item is reverse coded and rated on a scale that
ranges from 1—"Very inaccurate" to 5—"Very
accurate."]

INDEPENDENT VARIABLES

CHANGE STRATEGIES

These items are rated in response to the following instructions:

Please indicate whether each statement is an *accurate* or

rate or *inaccurate* description of the change process in this plant [division/corporation].

1	2	3	4	5
Very inaccurate	Mostly inaccurate	Uncertain	Mostly accurate	Very accurate

Model Organizations in Company

A number of ideas for change in this plant [division] were influenced by the example of innovative plants elsewhere in *this* company.

[Corporate question] There are visible model organizations in this company (plants, branches, or divisions) that are used to make people aware of the types of changes desired and how to go about these changes.

Change Spread through Moving Committed Managers

A number of ideas for change in this plant [division] came to us from managers who were transferred in from other innovative parts of this company?

[Corporate question] The management of this company has tried to increase the spread of the new methods of organizing by transferring committed line managers from one organizational unit to another.

Conferences and Visits Spread Change

Members of this plant [division] have learned about successful new approaches to managing and organizing people through attendance at conferences and visits to leading-edge plants or companies.

[Corporate question] Mechanisms such as conferences, speeches, and visits to leading-edge plants, divisions, and branches have been used extensively in this company to spread the word about successful new approaches to managing and organizing people.

Network of Change Agents

The managers in this plant [division] are part of a network of managers in this company who are committed to the new methods of management and who communicate with one another regularly about their efforts, exchanging ideas and providing mutual support.

[Corporate question] There is a network of managers committed to the new methods of management who communicate with one another regularly about their efforts, exchanging ideas and providing mutual support.

Education in New Methods

Considerable time and money is being spent to educate managers at all levels in the new methods of organization and management.

Succession Used

Those individuals whose management style is more in line with the new philosophy of management in the plant [division/corporation] have been more apt to get pay increases, promotions, or other recognition.

A number of managers whose style does not fit the new approach to organization and management have left or been replaced.

Evaluation Used

You are being evaluated by your boss on how well your own management style fits the new methods of organizing and managing.

First-line managers and middle managers are being held accountable by upper management in this plant [division/corporation] for changing the approach to organizing and managing being used within their areas of responsibility.

REASONS FOR CHANGE

Improve Employee Welfare

The changes in organizing and managing employees came about primarily as a result of plant [division/corporate] management's attempts to improve employee welfare.

Improve Business Results

The changes in organizing and managing employees came about primarily as a result of plant [division/corporate] management's attempts to improve business results.

NATURE OF CHANGES EMPHASIZED

These items are rated in response to the following instructions:

To what extent do each of the following characterize the approach to organizing and managing people being implemented in your plant [division/corporation]?

1	2	3	4	5
Not emphasized at all		Somewhat emphasized		Emphasized to a very great extent

Lower costs through wage or people cuts

Decreasing costs through personnel reductions and/or wage and benefit reductions is emphasized.

Increased accountability for results

Increasing accountability for results—profitability, quality, customer service, and so forth—at all levels.

Increased employee input on task

Involving employees in decisions concerning their immediate job or task.

Improved intergroup coordination

Developing better organizational mechanisms for cooperation and coordination among interdependent organizational units.

Increased delegation of authority

Delegating authority for decisions to lower organizational levels.

Sharing power and equalizing status

Sharing power and equalizing status between plant [division] groups (such as between management and a union, managers and subordinates, or between different plant [division] departments) is emphasized.

[Corporate question] Sharing power and equalizing status between organizational groups (such as between unions and management, managers and subordinates, or between different functional areas).

Increasing employee influence over how treated

Giving employees greater influence and control over how they are treated in the organization.

Developing people skills

Developing the people skills of managers and workers

Increasing trust between groups

Developing more trusting and open relationships between organizational groups (such as between management and a
union, managers and subordinates, or between different
plant departments) is emphasized.

LEADERSHIP OF REVITALIZATION

These items are rated in response to the following instructions:

Please indicate whether each statement is an *accurate* or
inaccurate description of the change process in this plant
[division/corporation].

1	2	3	4	5
Very inaccurate	Mostly inaccurate	Uncertain	Mostly accurate	Very accurate

Top management espouses revitalization

The top management of the plant [division/corporation] spent
a lot of time discussing with all parties concerned why
changes in managing and organizing were necessary.

The major momentum for the new methods of organizing and
managing people was generated by the top management of
the plant [division/corporation].

Top management consistent in words and actions

The plant [division] manager and his staff have a real understanding of the changes in management they are asking
others to make.

[Corporate question] The top management of this company has a real understanding of the changes in management it is asking others to make.

The efforts to introduce new methods of management have
been accompanied by the plant [division] manager and staff
examining and modifying their own behavior.

[Corporate question] The efforts to introduce new methods of management have been accompanied by top corporate management examining and modifying its own behavior.

Even though the plant [division] manager and staff say they want to implement a new way of organizing and managing, they have often been perceived as acting in ways that are inconsistent with this approach. [reverse coded]

[Corporate question] Even though top management says it wants to implement a new way of organizing and managing, it has often been perceived as acting in ways that are inconsistent with this approach. [reverse coded]

Change from HR Initiatives

A number of the changes in how people are organized and managed in this plant [division/corporation] have resulted from the initiatives of plant [divisional/corporate] human resource/industrial relations personnel.

Sufficiently Skilled HR People

The plant [division/corporation] lacks sufficient numbers of human resource professionals with the skills to help institute the new model of management. [reverse coded]

Top Management Has Driven Change

The major momentum for the changes in organization and management was generated by the top management of the plant [division/company].

Middle Management Has Driven Change

The major momentum for the changes in organization and management came from the initiatives of a few innovative middle managers in the plant [division].

[Corporate question] The major momentum for the changes in organization and management came from the initiatives of a few innovative line managers in various parts of the company (plant, branch, or division).

Unions Have Driven Change

Our unions have been a major driving force for the changes in how people are managed in this plant [division/corporation].

Index

[1]Names of fictionalized companies and personnel are italicized.

Index

Product quality, 47, 117, 124–127
  See also Quality circles; Quality control
Programmatic change
  corporate culture and, 25–30
  critical path and, 148–150
  definition, 24
  implementation, 23, 30–37
  reasons for failure, 37–39, 41–42, 50–51
  reasons for use, 39–40
  task alignment and, 53, 55–56, 60–65
Project teams
  implementation, 86–89, 102
  revitalization and, 72–77, 82–83, 106, 212
  task alignment and, 51–52

Quality. *See* Product quality
Quality circles, 33–34
Quality control
  revitalization and, 72, 75, 85
  task alignment and, 48–50, 52–53, 57, 59–61

Reidsville box plant. *See Continental Glass & Container*
Renewal. *See* Revitalization
Replacement (personnel), 73, 88–89, 101–102
Research Design
  methodology, 2–4, 239–242
  quantitative results, 25, 54, 121, 160, 165, 183, 192, 196, 243–262
  variables for questionnaires, 275–285
  variables for ratings, 263–273
Revitalization
  goals, 8–9, 11–21, 54, 80, 85, 153–154
  implementation, 91–94, 119–120, 145–150, 223–231
  monitoring and evaluating, 143–145
  sequence of interventions, 145–148
  See also Case studies; Critical path; Employees; Management; Organizational structure; Programmatic change; Task alignment
Rockwell International Corp., 1

Scott Paper Co., 1
Scranton Steel
  competitive environment, 127–128
  cost control, 160, 162–163
  human resources, 165, 170, 172–173
  management role, 92–93, 128, 163, 186–187, 192, 196–200, 206

organizational structure, 16
overview, 236–237
programmatic change, 25
quantitative results, 251–262
revitalization performance, 4, 113, 121–122
union-management relations, 18, 89–91
Shields, Ed, 163, 186–187, 237
Simpson, Jerry
  identification, 235
  leadership, 193–194, 200, 213
  revitalization performance, 70–76, 79–89, 91, 94–96, 98, 106, 206
  union-management relations, 123
Singer, Donald
  identification, 237
  leadership, 163, 186–187, 195–198, 200
  revitalization performance, 128, 206
  role in human resource utilization, 170
Specialized Products. *See Fairweather Corporation*
Steel industry, Japanese, 127
Succession planning, 101–102, 141–143
Survey of Organizations, 242

Task alignment
  asset rationalization and, 62–63
  definition, 7, 45–47
  implementation, 47–54, 73–74
  leadership in, 187, 199
  problems, 77, 92–93
  programmatic change and, 60–65
  reasons for success, 54–60
  revitalization and, 52, 82–85, 154–155, 224
Task-driven organizations, 19–21
  See also Task alignment
Taylor, Jim, 31, 185, 234
Teams. *See* Project teams
Teamsters Union, 73, 89, 123
Technical Center. *See General Products*
Top management. *See* Management
Training programs, 30–33, 73, 86, 102, 136–141, 206–208
  See also Consultants
Tutt, Ben, 26–28, 34–35, 238

Union-mangement relations
  post–World War II, 17–19
  revitalization and, 71, 89–91, 113, 118, 120–123, 182–184, 228–229
Unions. *See* Teamsters Union; United Auto Workers Union; United Steelworkers of America